Intercultural Studies in Education

Series Editor
Paul Miller
School of Education & Professional Development
University of Huddersfield
Huddersfield, West Yorkshire
United Kingdom

The book series takes as its starting point the interrelationship between people in different places and the potential for overlap in the experiences and practices of peoples and the need for education to play a larger role in expanding and in these expanding discourses. This proposed book series is therefore concerned with assessing and arriving at an understanding of educational practices in multiple settings (countries), using the same methods of data collection and analysis for each country level analysis contained in each chapter, thereby leading to the production of "Cultures" [of understanding] on different topics. "Cultures" of understanding results from and leads to a deeper appreciation and recognition of educational practices, issues and challenges, (a) within a country (b) between & among countries and (c) between and among traditions and other specificities within and between countries.

More information about this series at
http://www.springer.com/series/15066

Paul Miller
Editor

Cultures
of Educational
Leadership

Global and Intercultural Perspectives

Foreword by Clive Dimmock

Editor
Paul Miller
School of Education & Professional Development
University of Huddersfield
Huddersfield, West Yorkshire
United Kingdom

Intercultural Studies in Education
ISBN 978-1-137-58566-0   ISBN 978-1-137-58567-7 (eBook)
DOI 10.1057/978-1-137-58567-7

Library of Congress Control Number: 2016950441

Cover image © Lev Dolgachov / Alamy Stock Photo

Printed on acid-free paper

This Palgrave Macmillan imprint is published by Springer Nature
The registered company is Macmillan Publishers Ltd.
The registered company address is: The Campus, 4 Crinan Street, London, N1 9XW,
United Kingdom

FOREWORD

It is a privilege to write the foreword to this book on cultural contexts to educational leadership. Paul Miller—as editor—has courageously set out to bring together an original set of comparative studies that are genuinely cross-cultural. He and his authors have generated a wide range of chapters, each of which relates to a minimum of three countries, one of which at least is a developing country and at least two of which are from different continents. In addition, each chapter is grounded in original empirical research. In these ways, Miller has guaranteed making a unique contribution to our understanding of educational leadership around the globe.

Brought together under one cover are chapters that embrace a large number of countries and themes, some of which are traditionally given little attention in the literature. For example, if I selectively refer to three chapter examples from among the 11 chapters, one study compares Pakistan, England and Malaysia and looks at how ethnicity, culture, gender and class play out amongst school leaders. Another chapter looks at the intersections of gender and race amongst black school leaders in South Africa, the United States and the United Kingdom. A third study focuses on a social justice perspective of women in educational leadership in Scotland, England, New Zealand and Jamaica.

In organizing the book in this way, Paul Miller deserves an accolade. This book makes an invaluable contribution to our knowledgebase on cross-cultural educational leadership. It does so by first, alongside studies of well-studied systems such as the United States and the United Kingdom; he has included comparative studies of countries in the Caribbean, Africa and Southeast Asia, about which little has been written.

Second, each chapter takes a theme that is topical, such as women in leadership, and leadership and social justice, and uses the same methods of data collection across the studies, to render authentic comparisons amongst three or more countries. Such an approach makes cross-cultural comparison feasible and meaningful. It avoids the typical country-by-country comprehensive accounts of educational leadership that while claiming to be comparative, often fail to yield genuine comparisons.

Unquestionably, students and scholars of educational leadership will benefit from this unique text. They will do so by extending their understanding of educational leadership across and within different cultures, and by experiencing an approach to authentic cross-cultural analysis that is thematic, focused, authentic and meaningful. Paul Miller has made a weighty contribution to our field for which he deserves much credit, and our respect.

Glasgow, Scotland, UK   Clive Dimmock
April 2016

CONTENTS

Cultures of Educational Leadership: Researching and Theorising Common Issues in Different World Contexts

Paul Miller

INTRODUCTION AND CONTEXT

While the need for leadership is perhaps universal across cultures, the practice of leadership is generally believed to be culturally situated. Different views exist in the leadership literature regarding the extent to which specific leader behaviours are transferable across cultures, leading some researchers to suggest that effective management and leadership processes should normally take account of the cultural and other contexts (Ayman 1993). Linked to this is an assumption that unique cultural features, for example, language, beliefs, values, religion and social organisation, demand that different leadership approaches are taken in different nations (Dorfman et al. 1997). Increasingly however, there has been a rise in recent research on educational leadership that includes a cross-cultural element, acknowledging that in addition to culture-specific tendencies, there may be more universal or broad-based approaches to understanding and practising leadership.

P. Miller (✉)
School of Education & Professional Development, University of Huddersfield,
Huddersfield, West Yorkshire, United Kingdom
e-mail: P.Miller@hud.ac.uk

© The Author(s) 2017
P. Miller (ed.), *Cultures of Educational Leadership*, Intercultural
Studies in Education, DOI 10.1057/978-1-137-58567-7_1

1

In the first edition of *The Handbook of Leadership* (Stogdill 1974), cross-cultural leadership received only limited attention. In the second edition (Stogdill and Bass 1981), a chapter on cross-cultural issues in leadership was included. In the third edition (Bass 1990), the 1981 chapter was revised and expanded, moving from circa 25 to circa 40 pages. In 2003, Dickson et al. proposed that 'it would be essentially impossible to prepare a single chapter that presented an exhaustive account of the research on cross-cultural issues and leadership' (p. 730). Now, in 2016 the intention of this edited volume is to highlight the need for and relevance of intercultural and cross-cultural research in guiding our understanding of common issues in the practice of educational leadership in different educational contexts globally.

A starting point for our discussion is the mid- to late 1990s, a period in which House and Aditya (1997) produced a comprehensive review of issues pertinent to cross-cultural research in the area of leadership. This was accompanied by insightful commentaries by Smith (1997) and Dorfman et al. (1997). This book is not to provide an update of advances in cross-cultural leadership research. Rather, it is to highlight the necessity of such research, in a time of increased globalisation and the continuing narrowing of cultural and other spaces. We are certainly not the only researchers to undertake inter-cultural and cross-cultural studies in educational leadership. However, we are the first to examine educational leadership practices and issues in the way we have. These will be discussed further in the methodo-logical approach. In their review in a special issue of *The Leadership Quarterly* on 'International Leadership', Peterson and Hunt (1997) raised concerns about the American bias (and arguably the Anglo-American bias) in several existing theories of leadership and high-lighted the importance of scientific approaches to studying leadership. In producing this book, we do not present a simple collection of articles. Instead we present empirical research organised and grouped by related themes, although each chapter can stand on its own, debat-ing an issue or an element of practice or research in educational leadership that has been examined across different countries and edu-cational contexts. In organising our work in this way, it is proposed this approach is both an innovative and sophisticated way of examining and incorporating intercultural and cross-cultural issues in educational leadership.

CONCEPTUAL ISSUES: INTERCULTURAL AND CROSS-CULTURAL

Intercultural and cross-cultural understanding is about taking an interest in and showing empathy towards people from other groups (Alred et al. 2003, p. 3). Intercultural and cross-cultural understanding was, traditionally, a part of foreign language education, concerned with the 'foreign' and 'the strange'. Over time, however, and with the advance of globalisation, intercultural and cross-cultural education has become an important role in promoting global harmony and global social justice (Besley and Peters 2012). In its White Paper, *Intercultural Dialogue: Living Together as Equals in Dignity*, The Council of Europe (2008) emphasised the need for Europe to more purposefully engage in interculturalism in order to cope with diversity in the age of globalisation (Besley et al. 2011).

Without question, increased interconnectedness is fuelling intercultural awareness and understanding. As Dimmock and Walker (2005) proposed: 'Understanding what a culture is and why it is so important in determining our relationship with other people are key elements of global citizenship...' (p. 25). Nevertheless, as Rule (2012, p. 336) asserts, there are a number of obstacles to intercultural understanding, including the imposition of Western languages and a broadly Eurocentric world view. Martin and Griffiths (2012) question whether intercultural understanding is possible within a global context of domination and inequality. Allmen (2011) acknowledges inequality of educational opportunity and cultural exchange by pointing out that 'Intercultural pedagogy tries to encompass the World by deploying "the other as the supplement of knowledge"' (p. 35). Sealey and Carter (2004) suggest that individuals can position themselves in intercultural conversations, thus influencing what is heard and how this is translated.

Intercultural, Cross-Cultural, Culture

There is some confusion in the available literature concerning the meaning of the terms cross-cultural and intercultural. As a result, it is important to clarify how these feature in this important work. Cross-cultural connotes a comparison or contrast between two or more cultural groups (Lustig and Koester 1993). On the other hand, intercultural means 'equitable exchange and dialogue among civilizations, cultures and peoples based on a mutual understanding and respect and the equal dignity of all cultures is the essential prerequisite for constructing social cohesion, reconciliation among peoples and peace among nations' (United Nations 2005). In other words, inter-cultural refers to what happens when people from two (or more) culturally different groups come together, interact and communicate (Lustig and Koester 1993). Both terms, intercultural and cross-cultural, are important to our work in this book.

Culture is a contested term. Hofstede (1991) defined culture as 'the collective programming of the mind which distinguishes the member of one group or category of people from another' (p. 5). Spencer-Oatey (2000) extends this notion by suggesting: 'Culture is a fuzzy set of attitudes, beliefs, behavioural norms, and basic assumptions and values that are shared by a group of people, and that influence each member's behaviour and his/her interpretations of the "meaning" of other people's behaviour' (p. 4). These definitions position culture as both a product and a process, which are important notions in this book.

INTERCULTURAL AND CROSS-CULTURAL RESEARCH IN EDUCATIONAL LEADERSHIP

Intercultural and cross-cultural research is not as straightforward as one may think. As noted by Gill (2011) and Earley (2013), leadership is a contested term with no universally agreed definition. As discussed previously, 'culture' is also a contested term with different shades of meanings. Dickson et al. (2003) argue that the term 'leadership' presents 'no clear understanding of the boundaries of the construct...' (p. 732). In adding intercultural and cross-cultural dimensions to the mix in educational leadership research, far from simplifying matters, this makes identifying a precise definition a more complex and confusing one. Without a workable framework that helps to narrow and guide intercultural and cross-cultural research in educational leadership therefore, it is possible for research in this area to be fragmented and incoherent. In *Cultures' Consequences* (1980), Hofstede argues for such a framework and proposes that cultural differences are primarily about shared values or about values believed to be preferred by some in certain cases, although not all, in all cases. Hofstede also argues that in cross-cultural research, three fundamental questions are to be considered: 'What are we comparing? Are nations suitable units for this comparison? Are the phenomena we look at functionally equivalent?' These are important questions that align with the aims, methodology and design of this book.

Graen et al. (1997) assert that the focus of cross-cultural research is on comparability. They argue, 'Emics are things that are unique to a culture, whereas etics are things that are universal to all cultures. Emics are by definition not comparable across cultures. One task of cross-cultural researchers, hence, is to identify emics and etics' (p. 162). By design, this book is about examining intercultural and cross-cultural leadership through both emics and etics perspectives.

Despite the growing importance and appeal of intercultural and cross-cultural research, only 'few researchers and educators rely on empirical cross cultural and intercultural research to interpret their observations' (Dahl 2003, p. 1). A commonly acknowledged example of a large research project on cross-cultural issues in leadership is the Global Leadership and Organizational Behavior Effectiveness (GLOBE) Project (House et al. 2004). In their project, covering 60 countries and over 180 researchers, House et al. examined the relationship between leadership, societal culture and organisational culture. Crucially, what we attempted to do and indeed have been successful in doing with this work, *Cultures of Educational Leadership*, has never before been done in the field of educational leadership. That is, whereas the GLOBE Project focused on leadership in organisations, the focus of our work in this book is on educational leadership.

Before this book however, other researchers have undertaken work in educational leadership that has been described as 'international' or 'comparative' or both. In doing so, such works have broadened the scope of research in educational leadership from the usual developed countries in the English-speaking world to countries in the developing world, and in doing so 'other voices' have entered into the debates and literature providing possibilities for more inclusive evaluation of issues to be undertaken. For example in 2012, the *Journal of the University College of the Cayman Islands* carried a special issue on *The Changing Nature of Educational Leadership: Caribbean and International Perspectives*. In its editorial, Miller (2012) positions the special issue as contributing to our understanding of educational leadership within, across and beyond the Caribbean region. This special issue was followed by *School Leadership in the Caribbean: Perceptions, Practices and Paradigms* (Miller 2013), which provides multiple insights of school leadership and practices within, between and among English-speaking Caribbean countries. Practices are examined through lens of religious, cultural, social and historical foundations adding useful dimensions to our study and understanding of school leadership practice. In *Multidimensional Perspectives on Principal Leadership Effectiveness*, Beycioglu and Pashiardis (2014) provide crucial exploration of challenges faced by principals, as well as the impact of new managerial tactics being employed by education ministries/departments in multiple contexts. In *Building Cultural Community through Global Educational Leadership*, Harris and Mixon (2014) underline how globalisation can impact educational leadership and practice. In the main, they highlighted the role of a global leader in the education setting in a time of complexity in tackling social, political, economic and especially social justice issues. A main limitation of all these works however is that chapters, except in a small number of cases, tend to focus on a single country, thereby limiting opportunities for deep cross-cultural analysis based upon a common methodological frame.

Nevertheless, in *Educational Leadership: Culture & Diversity*, a precursor to these works, Dimmock and Walker (2005) provide a thorough treatment and an integrated analysis of the importance of understanding culture, leadership and their interaction in different contexts through comparative accounts of Anglo-American and Asian schooling systems. They also highlight cultural differences between societies, leadership practices associated with multicultural schools and cultural and contextual factors influencing teaching and learning. Things also moved further forward with the publication of *Exploring School Leadership in England & the Caribbean: New Insights from a Comparative Approach* (Miller 2016), which used a common methodological frame between the countries involved in the study, and in *Successful School Leadership: International Perspectives*, (Pashiardis and Johannson 2016), which presents chapter analysis based on regions of the world examined. A limitation of Miller's work is that, despite focusing on common issues between very different countries and educational systems, its coverage only extends to two countries—England and Jamaica. A limitation of Pashiardis and Johannson's work, on the other hand, is that although chapters are nominally based on regions, some chapters include only one or two countries, though not all.

This book, *Cultures of Educational Leadership*, therefore goes furthest in providing a comprehensive evaluation of issues related to educational leadership in different parts of the world in an integrated manner in that each chapter:

- Uses a single method/approach to gather data per chapter regardless of the number of countries included in that chapter
- Includes a minimum of three countries per chapter, one of which must be a developing country

- Includes a mix of developed and developing countries per chapter
- Includes countries from at least two continents per chapter
- Includes countries from the six world continents

Our work, articulated in 11 chapters presents research data on 18 countries located on the six continenets of the world, undertaken by a team of 35 researchers. This book is intended to provide an authentic, critical insight into the social construction and practice of educational leadership in multiple contexts since, as we have come to agree, the practice and enactment of leadership is culturally and contextually situated. This idea is illustrated by Bordas (2007), who argues that 'Only by becoming aware of how society is structured to perpetuate the dominance of some groups and to limit access to others, will leaders be able to create a framework for the just and equal society in which diversity can flourish' (p. 112).

CULTURES OF EDUCATIONAL LEADERSHIP

Globalisation has led to the narrowing of physical and cultural spaces, the result of which has been the creation of multicultural societies and communities, providing opportunities for bidirectional and multi-directional sharing of knowledge, values and understandings. Notwithstanding, as countries and regions collaborate and cooperate, our understanding of national and regional cultures, cultural spaces and cultural practices is arguably not as developed as one might expect, and our attitudes are sometimes premised on differences and not on similarities. Some studies, although providing 'authority' through their 'global' and 'international' labels, have only included countries from the developed world in their analyses, and in many others, where developing countries have been included, these countries are often typecast as problematic and in need of assistance to raise them up to standard. Research conducted in this way sustains negative tension between the intellectual needs of developing countries and Western intellectual hegemony, where developing countries are treated as intellectual dumping grounds for international ideas (Bristol 2012). This book is therefore a simultaneous attempt to re-balance and balance current discourses in educational leadership through a global integrated issues-based research approach.

Globalisation is a rapid, highly interactive phenomenon that has simultaneously reset and surpassed the boundaries of economics and is actively setting new challenges within all aspects of life, including in education.

Increasingly, educational institutions in both developed and developing countries are expected to account for and respond to the impacts of this phenomenon that has frustrated scientific precision (Croucher 2004). Furthermore, as global interconnectedness intensifies, educational institutions, from nursery to university, are tasked with equipping learners to live and work in a much narrower world economy. Because of this, education itself and schooling can no longer be seen as the preserve of a nation but as an international tool for individual and social transformation (Bristol 2012). Similarly, educational leadership can no longer be seen as delivering outcomes for a nation state but rather for a globalised economy, although in the process one might expect the exercise of leadership to increase a nation's competiveness. Educational leadership therefore may be thought of as both a lock and a key, to be used to secure and safeguard and to release and reassure.

But globalisation is not about to disappear and should therefore be seen as an important element in any debate on intercultural and cross-cultural research in educational leadership. As Miller puts it, 'Faced with external factors such as the recent economic meltdown, globalisation and changing borderland narratives and shifts in government policy, education institutions the world over are being forced to "do education differently". This shift is as much about the leadership of policymakers in education departments and ministries as it is about the practice of leadership by school leaders and teachers at all levels' (2012, p. 10). Miller's observations bring to light three important things. First, globalisation has had and continues to have an impact on the policy, practice and research of educational leadership in countries all over the world. Second, educational leadership (policy, practice) must respond to changes in the environment with new, different and innovative practices and ideas. Third, ongoing environmental changes to life and work provide opportunities for researchers to engage in integrated issues-based inquiry. It is these underpinnings that lay the foundation for this book—the main content of which is summarised next, based upon the two dominant themes of chapters received.

Social Justice, Gender, Intersectionality

The theme of empowerment and social justice is quite dominant throughout the book—acknowledging its importance for countries and individuals, although simultaneously underlining the struggles and (structural) imbalances inherent in all societies. In their chapter on *Social Justice Perspective on Women in Educational Leadership in Scotland, England, New Zealand, Jamaica*, Torrance et al. (this volume) propose, 'In truth, we still know very little about women in educational leadership as a social justice issue within any individual country's context and far less across countries and continents.' Walrond (2009) argues that research within minority, and arguably minoritised communities, helps to give voice to others previously silenced. This chapter did not seek to highlight victimisation among women school leaders, but rather for their experiences and perceptions to be acknowledged and documented. As Murakami et al. proposed, 'There is no silver bullet or a one size fits all approach,' although what is noticeable from the stories of women school leaders in the chapter by Torrance et al. (this volume) is that 'At the core of these women's vulnerable selves is an articulated dynamism and energy that expertly toggles between the social, scientific, and political' (Murakami et al., this volume), underlining Blackmore's (2009) point that 'The challenge for any transnational dialogue is understanding the new global terrain beyond national borders' (p. 4) and Hall's (1993) suggestion that 'we all write and speak from a particular place and time, from a history and culture, which is specific' (p. 222).

It is of note that the study by Torrance et al. included interviewing school leaders in environments where women make up the majority of the teaching profession and in some cases both teaching and leadership roles (as in the case of Jamaica). This is important, since, to date, studies on women in leadership and minority-related issues of identity and alienation have tended to be located in developed countries, in particular the United Kingdom, the United States and Canada. Nevertheless, as the authors have acknowledged, the emerging findings from their chapter reflect the view of Bogotch (2014, p. 62) that 'Social justice as an educational practice is inclusive of all members of the world's population regardless of governmental structures, cultures, or ideologies, and it accounts for innumerable contingencies of life-influencing individual outcomes or unpredictable consequences of our actions'.

In their study on *Educational Leadership among Women of Colour in United States, Canada, New Zealand*, Murakami et al. (this volume) highlight how important these issues are by drawing on positive attributes from the particular ethnic, cultural, linguistic and, sometimes, national identities of women leaders advancing social justice (Santamaría and Jean-Marie 2014) to explore the meaning of social justice leadership for women of colour, recognising their role in challenging hegemonic practices and in forging new paths through their research. The activist approach taken by Murakami et al. is consistent with the view that recognising [and challenging] the relationship between leadership and cultural and contextual influences can lead to improvements in practice (Dimmock and Walker 2005). Such improvements are sometimes delayed or restricted and may be due to several reasons. For example, in 1997 Motzafi-Haller argued that the experiences of women and people of colour were considered less authentic and unscientific in attempts to theorise issues of difference. Showing some movement in this area, Murakami et al. (this volume) instead propose:

> In this chapter, women leaders of color in different contexts reimagine a new leadership discourse toward social, political and scientific rejuvenation and reclamation. Scholars do this by looking inward and outward simultaneously taking the position that their realization and manifestation of leadership practice is irreconcilably intertwined with their social, political, and scientific identities. The authors' individual and collective critical stances are on the cutting edge of scholarship in educational leadership arguably pushing beyond what is known and currently practiced in the field.

Moorosi et al. (this volume) disrupt the geographical imbalance on research on social justice and intersectionality issues by including South Africa in their chapter on race, gender and leadership in South Africa, the United States and the United Kingdom. They found that the women had more in common around early family support, their socialisation towards dreaming and a desire to give back to students 'like them', to be overwhelming drivers and levers in their professional lives. Like Torrance et al., Moorosi et al. have been 'struck by the similarities between diverse countries' (Torrance et al., this volume) in the experiences of the school leaders. In producing the evaluation in the way they have, Moorosi et al. foregrounded Norberg et al.'s (2014) conclusions that 'social justice leadership in practice, despite the national context, offers more commonalities than differences' (p. 101). Furthermore, as Moorosi et al. (this volume) put it 'By crossing boundaries, including breaking out of the powerful structures of inequalities such as poverty, racism and sexism, to succeed in education and by breaking out of the powerful discriminatory attitudes in education to succeed in educational leadership, these women demonstrated their exercise of agency.' This is an important finding for women everywhere who have faced racial, gendered and/or other discrimination, opening up possibilities for further research on intersectionality and educational leadership in different cultural and country contexts. As the authors also propose, the success of these women school leaders should not be seen as 'colluding with the mainstream' but instead as 'collectively opening up transformative possibilities for their community' by 'the power of education to transform and change the hegemonic discourse' (Mirza 1997, p. 276).

In their chapter, Showunmi and Kaparou (this volume) also highlight intersectional and social justice issues in Pakistan, England and Malaysia in relation to ethnicity, culture, gender and class among school leaders. Issues such as role stereotyping and discrimination, debated by the authors, conclude that facets of intersectionality presented in the chapter appear only to receive surface-level treatment from those responsible for implementing change. This important finding simultaneously widens the debate on social justice and intersectionality and underlines the fact that '[I]n the field of educational leadership, intersectionality approaches have not generated either ideas or drive for policy or behaviour change' (Lumby 2014, p. 20). Shields (2003, p. 8) argues, 'commitment and good intentions are not enough' and where such exists, these must be matched by activism described by Murakami et al. (this volume) as 'social, political and scientific', or put another way: people, leverage and research.

García-Carmona et al. (this volume) intensify the debate on women in leadership; social justice and leadership; race and leadership; and leadership and intersectionality in their chapter on gender and leadership through a secondary analysis of Teaching and Learning International Survey (TALIS) data for Brazil, Singapore and Spain. Citing a plethora of literature on aspects of leadership practice, the authors argue that 'there are very few studies aimed at helping our understanding of school leadership at a multiple country level'. Such recognition not only affirms the need for cross-cultural and intercultural research in educational leadership, but underlines the important role this book has in bridging the gap in literature and research design, thereby adding to the field. From their detailed analysis across three countries, the authors argue that although there were differences in the experiences of school leaders within and across the countries, there were many more similarities. For example, 'women show a tendency to leader in schools through a distributed leadership which is a disadvantage if we consider that they should master both instructional and distributed leadership styles' (García-Carmona et al., this volume) and 'successful school leaders must master both the leading and the learning environments and they must navigate and shape the school-level context in order to reform the teaching and learning context. For that reason, it should be considered a necessity for training in both distributed and instructional leadership for principals before to occupy their positions.' As observed by Torrance et al. (this volume), 'It is hoped these case studies provide potential for a cross-phase comparison (primary and secondary contexts) as well as a cross-national comparison of contexts, influences, possibilities and challenges' of the kind that situates sound leadership at the heart of successful educational systems (Miller 2012) whether exercised by male or female.

Policy, Whole School Development and Sustainability

As we know, the practice and enactment of school leadership is individually, culturally and contextually bound. Nevertheless, global discourses and debates within and outside education can have a direct impact on the practice of school leaders in every corner of the globe. From performativity to benchmark standards, and accountability to high-stakes testing—these and other factors are having a significant impact on what goes on inside schools, and both developing and developed countries appear to be caught up in the race to driving up performance and achievement standards. In their chapter on *Policy Leadership, School Improvement and Staff Development in England, Tanzania and South Africa*, Middlewood et al. (this volume) summarise:

> In developed countries, where a market-led school choice model operates, schools have inevitably become dislocated from their own communities and in many less developed countries, issues of lack of resources, vast distances and historical divisions hinder opportunities for much national cohesion. Effective change, we suggest, is most likely to happen when a number of schools work or operate within networks or partnerships of various kinds, where they can together devise their own system(s) for innovation and development in learning and teaching.

These important observations confirm two important issues. First, a market-led model of schooling is affecting schools in the developing world, albeit in different ways. Second, to remain relevant for the times we live in, schools in both the developed and developing world must engage in innovative teaching and learning, and collaborative partnership arrangements that extend current opportunities for those who work and study in them.

Meaningful change that engages with and embraces diversity of cultures, peoples and regions is easier said than achieved. Nevertheless, and being mindful of the apparent dilemma, the authors suggest:

> With research evidence over a period of years indicating that cross-nation practice was erroneously based on the concept of successfully transposing lessons from one culture to another, especially western culture onto eastern culture, (Stephens, 2012) ideas are needed for practice which can have positive effects in a range of countries. It is necessary therefore to seek ideas about practices which are universal to the way people operate, and at the same time applicable to contexts in countries which may have widely different geographical, political and resource issues.

This is an important observation aimed at inviting voices previously 'silent', 'uninvited' or 'disempowered' to contribute to debates and a field of knowledge that needs to be inclusive in order to be relevant and in which being relevant means to be inclusive.

School principals across the world are, more and more, being required to lead successful schools—usually measured in terms of students' outcomes. In their chapter, Abawi et al. (this volume) discuss the importance and process of leadership in high-achieving contexts in Brazil, Malta and Australia through a research-based framework. Although the importance of leadership is not in doubt, the process of leadership is less straightforward, that is, 'how to do leadership'. Torrance and Humes (2015) allude to this difficulty in positioning school leadership as 'embedded both horizontally and vertically...within a distributed perspective' (p. 793). From his work on high-performing principals, Hutton (2011) asserts that effective principals often navigate conundrums brought about by factors in a school's external environment and those in a school's internal environment. These conundrums, however, are important in shaping, and perhaps in determining, the kind of leadership exercised by principals and received by their publics. Hutton further proposes that it is the degree and intensity to which the internal and external factors intersect that will determine the quality of leadership success.

Hutton's observation extends the notion of successful leadership as a practice driven by 'outcomes' for students, but a practice that is fraught with external and internal challenges, which, in the process of negotiating outcomes for students, principals sharpen the quality of leadership they provide. Holden describes this improvement in leadership quality as 'a personal sense of personal agency, empowerment' emanating from a principal's 'conscious and deliberate interaction with the culture of the school' (2002, p. 12). As Sirotnik and Clark (1988) underline:

> [T]he schools that make a difference are those that extend the leadership to include others that focus not only on academic issues but also address the affective domain. Rather than merely following prescription or the dictates of central authorities, quality change and quality improvement depends on the inner potential of school staff—on the 'heads, hands and hearts' of educators who work in schools. (p. 660)

As Miller and Hutton (2014) argue, school leadership is 'situated' within an individual but emerges from how they engage with and manage, negotiate and navigate factors in a school's internal and external environments. Nevertheless, by focusing on 'heads, hands, and hearts' (Sirotnik and Clark 1988, p. 660), school leaders are making the point that capacity exists at different levels within their school organisation and making use of this capacity has potential to enhance individual and organisational growth.

Without question, teachers play an important role in the success of schools. In his economic-motor model of schooling, Miller (2016) characterised teachers as 'mechanics' (p. 144), 'providing students, through their skills, knowledge and experience the knowledge and skills they need to function effectively and independently in society' (ibid). Yet, the needs of teachers, in particular those newly qualified, can be overlooked as schools press forward to achieving goals for students. Nevertheless, where systems are in place to support their professional development, teachers are more likely to grow and to thrive. As one teacher in the study by Majocha et al. puts it: 'Communicating and sharing what I am struggling with helps me analyze the problems I am facing and develop different methods to deal with old problems we have in public teaching context' (in this volume). In their study of teacher development in Brazil, Canada, Pakistan and South Africa, Majocha et al. highlight that investment in people development is not only smart human resources management but smart public policy. As Clutterbuck (1992) states, 'A mentor is a more experienced individual, willing to share his/her knowledge with someone less experienced in a relationship of mutual trust' (p. 12).

The idea of mentoring and coaching for and among teachers is not new and its benefits are well documented. Kram (1985) notes that mentoring is about the career progression as well as the psycho-social development of individuals. From the case studies presented, Majocha et al. note:

> The commonality shared by all the participants from Brazil, Canada, South Africa, and Pakistan is that their more experienced colleagues are supportive and encouraging during their first years of teaching. When novice teachers are struggling, they go to their colleagues to seek support for their teaching strategies to overcome student learning. Therefore, in order for them to learn well among their colleagues, there is an availability of collaborative dialogue which will make their individual learning accessible and personal through their supportive colleagues.

Increasing individual, team and, ultimately, organisational capacity (Mitchell and Sackney 2009) appeared to have been an important outcome for both mentors and newly qualified teachers. The overriding argument by Majocha et al. however was that 'when novice teachers are supported through professional learning communities, and there are opportunities for dialogue with colleagues within their school districts, the ultimate winners are the students. The students gain in achievement when their teachers gain confidence and efficacy'. The implications for teacher development vis-à-vis staff mentoring and staff involvement in communities of practice and in learning communities are quite clear, be they local and/or international communities.

Intercultural and cross-cultural learning are examined through Miller and Potter's (in this volume) account of whole school learning across borders. Highlighting how bidirectional flows of students and staff can contribute to individual, team and organisational development (Mitchell and Sackney 2009), the confluence of human, social and decisional capitals (Hargreaves and Fullan 2012, p. 88) is examined. This sense of professional community underpins their work with a view that working together is ultimately better for the whole since this provides opportunities for cross-fertilisation of skills and knowledge to take place. Dimmock (2012) argues for 'A new conceptualisation of educational leadership for the twenty-first century' (p. 18), where leadership is 'aimed at marshalling resources in ways that maximise capacity' (ibid). This view of organisational development is one that is inclusive and that suggests that capacity and capital can be increased through partnership. Conway et al. sustain the narrative on whole school development by an examination of stories from school leaders in Australia, South Africa and Canada. Turning to a well-ventilated debate about whether leaders are born or made, the authors appropriately remind us that 'the complexity of leadership is far more than adhering to predetermined frameworks and standards'. The professional development of school leaders matters, perhaps more so in cultures of performativity. While Miller and Hutton (2014) remind us that effective school leadership is 'situated' within an individual, Addison (2009) reminds us of a game in which principals appeared to have been seduced, 'a game in which market-based economic imperatives have become central to both their professional success and professional leadership' (p. 335). Principals have been described extensively as 'drivers' and as such they have huge responsibility to learners, their families and a nation's education system. In his economic-motor model of schooling, Miller (2016) argues, 'principals are the "drivers" of government policy at the operational level, and they do so in relation to their school's context, their vision for the school, the resources available to the school and in relation to where the school is currently "at"' (p. 143).

The importance of policy, context, personal values and resources is all important to how a principal will (be able to) lead. In foregrounding the peculiarities of context and through the stories of principals in multiple contexts, Conway et al. confirm:

> The greatest value in this relatively small study has been the richness of the principals' voices. Each principal generously shared their perspectives and provided opportunity for valuable conclusions within the parameters of this chapter. Of significance is the interpretation of the principals' roles in relation to the context categorised as structural, relational, and cultural. In conclusion, there is evidence to suggest that two specific factors contribute to the way in which the individual principal perceives the role of school leadership—the nature of the context, and the relationship between the system and the school (in this volume). The implications for successful school leadership are clear when one considers the changing nature of school leadership in response to local and global performativity pressures.

Fullan (2004) argues that 'Nothing beats learning in context' (p. 16)—which is an important consideration for organising cross-border collaborations aimed at capacity building. Fullan's point is further elaborated by Wilkins (2013) that transformational leaders create infrastructure for capacity building that connects homes, workplaces and civic spaces through the school networks—a realisation borne out by Miller and Potter in their chapter on study tours between England, Jamaica, Albania and Malawi. They argue, 'The objectives of the study tours have been achieved. There has been a narrowing of the gap between peoples and places and there has been a cultural introduction (and immersion) for participants, not obtainable from textbooks.' Dimmock (2012) argues that 'one is able to arrive at a fuller and more holistic understanding of leadership and schooling by placing them in the larger social context of which they are a part' (p. 202). This point was amplified by Miller and Potter's overarching conclusion that '*The* greatest value in this study has been the richness of the participant's voices. Of significance is the participant's understanding that through their capacity building tours to other countries, their contextualised (situated; original) knowledge has been de-contextualised (disrupted; altered based on the introduction of new information) and as a result, attitudes and actions are set to be re-contextualised.' These findings reflect important personal and cross-cultural shifts for staff and students who've simultaneously experienced a 'contextualised' and 'de-contextualised' educational experience that will go some way in preparing them to more successfully and competently function in an increasingly global environment.

Cross-Cultural Research and Theory Building

Through our examination of the range of issues presented in this book from national, cultural, intercultural, international and cross-cultural perspectives, one cannot escape the similarities between developed and developing country contexts and Western and non-Western countries. While more Western countries are represented in the book, the inclusion of countries from the six world continents and the treatment given to non-Western countries, particularly smaller developing countries, represent a significant move towards narrowing the gap in studies in educational leadership. Although Western countries in this book tend to produce practices that are largely similar, the findings from non-Western countries have added new and useful insights into the practice and research of educational leadership. Nevertheless, there were several issues that appeared equally between and among all countries. For example, social justice issues, in particular female participation in leadership, especially among black, Asian and minority ethnic women, are areas of concern and research interest in developed and developing countries alike. Similarly, whole school development, in particular teacher and principal development, remains an area of focus for all countries. Furthermore, the enthusiasm and 'drive' among principals in navigating internal and external factors in the forms of cultural, relational and structural challenges to better enable them to 'best' serve their publics is a matter for practice and research in both developed and developing countries. Other issues that emerged include leadership approaches among women, in particular distributed and instructional leadership, and whether or how these approaches influence attainment among students. The use of cross-border experiential learning to engage individuals, groups and schools in cross-cultural and intercultural learning for both staff and students is a matter for policy, research and practice.

In returning to the debate about cultural specifics and cultural universal aspects of leadership, one is reminded of Bond and Smith's (1996) exposition that '*The search* for universals and an emphasis upon indigenous culture-specifics are often cast as contradictory enterprises that exemplify contrasting etic and emic approaches. Yet these concepts are no more separable than nature and nurture' (p. 226). The result of our examination provides that similarities and differences between and among cultures can be sensibly incorporated into appropriate theoretical frameworks, thereby adding to our understanding of the specific cultures being studied. Furthermore, it is possible that through hybrid research designs (Earley and Singh 1995), such as the approach used in this book, there is opportunity for meaningful cross-cultural comparisons to be made and for cultural differences and variations to be more appropriately understood.

Conclusions

Samoff (1999) highlights the global diffusion of Western ideas, highlighting assumptions about how knowledge should be ordered from the Western core to Southern periphery, with the 'core' maintaining its authority and leaving the periphery to mimic discourses and practices established by the core. Knowledge organised along these lines reinforces the continuance of powerful social forces along Anglo-American elitist lines and ignores calls from the United Nations (2005) for 'equitable exchange and dialogue among civilizations, cultures and peoples based on a mutual understanding and respect and the equal dignity of all cultures...'.

In this post-colonial era, cultural domination as well as knowledge domination are as problematic as economic domination, and every attempt should be made to promote activism through research and policy which can lead to 'social cohesion, reconciliation among peoples and peace among nations' (United Nations 2005) through our work. Within and among developing and developed countries, globalisation continues to present opportunities for intercultural and cross-cultural collaboration where our research will be a tool for attempting to dismantle hegemonic discourses and for promoting global inclusion and mutual understanding. Intercultural and cross-cultural research in educational leadership is significant to our achieving an informed understanding of each other, no matter where in the world we live, work or go to school. Cross-cultural and intercultural research promotes [global] citizenship and the ability within, between and among individuals to collaborate with people who are different from themselves and who live and work in different cultural contexts and spaces. In this edited volume, we have started a conversation that through our research we hope will go some way to promoting mutual understanding of each other and a sense of global citizenship—in terms of both our research design and our findings. Put differently, our research provides a 'conceptual framework for transcending the nation or the barriers of ethnic, religious or racial difference to include all within a global community' (Jefferess 2012, p. 29). Furthermore, in researching and theorising educational leadership through an intercultural and cross-cultural approach, we affirm our commitment to global interdependence in terms of learning with, learning from, learning through and learning about each other.

REFERENCES

Addison, B. (2009). A feel for the game—A Bourdieuian analysis of principal leadership: a study of Queensland secondary school principals. *Journal of Educational Administration and History, 41*(4), 327–341.

Allmen, M. (2011). The intercultural perspective and its development through cooperation with the Council of Europe. In C. Grant & A. Porter (Eds.), *Intercultural and multicultural education: enhancing global interconnectedness.* New York: Routledge.

Alred, G., Byram, M., & Fleming, M. (Eds.) (2003). *Intercultural experience and education.* USA: Multilingual Matters.

Ayman, R. (1993). Leadership perception: the role of gender and culture. In M. M. Chemers & R. Ayman (Eds.), *Leadership theory and research.* San Diego: Academic Press.

Bass, B. M. (1990). *Bass and Stogdill's handbook of leadership. Theory, research and managerial applications* (3rd ed.), New York: Free Press.

Besley, A. C., Peters, M. A. & Jiang, X. (Eds.) (2011). The Council of Europe's *White Paper on Intercultural Dialogue*, Special Issue. *Policy Futures in Education*, 9(1), 1–12.

Besley, A. C., & Peters, M. A. (Eds.) (2012). *Interculturalism, education and dialogue*. New York: Peter Lang.

Beycioglu, K., & Pashiardis, P. (Eds.) (2014.) *Multidimensional perspectives on principal leadership effectiveness*. Hershey, PA: IGI Global.

Blackmore, J. (2009). International response essay, leadership for social justice: a transnational dialogue. *Journal of Research on Leadership Education*, 4(1), 1–10.

Bogotch, I. (2014). Educational theory: the specific case of social justice as an educational leadership construct. In I. Bogotch & C. Sheilds (Eds.), *International handbook of educational leadership and social [In]Justice* (Vol. 1, pp. 51–65). London: Springer.

Bond, M. H., & Smith, P. B. (1996). Cross-cultural social and organizational psychology. *Annual Review of Psychology*, 47, 205–235.

Bordas, J. (2007). *Salsa, soul and spirit: leadership for a multicultural age* Oakland, CA: Berrett-Koehler Publishers.

Bristol, L. S. M. (2012). *Plantation pedagogy: a postcolonial and global perspective*. New York: Peter Lang.

Clutterbuck, D. (1992). *Mentoring*. Henley: Henley Distance Learning.

Council of Europe (2008). White paper on intercultural dialogue "living together as equals in dignity". http://www.coe.int/t/dg4/intercultural/source/white%20paperCouncilofEurope_final_revised_en.pdf. Accessed 5 May 2016.

Croucher, S. (2004). *Globalization and belonging: the politics of identity in a changing World*. USA: Rowman and Littlefield Publishers.

Dahl, S. (2003). *An overview of intercultural research*. Middlesex University Business School London: Society for Intercultural Training and Research UK 1/10 (2/2003), London.

Dickson, M., Den Hartog, D. N., & Mitchelson, J. K. (2003). Research on leadership in a cross-cultural context: making progress and raising new questions. *The Leadership Quarterly*, 14(3), 729–768.

Dimmock, C. (2012). *Leadership, capacity building and school improvement: concepts, themes and Impact*. Leadership for learning series. London: Routledge.

Dimmock, C. A. J., & Walker, A. (2005). *Educational leadership: culture and diversity*. London: Sage.

Dorfman, P. W., Howell, J. P., Hibino, S., Lee, J. K., Tate, U., & Bautista, A. (1997). Leadership in Western and Asian countries: commonalities and differences in effective leadership processes across cultures. *The Leadership Quarterly*, 8(3), 233–274.

Earley, P. (2013). Foreword. In P. Miller (Ed.), *School leadership in the Caribbean: perceptions, practices, paradigms*. Didcot: Symposium Books.

Earley, P. C., & Singh, H. (1995). International and intercultural management research. What's next? *Academy of Management Journal, 38,* 327–340.

Fullan, M. (2004). *Leading in a culture of change.* London: Sage.

Gill, R. (2011). *Theory and practice of leadership* (2nd Ed.). London: Sage.

Graen, G. B., Hui, C., Wakabayashi, M., & Wang, Z.-M. (1997). Cross-cultural research alliances in organizational research. In P. C. Earley & M. Erez (Eds.), *New perspectives on international industrial/organizational psychology.* San Francisco, CA: Jossey-Bass.

Hall, S. (1993). Cultural identity and diaspora. In P. Williams & L. Chrisman (Eds.), *Colonial discourse and postcolonial theory: a reader.* London: Harvester Wheatsheaf.

Hargreaves, A., & Fullan, M. (2012). *Professional capital: transforming teaching in every school.* New York, NY: Teachers College Press.

Harris, S., & Mixon, J. (Eds.), (2014). *Building cultural community through global educational leadership.* Ypsilanti: NCPEA Publications.

Hofstede, G. (1980). *Culture's consequences: International differences in work-related values.* Beverly Hills, CA: Sage.

Hofstede, G. (1991). *Culture and organizations: the software of the mind.* New York: McGraw-Hill.

Holden, G. (2002). Towards a learning community: The role of mentoring in teacher-led school improvement. *Journal of In-Service Education, 28*(1), 9–22.

House, R. J., & Aditya, R. N. (1997). The social scientific study of leadership: Quo vadis? *Journal of Management, 23*(3), 409–473.

House, R. J., Hanges, P. J., Javindan, M., Dorfman, P. W., & Gupta, V. (Eds.) (2004). *Leadership, culture and organizations: the GLOBE study of 62 societies.* Thousand Oaks, CA: Sage.

Hutton, D. (2011). Revealing the essential characteristics, qualities and behaviours of the high performing principal: experiences of the Jamaican school system. *International Journal of Educational Leadership Preparation, 5,* 3.

Jefferess, D. (2012). Unsettling cosmopolitanism: global citizenship and the cultural politics of benevolence. In V. Andreotti & L. De Souza (Eds.), *Postcolonial perspectives on global citizenship education.* New York: Routledge.

Kram, K. (1985). *Mentoring at work: developmental relationships in organisational life.* Glenview, IL: Scott Foresman.

Lumby, J. (2014). Intersectionality theory and educational leadership: help or hindrance? Paper presented to the *British Educational Leadership, Management and Administration Special Interest Group,* Gender and Leadership, Birmingham, 31 March 2014.

Lustig, M. W., & Koester, J. (1993). *Intercultural competence: interpersonal communication across cultures.* Michigan: HarperCollins College Publishers.

Martin, F., & Griffiths, H. (2012). Power and representation: a postcolonial reading of global partnerships and teacher development through North–South study visits. *British Educational Research Journal, 38*(6), 907–927.

Miller, P. (2012). Editorial. *Journal of the University College of the Cayman Islands* Special Issue on 'Educational Leadership in the Caribbean & Beyond'. December, JUCCI 6.

Miller, P. (Ed.) (2013). *School leadership in the Caribbean: perceptions, practices and paradigms.* London: Symposium Books.

Miller, P. (2016). *School leadership in England and the Caribbean: new insights from a comparative approach.* Bloomsbury: London.

Miller, P., & Hutton, D. (2014). Leading from "within": towards a comparative view of how school leaders' personal values and beliefs influence how they lead in England and Jamaica. In S. Harris & J. Mixon (Eds.), *Building Cultural Community through Global Educational Leadership.* Ypsilanti: NCPEA Publications.

Mitchell, C., & Sackney, L. (2009). *Sustainable improvement: building learning communities that endure.* Rotterdam, The Netherlands: Sense Publishers.

Mirza, H. (Ed.) (1997). Black women in education: a collective movement for social change. In *Black British feminism.* London: Routledge.

Motzafi-Haller, P. (1997). You have an authentic voice: anthropological research and the politics of representation. *Teoriyah U'bikoret, 11,* 81–99.

Norberg, K., Arlestig, H., & Angelle, P. S. (2014). Global conversations about social justice: the Swedish-US example. *Management in Education, 28*(3), 101–105.

Pashiardis, P., & O. Johansson. (Eds.) (2016). *Successful school leadership: international perspectives.* Bloomsbury: London.

Peterson, M. F., & Hunt, J. C. (1997). International perspectives on international leadership. *The Leadership Quarterly, 8*(3), 203–231.

Rule, P. (2012). Intercultural dialogue, education and transformation: an African perspective. In A. C. Besley & M. A. Peters (Eds.) (2012), *Interculturalism, education and dialogue.* New York: Peter Lang.

Samoff, J. (1999). Institutionalizing international influence. In R. Arnove & C. Torres (Eds.), *Comparative education: the dialectic of the global and the local* (pp. 51–90). Lanham, MD: Rowman and Littlefield.

Santamaría, L. J., & Jean-Marie, G. (2014). Cross-cultural dimensions of applied, critical, and transformational leadership: women principals advancing social justice and educational equity. *Cambridge Journal of Education, 44*(3), 333–360.

Sealey, A., & Carter, B. (2004). *Applied linguistics as social science.* London, UK: Continuum.

Shields, C. M. (2003). *Good intentions are not enough: transformative leadership for communities of difference.* Lanham, MD: Scarecrow.

Sirotnik, K. A., & Clark, R. W. (1988). School-centred decision making and renewal. *Phi Delta Kappan, 69*(9), 660–664.

Smith, P. B. (1997). Cross-cultural leadership: a path to the goal? In P. C. Earley & M. Erez (Eds.), *New perspectives on international industrial/organizational psychology.* San Francisco, CA: Jossey-Bass.

Spencer-Oatey, H. (2000). *Culturally speaking: managing rapport through talk across cultures.* London: Continuum.

Stephens, D. (2012). The role of culture in interpreting and conducting research. In A. Briggs, M. Coleman, & M. Morrison (Eds.), *Research methods in educational leadership and management.* London: Sage.

Stogdill, R. M. (1974). *Handbook of leadership: A survey of theory and research.* New York: Free Press.

Stogdill, R. M., & Bass, B. M. (1981). *Stogdill's handbook of leadership: a survey of theory and research* (Revised and Expanded). USA: Macmillan.

Torrance, D., & Humes, W. (2015). The shifting discourses of educational leadership: international trends and Scotland's response. *Educational Management Administration & Leadership, 43*(5), 792–810.

United Nations (2005). United Nations alliance of civilizations. Many cultures. One humanity. http://www.unaoc.org/. Retrieved 19 March 2016.

Wilkins, R. (2013). Professional strengths in school leadership: Collaborating for knowledge generation, problem solving and policy influence. *Education Today, 93*(4), 308.

Walrond, J. (2009). In the diaspora, Black Caribbean Canadian culture matter: perspectives on education "Back Home". In G. A. Wiggan & C. B. Hutchison (Eds.), *Global issues in education: pedagogy, policy, practice, and the minority experience.* Toronto, ON: Rowman & Littlefield.

Paul Miller, PhD, PFHEA, is Professor of Educational Leadership and Management at the School of Education and Professional Development, University of Huddersfield, UK. He is President of the Institute for Educational Administration and Leadership, Jamaica (IEAL-J); a member of Council of the British Educational Leadership Management Administration Society (BELMAS); a member of the Board of the Commonwealth Council for Educational Administration and Management (CCEAM). He is an Associate Editor of *International Studies in Educational Administration* and *Educational Management Administration & Leadership.* He has taught in secondary schools and universities in both Jamaica and the United Kingdom, and his work in educational leadership and management is predominantly framed with comparative and cross-cultural perspectives. He is Principal Fellow of the Higher Education Academy.

CHAPTER 2

A Social Justice Perspective on Women in Educational Leadership

Deirdre Torrance, Kay Fuller, Rachel McNae, Carmel Roofe, and Rowena Arshad

INTRODUCTION

Internationally, social justice represents a major theme within the areas of leadership policy, research and literature. Related to this, there has been a resurgence of interest into the experiences and perceptions of women in educational leadership (Grogan and Shakeshaft 2011;

D. Torrance (✉) · R. Arshad
University of Edinburgh, Scotland, United Kingdom
e-mail: deirdre.torrance@ed.ac.uk; rowena.arshad@ed.ac.uk

K. Fuller
University of Nottingham, Nottingham, United Kingdom
e-mail: Kay.Fuller@nottingham.ac.uk

R. McNae
University of Waikato, Hamilton, New Zealand
e-mail: r.mcnae@waikato.ac.nz

C. Roofe
University of the West Indies, Kingston, Mona, Jamaica
e-mail: carmelg.roofe@gmail.com

© The Author(s) 2017
P. Miller (ed.), *Cultures of Educational Leadership*, Intercultural Studies in Education, DOI 10.1057/978-1-137-58567-7_2

McNamara et al. 2008; Reynolds 2002). Internationally, women are under-represented in school leadership and continue to face challenges that are both complex and not altogether understood. This under-representation of women in school leadership represents a key issue in unlocking leadership and management potential, as well as establishing equality with men. However, within the context of this broader policy environment, limited comparative empirical evidence is available on women in school leadership. Blackmore (2009a, p. 80) suggests 'research is needed to further explore the significance of the relations between context and leadership practice in order to comprehend how context shapes the practice of leadership'.

What Does the Literature Say About Women in Educational Leadership with a Social Justice Perspective?

Research literature on women and educational leadership continues to direct scholarly attention to women's over-representation in the teaching population and under-representation in headship positions (Grogan and Shakeshaft 2011; Fuller 2013). Much of this literature serves to remind us of the ever-present barriers, contradictions and achievements associated with women leading in education.

Women and Leadership

Research illustrates significant factors that impact on women's representation and leadership practice (Grogan and Shakeshaft 2011) and barriers to women's advancement (Coleman 2001). Despite the legitimacy of gender equity within official government discourse, institutionalised formations of bureaucracies informed by neoliberal political theories premised upon individual merit (Blackmore 2010) reproduce hierarchical structures. Such structures propel male leaders into senior positions (Shakeshaft et al. 2007), exclude many women from educational leadership opportunities, thus creating social injustice. Women's representation in leadership is a matter of social justice and 'we must never lose sight of the facts that the leaders we are discussing are women, that doing leadership may differ for women and men, and that leadership does not take place in a genderless vacuum' (Yoder 2001, p. 815).

What Is 'Social Justice'?

As a concept, social justice is 'inherently problematic' with usage of the term reflecting a 'broad range of philosophical and political traditions' (Barnett and Stevenson 2015, p. 520). Constructions of social justice are 'highly dependent on the context in which it is used' (Gairín and Rodriguez-Gómez 2014, p. 820), with perspectives 'inextricably linked to social contexts within which models of justice make sense to the people involved' (Harris 2014, p. 98). Attempts to define social justice are problematic since 'in pluralistic societies people understand it differently' (Taysum and Gunter 2008, p. 184). Thus, 'social justice has diverse, complex and dynamic meanings' (Davis et al. 2014, p. 7). Moreover, conceptions of social justice 'are not fixed, stable or uncontested across time, place and political context' (Hajisoteriou and Angelides 2014, p. 897).

Blackmore (2009b, p. 7) calls for 'greater conceptual clarification' of social justice, recognising that its current use includes terms such as equity, (in)equality, equal opportunity, affirmative action and diversity, each taking on different meanings dependent on national context. While social justice may well be 'an irreducibly complex concept' (Griffiths 2014, p. 234), Shields and Mohan (2008, p. 291) provide a helpful frame through which this chapter explores a social justice perspective on women in educational leadership:

> Our concept of social justice is one that identifies issues of power and inequity in schools and society and that challenges personal and systemic abuses of power as well as alienating and marginalizing beliefs, values, and practices.

How Does Social Justice Relate to Educational Leadership and Management?

Within the field of educational administration, leadership and management interest in '*issues of marginalization*' is relatively recent (Ryan 2010, pp. 358–359), with research mostly focused on the role of the school administrator and on principal preparation programmes (Insana et al. 2014).

Mullen (2008) considers democracy and accountability, power and authority, equity and opportunity as critical issues of social justice that are central to educational leadership. Richardson and Sauers (2014, p. 107) contend that social justice within schools begins with leaders since 'leaders recognize that inequalities exist within the system and focus their energies to ensure equity for all students'. Similarly, Bogotch and Shields (2014, p. 10) believe that 'educational leadership and social justice are, and must be, inextricably interconnected'. Indeed, Bogotch (2008, p. 94) perceives the onus for education as 'seeking a pedagogy and leadership that might guide us towards change and social justice', coming to perceive social justice as 'a moral responsibility in terms of how educational leaders used their power' (Bogotch 2014, p. 54). In discussing social justice as an educational leadership construct, Bogotch (2014, pp. 52–53) asks, 'Why insert educational leadership?' concluding that:

> ... the relationship between educational leadership and others is reciprocal, translating the lessons of power so as to create opportunities for others to better their lives.... the legitimacy of social justice as an educational construct lies in making tangible differences in other people's lives, not in how we, as educators, practice education, good, bad, or indifferently.

Thus, social justice leadership is to do with taking forward a sense of agency and responsibility for a better future for all pupils, regardless of their circumstances. Social justice involves political action to improve society (Mestry 2014). It cannot be left to a few formal leaders in a school but needs to permeate the culture of a school within which teachers consider themselves activists, as 'Teachers can be agents of change or they can be guardians of the status quo' (Arshad 2012, p. 4). Social justice leadership needs to be positioned in school organisations, with teacher leadership 'at the intersection of social justice and curriculum inquiry acted on in teachers' classrooms' (Lopez 2014, p. 478). Lopez argues that:

> teacher leadership represents the agency of teachers to disrupt existing norms and as social justice represents the pursuit of more equitable schooling, moving away from what I refer to as laminated equity and policies.... seek[ing] to implement social change, remove injustices and improve the lives and experiences of students.

Lopez (2014, p. 480) proposes 'a cadre of aspiring school administrators' will ensue, 'who understand how to meet the needs of diverse learners and ease the conundrum of retraining and training current school leaders and administrators who do not bring these experiences'. This is not to negate the role of head teachers in hierarchical school structures who 'retain[ing] overall power and influence and the strategic control over the direction of school improvement as well as providing legitimisation to staff leadership' (Torrance 2013, p. 368).

In What Ways Is 'Women in Educational Leadership' a Social Justice Issue?

A concern with women in educational leadership represents a social justice perspective in a number of ways. At a basic level, social justice represents a fundamental commitment to issues of equality (Dukes and Ming 2014). Not only are women under-represented in senior leadership but the discussion of gender in educational leadership is rare since it 'does not seem to be considered an essential component of the discussion and classification of leadership theory in education' (Coleman 2003, p. 326). That said, the under-representation of women in leadership positions 'has a well developed body of literature that explores different notions of social justice over time informed by liberal, radical, cultural and post structural feminisms' (Blackmore 2009b, p. 4). Women still experience barriers into headship (Coleman 2005). Despite a much higher proportion of teachers internationally being women than men, they hold a minority of secondary school management positions and in primary schools, males hold an over-representative proportion of management positions (Coleman 2002, 2005). Exploring why the potential for women to become 'the new source of talent for leadership positions' did not progress further beyond the turn of the millennium (Blackmore 2009b, p. 3) remains an equality issue. Coleman (2002) identified different pressures that female head teachers face in maintaining work–life balance, making career choices and choice of leadership style to conclude 'women experience headship differently' (Coleman 2002, p. 325). Of those women who do take up headships in English secondary schools, they are 'more likely to be single, separated or divorced; fulfill domestic responsibilities; move location to follow their partner's career; have fewer children; and draw on a wide range of carers to look after sick children than men' (Fuller 2010, p. 376). Women constantly negotiate their coexisting roles as professional and mother (Bradbury and Gunter 2006).

Traditionally, women 'are culturally expected to be caring, subjective and personal' (Oplatka 2001, p. 231) while working within 'a male-dominated organisational culture' (p. 230) within which 'orthodox leadership is male' (Coleman 2003, p. 325). The pervading presence of gender stereotyping of leadership styles is based on socially constructed gendered norms (Hoff and Mitchell 2008; Schmuck 1996). These norms frequently position men as natural candidates for leadership and marginalise women's ways of leading to exclude them from leadership (Blackmore 2002; Court 1994; Shakeshaft 1987). The equation of leadership with masculinity is not new (Alimo-Metcalfe 1998; Kezar and Moriarty 2000). Yoder (2001) draws our attention to the influence gender can have on leadership opportunities for women; when issues of gender are left unchallenged major limitations to encouraging young women into leadership can occur. Kezar and Moriarty (2000, p. 55) indicate:

> Traditional models of leadership tend to be exclusive and represent an orientation to leadership derived from those traditionally in positions of power that is mostly Caucasian, male, upper-middle-class orientation to leadership.

That said, Coleman (2003, 2005) found that there were no significant differences in female and male head teachers' descriptions of their leadership style or perceptions of their daily leadership practice. Whether men and women leaders behave differently in leadership is a highly debated topic (Eagly and Johannesen-Schmidt 2001). Eagly and Johnson's (1990) meta-analysis of over 350 gender comparison studies in the area of leadership found no differences in styles for men and women leaders in formal leadership positions. As such, it would be contentious to refer to female or male perspectives on and styles of leadership, since feminine and masculine styles can be enacted by both male and female head teachers. Indeed, as outlined previously, research on gender in educational leadership styles has had an increasing emphasis on androgyny (Pace and Pace 2005). In researching women leaders as if they are a homogenous group, some of the literature that explores women secondary head teachers 'is predicated on outmoded theories of gender' (Fuller 2010, p. 363) since 'Gendered leadership is more fluid and shifting than some research into differences between the sexes might suggest' (2010, p. 369). Indeed, Blackmore (2009a, p. 57) argues that 'the process of popularization of women's ways of leading discourse treats women as a homogeneous group without differences in race/class/gender or in beliefs' and does not necessarily consider the diverse contexts in which women lead. It is timely that Grogan and Shakeshaft (2011) synthesise the significant number of leadership studies related to ways in which women lead to highlight five key ways that women show their contextual approach to leadership—relational leadership, leadership for social justice, leadership for learning, spiritual leadership and balanced leadership.

In a sense, it is not surprising to find that women, who may or may not have experienced gender inequalities in the family, education and the workplace, choose to lead in such ways. Over the last decade, many researchers have reported that women tend to focus more on relationships and participation, sharing power and responsibility and deconstructing hierarchies, emphasising reciprocity and conceptualising leadership as collective rather than individualistic (Billing and Alvesson 2000; Blackmore 1989; Court 2003; Kezar and Moriarty 2000; McNae 2010, 2014). With women, there is often an emphasis on the need to empower and care for others, and work in consultation and collaboration with consensus (Eagly and Johannesen-Schmidt 2001).

We still know very little about women in educational leadership as a social justice issue within any individual country's context and far less across countries and continents. This study sets out to explore the feasibility and utility of such research, recognising that 'The challenge for any transnational dialogue is understanding the new global terrain beyond national borders' (Blackmore 2009b, p. 4). There is much to be explored since, as Fuller (2010) notes, schools are contexts that expose children and young people to gendered representations beyond the family context. The school is a context that can, in its actions and inactions, perpetuate gender inequities or seek to dispel them. There is a misconception of schools as 'feminised' workplaces. The majority of teaching staff may be women but men are over-represented in headship posts. The construction of schools as 'feminised' perpetuates the misapprehension that women's dominance in the workforce leads to opportunities for promotion should they choose to achieve senior posts. Thus, children and young people encounter a women-dominated workforce that is disproportionately managed and led by men that seemingly also goes largely unquestioned.

By exploring women's experiences across different contexts, it may be possible to illuminate some of the experiences which inform the ways in which women perceive their leadership, and also their contribution to leading in socially just ways.

METHODS AND SAMPLE

This study draws from four countries, loosely connected by being part of The Commonwealth; a group of 53 countries that span Africa, Asia, the Caribbean and the Americas, Europe and the Pacific. Case studies conducted in Scotland, England, Jamaica and New Zealand provide contrasting, cross-national contexts to explore the influences, possibilities and challenges that women school leaders experience. The researchers are mindful that 'educational administration and leadership are primarily a Western concept' (Bogotch and Shields 2014, p. 8) and that 'assumptions of Western, liberal democracies which tend to underlie many of the theoretical conceptions/definitions of social justice need to be recontextualized and then reconceptualized' (Bogotch 2014, p. 61). Moreover, in this study, the Jamaican context provides a contrast to the majority of international studies available to women in educational leadership. Caribbean society is matriarchal with a high proportion of both women teachers and head teachers although beyond the school level, it is argued that men still hold significant power and influence (Miller 2013).

This international project is exploratory and develops as understandings become clearer. As a small-scale multi-method investigation, it combines documentary analysis of policy documents and related research literature with semi-structured interviews. It aims to contribute to the limited comparative empirical evidence available on women in school leadership, within the context of a broader policy environment nationally and internationally. It seeks to make a modest contribution to knowledge in this area.

Each research team adopted purposive sampling of women head teachers. Many were known to the researchers and selected on the basis of their ability to critically reflect and articulate their experiences. There were head teacher/principals in a variety of schools as nursery (one), infant (two), primary (eight), intermediate (one), and secondary (four) schools. It is intended that their engagement will contribute to their professional development and assist them in clarifying their own thinking about their role as women school leaders. Participants are conceptualised as co-creators of the data. An in-depth approach was favoured, to gather narrative accounts of life story events as 'a way of recognizing and capturing others' sense of social justice . . . critiquing and reflecting upon the taken for granted assumptions' (Taysum and Gunter 2008, p. 190). This narrative approach was utilised as 'a critical method in the struggle for social justice' (Muzaliwa and Gardiner 2014, p. 194). The interviews were guided by six overarching questions, the first two drawn from more heavily for this chapter:

1. What motivates women to become head teachers?
2. Do women benefit from any supports or encounter any barriers en route to headship?

3. Do women perceive that they experience headship in the same or different ways from men and if so, in what ways?
4. Do women perceive that they enact leadership in the same or different ways from men and if so, in what ways?
5. Does educational policy contribute in any way to supporting or promoting women in school leadership?
6. How do the research findings contribute to developing understandings of women in school leadership to potentially inform a larger scale research project?

Procedures for the Recruitment and Selection of Principals/Head Teachers

Across the four countries, there exist key differences in the procedures used for the recruitment and selection of principals/head teachers. In Scotland, the 32 Local Authorities are responsible for this process with the Scottish Schools (Parental Involvement) Act 2006 ensuring procedures include parental involvement. From 2018 to 2019, the Scottish Government intends that all new head teachers will have completed a postgraduate qualification for headship.

In England, head teachers are selected by school governing bodies. From 2010, the further academisation of schools removed many schools from local authority control. Local authorities are not represented in the selection process. From 2012, the National Professional Qualification for Headship is no longer mandatory. The responsibility for selecting, training, preparing and developing teachers and school leaders has been devolved to Teaching School Alliances in a shift away from Higher Education Institutions.

In Jamaica, the recruitment and selection of head teachers/principals is governed by the Education Act of 1980, section 43. Each School Board, acting in support with the Ministry of Education, is responsible for the recruitment and selection of principals. For appointment as a principal, the individual must possess at least a first degree, be teacher trained with at least 3 years approved service as a trained teacher.

The governance responsibilities and decision-making processes of New Zealand schools are devolved to school principals and individual school boards of trustees. These boards comprise elected or co-opted community members and parents, and one member of the school staff. The process of head teacher/principal appointments is highly localised and there is a high level of autonomy overall with 'no accountability required at any level of central government in the appointment process' (Brooking 2003, p. 2), as no officials from the New Zealand Ministry of Education are involved in the process.

The 16 Head Teachers Involved in This Study

A small number of women head teachers in each country contributed to the first phase of this study (see Table 2.1). In Scotland, four head teachers participated with varying years of experience and number of headship posts to date. All four head teachers were born in Scotland: three were white British; one was British Asian. All four Scottish head teachers had children, three were married and one was divorced but living with a long-term partner. Their ages ranged from late 30s to late 50s. In England, the head teachers reflected the multiethnic urban population. However, there are so few Black and Global Majority heritage women in headship in England that their countries of origin and/or faith are omitted for purposes of anonymity. In Jamaica, the four head teachers had taught in primary schools and had over 10 years of classroom teaching experience. At the time of the study all four teachers were serving as head teachers in the primary school where they were first appointed as teachers. The participants' ages ranged from early 30s to mid-50s. In New Zealand, the length of service and leadership experience varied among the four head teachers. Two head teachers who led inner city primary schools were experienced teachers (11 and 15 years in their schools) and both relatively new to leadership. The ages for this group ranged from mid-30s to mid-50s.

EMERGING THEMES FROM THE DATA

The purpose was to investigate women's experiences and perceptions of leadership, locating these within a framework of leading for social justice. Common themes emerged across the Commonwealth countries, with a small number of contextual differences appearing. These common themes are presented in Table 2.2, along with an indication of which women leaders in each country raised each theme. Where all four of the women raised a theme, this is indicated by 'All'. Where fewer than four women raised a theme, the names of those who did so are presented in the table.

Table 2.1 Head teachers involved in this study

Country	Name	School	Time in post	Personal details
Scotland	Alison	Middle-sized infant school Rural town	4 years Third permanent headship	Born in Scotland Has children
	Louise	Large primary school Suburban area of city	2 years First permanent headship	Born in Scotland Has children
	Ann	Large secondary school Outer edges of city	1 year Second permanent headship	Born in Scotland Has children
	Claire	Large secondary school Within a city	9 years First permanent headship	Born in Scotland Has children
England	Susannah	Nursery school Urban setting	4 years	White British Married with children Mid-50s
	Hasna	Primary school Urban setting	1 year	First generation immigrant Married with children Mid-40s
	Dee	Secondary school Urban setting	2 years	British Asian Married with children Mid-40s
	Coleen	Secondary school Urban setting	12 years	Mixed heritage—British and faith Married with children Mid-50s
Jamaica	Gene	Primary school Inner city	12 years	Born in Jamaica Unmarried
	Sherett	Primary school Rural multigrade school	1 year	Born in Jamaica Married with children
	Kemma	Middle-sized primary school Urban	5 years	Born in Jamaica Unmarried
	Smerl	Middle-sized primary school Rural	8 years	Born in Jamaica Unmarried

(*continued*)

Table 2.1   (continued)

Country	Name	School	Time in post	Personal details
New Zealand	Maya	Primary school Rural	5 years	Born in New Zealand
	Kathy	Large primary school Urban	2 years	Born in New Zealand
	Sarah	Intermediate school Inner city	6 years	Born in New Zealand
	Aroha	Large high school	10 years	Born in New Zealand Of Māori descent (indigenous New Zealander)

Table 2.2   Overview of women leaders who raised each theme

	Scotland	England	Jamaica	New Zealand
Limited early career aspirations (linked to gender)	All	Susannah Hasna Dee	Gene Kemma Sherett	Maya Sarah Aroha
Pragmatic/altruistic reasons for seeking promotion	All	Hasna Dee	All	Kathy Aroha
Experience of discrimination	All	All	Gene Kemma Sherett	All
General sources of support	All	All	All	All
Specific support from husband and/or family	All	All	Sherett	Maya
Experience of personal challenges	All	All	All	All
Experience of wider challenges	All	Susannah Hasna Dee	Kemma Sherett	Sarah Aroha
Perceived differences between men and women's leadership styles	All	Susannah Dee Coleen	Gene Kemma	All
Perceived importance of national support and policy	All	All	None	Sarah
Suggestions for future research	All	Coleen	All	Sarah Aroha

The following four themes are highlighted to begin a conversation about women head teachers' similar and contrasting experiences of school leadership in Scotland, England, Jamaica and New Zealand:

- Limited career aspirations in early career phase (linked to gender)
- Experiences of discrimination (age, gender, ethnicity)
- Experiences of personal challenges
- Experiences of wider challenges

Limited Career Aspirations in Early Career Phase (Linked to Gender)

All four of the Scottish head teachers reported having limited career aspirations in the early phase of their careers, with none planning a career towards headship:

> it was never really on my radar at all. . . . it kind of made its way towards me. [Ann]

Similarly, three of the four English head teachers reported having limited career aspirations. Three started their working lives in other jobs with the fourth not immediately attracted to teaching:

> No plan whatsoever at the beginning and I'd say even to maybe two years ago, still not thinking about headship at all. [Dee]

In contrast, Coleen recounted:

> I've had my children. Gone straight back to work because I was absolutely driven about being a Head.

Three of the four Jamaican head teachers reported having limited career aspirations:

> No, not in my wildest dreams. [Gene]
> It was the furthest thing from my mind. [Kemma]

In contrast, Smerl had 'always wanted to become an education officer' and considered her head teacher role as 'preparation' for that.

Three of the New Zealand head teachers reported having limited career aspirations:

> I just did not know what was possible . . . what was out there for me. [Maya]
> The way forward was not always clear and I had time out. I think I had a different perspective to most, because for me, family always came first. [Sarah]
> I went into teaching to make a difference and did not really picture myself as one [a principal]. It was not until someone said to me that I should consider it [headship] that I thought seriously about it and actively pursued it. [Aroha]

However, Kathy had aspirations from the beginning of her teaching career and stated:

> I knew that was me . . . I wanted to leave a legacy right from when I was at uni . . . the way I could do this was through having my own school, being the decision maker . . . I've always been at the front, leading and making decisions from when I was a student. [Kathy]

Experience of Discrimination

All four of the Scottish head teachers reported experiences of discrimination. Alison in her mid-30s and Louise at age 27 experienced age discrimination on applying for a first promoted post:

> I saw that as quite a barrier, that I'd left it too late. And people were thinking I was too old to be a senior teacher. . . . people thought at school, that I was too old to start, to start the journey to become a school leader. [Alison]

Whereas Ann and Claire experienced discrimination returning to work after their first children were born:

> I think one of the biggest challenges for me if I go right back was when I decided to have children. And I remember at one point coming back from my first maternity leave and discussing things with the head teacher. And he

said to me at that point, 'I don't know why you're coming back to work. The most important thing that you have and is a challenge is bringing up your child. And what are you doing coming back to work?' And that shocked me a bit really...So that was a challenge but, you know, I knew within myself my family was important to me but so was my career. And I just rose above that and thought, 'I won't have his value system imposed upon me'. [Claire]

All four English head teachers raised examples of different types of discrimination. Susannah was not perceived as having leadership potential while Hasna had felt patronised. Hasna and Dee had experienced discrimination related to race, culture and/or religion. References were made to:

'Your community', and, 'In your area', and, 'The risks to your children', you know, I was fuming inside but I had to control it and I had to be professional about it, but it was a personal attack [on me as a Muslim]. [Hasna]

Coleen experienced discrimination directly related to being a working mother:

when I had my last child, when I came back from maternity leave my Head said to me, 'Oh you won't need to attend those meetings now because you've got your little one to look after. So don't worry about it.' Then I went away to my line manager and blew my top because I was so cross that she thought that because I'd had a child, I couldn't carry on operating at the level I had before. [Coleen]

Three of the Jamaican head teachers identified examples of age and/or gender discrimination. Gene raised a highly political example:

The Chairman of the School Board at the time wanted a male even though I did very well at the interview. I came out on top of all the interviewees but he was adamant he wanted a male while the other members of the board did not agree with him and so the MOE [Minister of Education] and the Member of Parliament had to step in and that is how they overrode his decision and I got the job. But I think he wanted a male as he felt it was a male who could bring strong leadership to the school. [Gene]

All of the women in New Zealand had experienced discrimination in various forms.

Kathy shared an example of age discrimination:

> ...and they looked at me and one asked, 'what life experiences could you possibly have in the relatively short life you have lived so far?' I could not believe they would ask a question like that. It really rocked me, I was gobsmacked and I felt like a child, having to justify my 'short existence' and lack of time teaching, although I knew I had the stuff to do the job.

Sarah and Maya shared instances of gender discrimination with Sarah venting her frustration with the number of inexperienced young male teachers being appointed to leadership roles ahead of other more experienced and qualified women who had applied:

> You see them come in, lap top under one arm, rugby ball under the other and you know the story...you just know...they are going to get it over you. Some people are like, 'we can't see why you did not get it'. But I know—it's that the Boards can't see past the penis, the man and what they think he's going to bring to the school. They [board of trustees] just assume he will be stronger, firmer, better role model for boys...you name it, they will spin any line to disguise their traditions and unfair and often wrong choices.

Aroha shared an interesting example of positive discrimination. She had been appointed to a role because 'they needed my brown face'. She described winning a position in a school with a high proportion of Māori students. The school had become alienated from its community and the board of trustees was looking for a leader to make reconnections. Aroha came from Māori lineage, highly respected in the area, and although relatively inexperienced in the area of formal educational leadership, she believed she had won the position over more experienced applicants because of her skin colour 'but they would never say that out loud'. Aroha also experienced discrimination, often feeling 'excluded and on the outer' at Principals' conferences and events because she was a woman and more so because she was a Māori woman. She stated:

> I stand there invisible mainly. They ignore me. I'm not invited onto committees. I don't drink, I don't play golf...so I don't really fit the mould and because of this I guess I miss out. I feel alone and mostly just stay in my room.

Personal Challenges Experienced

All four of the Scottish head teachers reported the personal challenges linked to work-life balance as working mothers:

> That's been my big barrier all the way through. [Ann]
> So there's always a constant pressure. And I think it's all about being, being the best mum you can be as well as being the best head you can be [Claire]

All four of the English head teachers reported having experienced similar challenges:

> being able to spend quality time with my family in the evenings and the weekends. Now that's not physically possible. [Coleen]

Dee, however, saw an advantage to this challenge:

> one of the things that has really helped me get the work-life balance was having children because you have limited time to do work. [Dee]

Maintaining a work–life balance as a working mother/carer was a challenge highlighted by the Jamaican head teacher who was a mother/carer while the others perceived it as a challenge for working mothers:

> The home gets neglected; children suffer everybody else suffer. [Gene]
> Definitely! ... and work takes the bigger share. [Smerl]
> Women school leaders face many challenges in maintaining a work and personal life balance. Women, are most times the person who have to ensure that the children are taken care of, the house is clean, the husband is taken care of, do grocery shopping, take the sick children to the doctor and be a good leader, mother and wife. Some female school leaders are also single parent and this poses a problem in terms of spending enough quality time with their children/child. [Sherett]

All of the participants from New Zealand experienced personal challenges associated with their leadership. Maya had returned to work having experienced fatigue and what she considered 'burn out':

> You try to be everything to everyone and still it is not enough ... people want more from you and my tank was empty. I had nothing left to give to anyone—my kids, my family, my job. My mind and body simply gave out.

Sarah explained a large number of challenges included the assumptions made by others:

> I was like the default—it was assumed that I would do kids, sports, dinner, washing—you name it! [Husband] and I had some big chats about how this was not fair and needed to change. He was like 'sure', then after a week or two it slipped back into the old ways ... I guess I am not good at letting go ... good at leading at school, not so much at home!

Kathy shared:

> They [staff] set you up against others. I remember the first run in I had ... some of the male staff just thought they could walk all over me. Maybe because I was new, but more likely because I was a woman ... not part of the old boys club. It was a hard culture to break ... and not easy to lead a team of males who don't want to play nicely.

Kathy had found it difficult to find a partner due to the long hours she worked; she felt 'wedded to the job', with little hope of finding a partner to share her life with.

Experience of Wider Challenges

All four of the Scottish head teachers reported having experienced a range of wider challenges associated with being a woman head teacher:

> So I think probably I have got myself into a number of situations which I'd have preferred not to have been in [with line managers in local authority]. Not through trying to cause trouble, but trying to do what's right. [Louise]
> It's probably not a deliberate decision to try and make an old boy's network. But I think what had happened in school leadership is a lot of the promoted posts were held by men. And as a result, you know, I suppose they did activities together which were kind of suitable for men ... And that created a mesh network in leadership which was particularly exclusive for a female leader unless you're into these particular areas [laughs]. So I think without really thinking about it they had created a network which was exclusive. [Ann]

Three of the four English head teachers provided examples of wider challenges. Susannah reflected on previous experience of organisational culture within Further Education, which she found was male dominated and no encouragement for her to lead or recognition of her potential. By contrast, Coleen was in danger of perpetuating a culture that might disadvantage other mothers:

> I guess that's about me believing that everybody should operate at my level and that's a weakness of mine I think. [Coleen]

Two of the four Jamaican head teachers reflected on wider challenges associated with being a woman head teacher:

> I encountered information withholding, things I should be told I was not told and also some teachers were not too cooperative. For example one teacher who was the signatory to the bank account for the school failed to turn up at the end of one term to sign cheques even though arrangements were made for her to sign some cheques and she did not respond to calls and text messages I sent to her. [Sherett J]

Two of the New Zealand women had experienced wider challenges. Sarah shared:

> For me it was breaking traditions and rituals what seemed like such normal practice, but until questioned, were not even considered to be damaging, to the school, the staff, the students and to me. They [rituals] created a culture of sexism and judgment which no one deserved to be on the receiving end of.

Aroha expressed the challenges of leading in her school context, and the tensions of stepping back in her family and cultural context where women leaders were not seen 'at the front'. She described how it was difficult to embody leadership in its full sense when the cultural protocol and expectations had a significant impact on her leadership outside the school creating a tension with her leadership in school. One example was when she felt she should speak on the school Marae (cultural meeting place), but cultural protocol prevented women from doing so. This impacted on how others saw her as a leader and how 'walking in two worlds' was confusing and lacked authenticity.

DISCUSSION

This chapter began with a discussion of social justice representing a major theme within leadership policy, research and literature internationally before identifying women in educational leadership as a social justice issue. A preliminary analysis of data gathered across four contrasting Commonwealth countries supports this view. Although there were differences in the experiences of women head teachers within and across the countries, there were more similarities. Almost all of these women said they experienced headship differently from male head teachers and had been treated differently in their careers. Many examples of discrimination and additional challenges were identified. We might have hoped our findings would contrast Coleman's from 20 years ago (2002) and Bradbury and Gunter (2006) with regard to negotiating coexisting roles as professional and mother. Instead, these findings point to entrenched social and cultural traditions that prescribe gender roles and 'spill over to influence leadership behaviour in organisations' (Eagly and Johannesen-Schmidt 2001, p. 787).

Despite decades of legislation and various initiatives such as mentoring, capacity building programmes aimed at assisting women into leadership, it would appear that gender still has a significant impact on leadership opportunities for women. Left unchallenged, this could create significant limitations to encouraging young women into leadership opportunities (Yoder 2001).

In overcoming challenges, and in many cases issues of power and inequality (Shields and Mohan 2008), these head teachers had prevailed. In the main, their early career aspirations were limited; they often took up headship for pragmatic or altruistic reasons rather than seeking status or power. This reflects Curry's (2000) assertion that through socialisation, many women come to believe that leadership is unacceptable for their gender. Certainly, there were examples of these women head teachers encountering organisational cultures that significantly impacted on them (Walker and Dimmock 2002), for example, as young leaders and when returning to leadership positions from maternity leave.

CONCLUSION

Social justice leadership represents a major theme within policy, research and literature. As part of this, the resurgence of interest into the experiences and perceptions of women in educational leadership (Grogan and Shakeshaft 2011; McNamara et al. 2008; Reynolds 2002) demonstrates internationally women remain under-represented in school leadership. Reasons vary from one country to another; however, it has been suggested from previous empirical studies (Bradbury and Gunter 2006; Coleman 2002, 2003, 2005; Oplatka 2001) that family and personal roles, social, cultural, orthodox stereotypes as well as systemic and policy-based actions all contribute.

Through participating in this study, the head teachers were encouraged to reflect on their experiences. Reflection is an important part of developing a conscience of social justice, and Whyte (2001, p. 157) advocates for more focused reflection suggesting 'we must go to the roots of our abilities, a journey into the core sense of ourselves where we can put together an understanding of how we are made, why we have the responsibilities we have, and, just as important, the images that formed us in our growing'. Indeed, one important facet of educational leaders leading in socially just ways is to ensure they critically reflect and understand how their 'underlying beliefs, values, and attitudes may be counterproductive in our quest for education that is both just and excellent' (Shields 2004, p. 8).

As researchers, like Slater, Potter, Torres and Briceno (2014, p. 114), we have been struck by the similarities between diverse countries, in the experiences of the 16 head teachers, reflecting the conclusions of Norberg et al. (p. 101) that 'social justice leadership in practice, despite the national context, offers more commonalities than differences'. Indeed, the emerging findings from this study reflect the view of Bogotch (2014, p. 62) that 'Social justice as an educational practice is inclusive of all members of the world's population regardless of governmental structures, cultures, or ideologies, and it accounts for innumerable contingencies of life-influencing individual outcomes or unpredictable consequences of our actions.'

We have gained much from considerations of local manifestations of global issues, moved individually and collectively to leadership commitments that emphasise social justice (Lyman et al. 2012). However, as Shields (2004, p. 8) argues, 'commitment and good intentions are not enough'. It is hoped these case studies provide potential for cross-phase comparison (primary and secondary contexts) as well as cross-national comparison of contexts, influences, possibilities and challenges. In addition, the study wishes to explore the intersection of gender with characteristics such as ethnicity/'race' and age to consider how these impact on the shape and realities of women's leadership in the twenty-first century.

The vast majority of women head teachers in this study experienced discrimination, personal challenges and wider challenges during their journey into headship and on appointment to headship. 'Women in educational leadership' is a social justice issue. If the under-representation of women in school leadership is to be addressed, then this reality needs to be faced, further explored and acted upon both nationally and internationally.

REFERENCES

Alimo-Metcalfe, B. (1998) Are there gender and cultural differences in constructs of transformational leadership? Toward the development of a new gender-inclusive model of transformational leadership. Paper presented at the 24th International Conference of Applied Psychology, San Francisco, CA.

Arshad, R. (2012). Shaping practice: the impact of personal values and experiences. In R. Arshad, T. Wrigley, & L. Pratt (Eds.), *Social justice re-examined: dilemmas and solutions for the classroom teacher* (pp. 3–17). London: Trentham.

Barnett, B., & Stevenson, H. (2015). International perspectives in urban educational leadership: social justice leadership and high-need schools. In M. Khalifa, N. W. Arnold, A. F. Osanloo, & C. M. Grant (Eds.), *Handbook of urban school leadership* (pp. 518–531). Landham, MD: Rowman and Littlefield.

Billing, Y. D., & Alvesson, M. (2000). Questioning the notion of feminine leadership: a critical perspective on the gender labeling of leadership. *Gender, Work and Organization, 7*(3), 144–158.

Blackmore, J. (1989). Educational leadership: a feminist critique and reconstruction. In J. Smyth (Ed.), *Critical perspectives on educational leadership* (pp. 93–129). London: Falmer Press.

Blackmore, J. (2002). Troubling women: the upsides and downsides of leadership and the new managerialism. In C. Reynolds (Ed.), *Women and school leadership: international perspectives* (pp. 49–69). Albany, NY: State University of New York Press.

Blackmore, J. (2009a). Re/positioning women in educational leadership: the changing social relations and politics of gender in Australia. In H. Sobehart (Ed.), *Women leading education: across the continents* (pp. 73–83). Lanham: Rowman and Littlefield.

Blackmore, J. (2009b). International response essay, leadership for social justice: a transnational dialogue. *Journal of Research on Leadership Education, 4*(1), 1–10.

Blackmore, J. (2010). Educational organizations and gender in times of uncertainty. In M. W. Apple, S. J. Ball, & L. A. Gandin (Eds.), *Routledge international handbook of the sociology of education* (pp. 306–317). New York: Routledge.

Bogotch, I. (2008). Social justice as an educational construct. In I. Bogotch, F. Beachum, J. Blount, J. Brooks, & F. English (Eds.), *Radicalizing educational leadership: dimensions of social justice* (pp. 79–112). Rotterdam and Taipei: Sense Publishers.

Bogotch, I. (2014). Educational theory: the specific case of social justice as an educational leadership construct. In I. Bogotch & C. Shields (Eds.), *International handbook of educational leadership and social [in]justice* (Vol. 1, pp. 51–65). London: Springer.

Bogotch, I., & Shields, C. M. (2014). Introduction: do promises of social justice trump paradigms of educational leadership? In I. Bogotch & C. Shields (Eds.), *International handbook of educational leadership and social [in]justice* (Vol. 1, pp. 1–12). London: Springer.

Bradbury, L., & Gunter, H. (2006). Dialogic identities: the experiences of women who are headteachers and mothers in English primary schools. *School Leadership and Management, 26*(5), 489–504.

Brooking, K. (2003). Boards of trustees' selection practices of principals in New Zealand primary schools: will the future be females? [online] Paper presented at BERA Conference, Edinburgh, 11–13 September. http://www.google.co.uk/url?sa=t&rct=j&q=&esrc=s&source=web&cd=1&ved=0ahUKEwiRyPeh07PLAhXh7HIKHXBGBC0QFgggMAA&url=http%3A%2F%2Fwww.educationalleaders.govt.nz%2Fcontent%2Fdownload%2F1189=2F9079%2Fkeren_brooking.pdf&usg=AFQjCNFk4gd6ejagKblkyiZDYjZiIaQDzw. Accessed 9 March 2016.

Coleman, M. (2001). Achievement against the odds: the female secondary headteachers in England and Wales. *School Leadership & Management: Formerly School Organisation, 21*(1), 75–100.

Coleman, M. (2002). *Women as headteachers: striking the balance.* Oakhill: Trentham Books.

Coleman, M. (2003). Gender and the orthodoxies of leadership. *School Leadership and Management, 23*(3), 325–339.

Coleman, M. (2005). *Gender and headship in the 21st century.* Nottingham: National College for School Leadership.

Court, M. R. (1994). *Women transforming leadership.* Palmerston North, New Zealand: Massey University ERDC Press.

Court, M. (2003). Towards democratic leadership: co-principal initiatives. *International Journal of Leadership in Education, 6*(2), 161–183

Curry, B. K. (2000). *Women in power: pathways to leadership in education.* New York: Teachers College Press.

Davis, J., Hill, L., Tisdall, K., Cairns, L., & McCausland, S. (2014). *Social Justice, the Common Weal and Children and Young People in Scotland.* Edinburgh: The Jimmy Reid Foundation in association with the Institute of Education,

Community and Society and in association with the Centre for Research on Families and Relationships University of Edinburgh.

Dukes, C., & Ming, K. (2014). Who among us may be literate? Closing the gap between literacy and diversity. In I. Bogotch & C. Shields (Eds.), *International handbook of educational leadership and social [in]justice* (vol. 1, pp. 117–137). London: Springer.

Eagly, A. H., & Johnson, B. T. (1990). *Gender and leadership style: a meta-analysis.* CHIP Documents. Paper 11 [online]. http://digitalcommons. uconn.edu/chip_docs/11. Accessed 9 March 2016.

Eagly, A., & Johannesen-Schmidt, C. M. (2001). The leadership styles of women and men. *Journal of Social Issues, 57*(4), 781–797.

Fuller, K. (2010). Talking about gendered headship: how do women and men working in schools conceive and articulate notions of gender? *Journal of Educational Administration and History, 42*(4), 363–382.

Fuller, K. (2013). *Gender, identity and educational leadership.* London: Bloomsbury.

Gairín, J., & Rodriguez-Gómez, D. (2014). Leadership, educational development, and social development. In I. Bogotch & C. Shields (Eds.), *International handbook of educational leadership and social [in]justice* (vol. 2, pp. 819–843). London: Springer.

Griffiths, M. (2014). Social justice in education: joy in education and education for joy. In I. Bogotch & C. Shields (Eds.), *International handbook of educational leadership and social [in]justice* (vol. 1, pp. 233–251). London: Springer.

Grogan, M., & Shakeshaft, C. (2011). *Women and educational leadership.* San Francisco: Jossey Bass.

Hajisoteriou, C., & Angelides, P. (2014). Education policy in Cyprus: from decision-making to implementation. In I. Bogotch & C. Shields (Eds.), *International handbook of educational leadership and social [in]justice* (vol. 2, pp. 895–909). London: Springer.

Harris, E. (2014). A grid and group explanation of social justice: an example of why frameworks are helpful in social justice discourse. In I. Bogotch & C. Shields (Eds.), *International handbook of educational leadership and social (in)justice* (vol. 1, pp. 97–115). London: Springer.

Hoff, L. D., & Mitchell, N. (2008). In search of leaders: gender factors in school administrators. *Advancing Women in Leadership Journal* [online]. http:// awljournal.org/awl_wordpress/in-search-of-leaders-gender-factors-in-school-administration/ Accessed 9 March 2016.

Insana, L., Mardones, D. J., Welsh, H., & Johnston-Parsons, M. (2014). Narrative dialogue and teacher leadership for social justice: re-storying to understand. In I. Bogotch & C. Shields (Eds.), *International handbook of educational leadership and social [in] justice* (vol. 1, pp. 447–464). London: Springer.

Kezar, A., & Moriarty, D. (2000). Expanding our understanding of student leadership development: a study exploring gender and ethnic identity. *Journal of College Student Development, 41*(1), 55–69.

Lopez, A. E. (2014). Re-conceptualising teacher leadership through curriculum inquiry in pursuit of social justice: case study from the Canadian context. In I. Bogotch & C. Shields (Eds.), *International handbook of educational leadership and social [in]justice* (vol. 1, pp. 465–484). London: Springer.

Lyman, L., Strachan, J., & Lazaridou, A. (2012). *Shaping social justice leadership: insights of women educators worldwide*. Lanham, MD: Rowman and Littlefield.

McNae, R. (2010). Young women and leadership: sharing conversations to create meaningful leadership learning opportunities. *Journal of Educational Administration, 48*(6), 677–688.

McNae, R. (2014). Educational leadership for social justice: engaging relational pedagogies. In C. Branson & S. Gross (Eds.), *Handbook of ethical educational leadership* (pp. 93–111). London: Routledge.

McNamara, O., Howson, J., Gunter, H., & Fryers, A. (2008). *No job for a woman the impact of gender in school leadership*. Birmingham: NASUWT.

Mestry, R. (2014). The state's responsibility to fund basic education in public schools. In I. Bogotch & C. Shields (Eds.), *International handbook of educational leadership and social [in]justice* (vol. 2, pp. 1081–1101). London: Springer.

Miller, P. (Ed.) (2013) *School leadership in the Caribbean: perceptions, practices and paradigms*. Oxford: Symposium Books Ltd.

Mullen, C. A. (2008). Theories and applications of social justice leadership. *Teacher Development: An International Journal of Teachers' Professional Development, 12*(4), 275–278.

Muzaliwa, A. I. I., & Gardiner, M. E. (2014). Narrative inquiry (NI) as an exemplary method for social justice leadership. In I. Bogotch & C. Shields (Eds.), *International handbook of educational leadership and social [in]justice* (vol. 1, pp. 183–198). London: Springer.

Norberg, K., Arlestig, H., & Angelle, P. S. (2014). Global conversations about social justice: the Swedish-US example. *Management in Education, 28*(3), 101–105.

Oplatka, I. (2001). 'I changed my management style': the cross-gender transition of women headteachers in mid-career. *School Leadership and Management, 21*(2), 219–233.

Pace, A., & Pace, J. (2005). Gender differences in headteacher leadership and management styles: a study of a number of headteachers in Maltese secondary schools. *Journal of Maltese Education Research, 3*(1), 61–79.

Reynolds, C. (Ed.) (2002). *Women and school leadership: international perspectives*. Albany, NY: State University of New York.

Richardson, J. W., & Sauers, N. J. (2014). Social justice in India: perspectives from school leaders in diverse contexts. *Management in Education, 28*(3), 106–109.

Ryan, J. (2010). Promoting social justice in schools: principals' political strategies. *International Journal of Leadership in Education: Theory and Practice, 13*(4), 357–376.

Schmuck, P. A. (1996). Women's place in educational administration: past, present and future. In K. Leithwood, J. Chapman, D. Corson, P. Hallinger, A. Hart (Eds.), *International handbook of educational leadership and administration* (pp. 337–368). Boston: Kluwer Academic.

Shakeshaft, C. (1987). *Women in educational administration.* New York: Sage.

Shakeshaft, C., Brown, G., Irby, B. J., Grogan, M., & Ballenger, J. (2007). Increasing gender equity in educational leadership. In S. Klein (Ed.), *Handbook for achieving gender equity through education* (pp. 103–130). Mahwah, NJ: Laurence Erlbaum Associates.

Shields, C. M. (2004). Dialogic leadership for social justice: overcoming pathologies of silence. *Education Administration Quarterly, 40*(1), 109–132.

Shields, C. M., & Mohan, E. J. (2008). High-quality education for all students: putting social justice at its heart. *Teacher Development, 12*(4), 289–300.

Slater, C., Potter, I., Torres, N., & Briceno, F. (2014). Understanding social justice leadership: an international exploration of the perspectives of two school leaders in Costa Rica and England. *Management in Education, 28*(3), 110–115.

Taysum, A., & Gunter, H. (2008). A critical approach to researching social justice and school leadership in England. *Education, Citizenship and Social Justice, 3*(2), 183–199.

Torrance, D. (2013). Distributed leadership: challenging five generally held assumptions. *School Leadership and Management, 33*(4), 354–372.

Walker, A., & Dimmock, C. (2002). Educational leadership: taking account of complex global and cultural contexts. In A. Walker & C. Dimmock (Eds.), *School leadership and administration: adopting a cultural perspective* (pp. 33–44). New York: Routledge Falmer.

Whyte, D. (2001). *Crossing the unknown sea: work as a pilgrimage of identity.* New York: Riverhead Press.

Yoder, J. D. (2001). Making leadership work more effectively for women. *Journal of Social Issues, 57*(4), 815–828.

Deirdre Torrance, PhD, is Director of Teacher Education Partnerships and Director of the Masters in Educational Leadership and Management in the School of Education, University of Edinburgh, UK. Deirdre has a substantial professional background across primary, secondary and special education, as well as local government, developing important perspectives in educational leadership and leadership development. She is engaged in a number of collaborative research and writing projects. Her primary research interests include leadership preparation, school leadership and management, teacher leadership, middle leadership, distributed leadership and social justice leadership. Deirdre is lead for Scotland in the International School Leadership Development Network's (ISLDN) social justice strand.

Kay Fuller, EdD, is Associate Professor of Educational Leadership and Management at the University of Nottingham, UK. Her research interests are centred in gender in educational leadership, and she is a member of the International Women Leading Education Network. Kay is also an elected member of the British Educational Leadership, Management and Administration Society (BELMAS) and co-convenor of the Gender and Leadership Research Interest Group. She is a former English teacher, a deputy head teacher of mixed comprehensive schools, a former Initial Teacher Educator and currently leads the MA in Educational Leadership and Management at the University of Nottingham.

Rachel McNae, PhD, is Associate Professor of Educational Leadership and Director of the Centre for Educational Leadership Research at the University of Waikato, New Zealand. Rachel's research agenda is founded on a firm belief for social justice. Through numerous research projects Rachel seeks out and interrogates the relational aspects of leadership, so that leadership encounters are authentic, culturally responsive and meaningful. Rachel has developed, taught and coordinated a range of postgraduate and higher degrees in educational leadership. In 2016 Rachel received the New Zealand Educational Administration and Leadership Society (NZEALS) Meritorious Service Award and currently holds the position of NZEALS Visiting Scholar.

Carmel Roofe, PhD, is a teacher educator at the University of the West Indies, Mona, Jamaica, in the School of Education, where she currently serves as a programme leader for the Curriculum and Instruction graduate course of study. Dr Roofe has several years of experience working in the area of pre-service and in-service teacher preparation. Her research interests include issues related to teacher quality, teacher preparation, curriculum leadership, curriculum change, mentoring, and online teaching and learning. She has widely published in national and international journals in these areas. Dr Roofe is also a Vice President in the Institute of Educational Administration and Leadership, Jamaica (IEAL-J), with responsibility for outreach and public engagement.

Rowena Arshad, EdD, OBE, is Dean of the Moray House School of Education, University of Edinburgh and Co-Director of the Centre for Education for Racial Equality in Scotland, UK. Rowena began her professional life in business and banking, before moving into youth and community work. Over the past 25 years, she has served on many government committees and advisory panels in Scotland and the UK, holding the position of Equal Opportunities Commissioner for Scotland from 2001 to 2008. She received an OBE (Officer of the Order of the British Empire) in 2001 for services to race equality and an honorary doctorate in 2010 for her work on gender. Her primary research interests include equity and anti-discrimination issues and how these issues are taken forward in education (school, community education and tertiary) policy and practice. Her latest research has been on the everyday geopolitics of minority ethnic young people.

CHAPTER 3

Educational Leadership Among Women of Colour in United States, Canada, New Zealand

Elizabeth T. Murakami, Gaëtane Jean-Marie, Lorri J. Santamaría, and Ann E. Lopez

The examination of cultures of leadership across countries inspires this chapter's focus on women scholars and female school leaders of color. As scholars from different countries (who once held positions as school educators and leaders), we analyze the rationale behind our shared interest in the generation

E.T. Murakami (✉)
Texas A&M University, San Antonio, United States
e-mail: Elizabeth.Murakami@tamusa.edu

G. Jean-Marie
University of Northern Iowa, Louisville, United States
e-mail: leadwithme@gmail.com

L.J. Santamaría
University of Auckland, Symonds St, New Zealand
e-mail: l.santamaria@auckland.ac.nz

A.E. Lopez
University of Toronto, Toronto, Canada
e-mail: Ann.Lopez@UTORONTO.CA

© The Author(s) 2017   53
P. Miller (ed.), *Cultures of Educational Leadership*, Intercultural
Studies in Education, DOI 10.1057/978-1-137-58567-7_3

of knowledge about women school leaders of color. This chapter presents a two-layered examination of cross-cultural women of color as enacting leadership for social justice in scholarship and practice.

Having experienced the challenge of being students of color in diverse school contexts, we reflect on the importance of studies focusing on the knowledge, wisdom, and potential of women of color in leadership. It relates to the improvement of children, families, and communities. Later, as we joined academia, we continued this advocacy by asking: is it possible that the limited number of women *scholars* of color in academia restricts the significant knowledge reporting on the contributions of women school leaders of color?

A critical examination of women in educational leadership has been developed by scholars indicating that education is a respectable career option for women (Acker 1995; Grogan 2010). However, the research has not been explicit about supporting women of color in educational leadership positions (Blackmore 1999; Coleman 2001, 2005; Jean-Marie and Normore 2010; Krüger et al. 2005; Shakeshaft 1989). Thus, we perceive social justice as the theoretical foundation, illuminating studies of educational leadership among women of color.

Leadership for social justice is perceived as generative power, emanating from the women leaders of color breaking patterns of inequities. Perceived as distinct from self-aggrandizing and traditional great-man paradigms (Adair 1989; Crevani et al. 2007), these women's leadership may be moved by the authority given by the people they serve (Bordas 2007). Bordas exemplifies this idea when she asserted that,

> Only by becoming aware of how society is structured to perpetuate the dominance of some groups and to limit access to others, will leaders be able to create a framework for the just and equal society in which diversity can flourish. (p. 112)

We share empirical studies related to women school leaders generated by this chapter's authors and ask: How do women school leaders of color engage in advocacy and leadership for community uplift to create change in diverse contexts? And in what ways do women researchers of color connect to the experiences of their participants within the intersection of race, gender, and advancing social justice?

In this cross-country study, we draw on positive attributes from the particular ethnic, cultural, linguistic identities of women leaders advancing social justice (Santamaría and Jean-Marie 2014), recognizing the researchers as a vibrant and significant element that connects the personal and the political in research (Denzin 2003). Individually, we examined our research scholarship with examples of empirical studies developed. Using a qualitative secondary analysis (QSA) (Gladstone et al. 2007), we reveal in what ways and under which conditions cross-cultural women of color embody and enact leadership for social justice in four spaces: two in the United States (one focusing on Latina women and one focusing on African-American women), one in Canada, and one in New Zealand (focused on Māori women).

Social Justice Leadership

Social justice leadership is increasingly significant for educational scholars and practitioners (Furman 2012). The K-12 (kindergarten to secondary school) student population is becoming increasingly culturally, economically, and racially and diverse in many Western nations. As Young and López (2005) asserted, there is a need for broader frameworks aimed at understanding leadership that includes alternative theories and practices to disrupt taken-for-granted assumptions of what leadership is, what it can do, and what purposes it serves.

As scholars in the field, we examine what constitutes the nature of leadership under a social justice lens. For example, Jean-Marie et al. (2009) argue that defining social justice is not an easy task. For example, it is argued that greater equity and inclusion in policies, curricula, and school environment is needed, which may positively affect greater academic achievement for students often pushed to the margins. Furman (2012) argues that leadership for social justice is 'action-oriented and transformative, committed and persistent, inclusive and democratic, relational and caring, reflective and oriented toward socially-just pedagogy' (p. 195).

Seeking to further deconstruct and theorize what it means to engage in leadership that is socially just, we explore ways in which cross-cultural women of color embody and enact leadership for social justice from different 'leadership spaces' and contexts across countries. As scholars of color, we deconstruct 'leadership spaces', defining it as a respectful and fluid space embodying experiences, navigations, empowerment, resistance, agency, and ways of being. This 'leadership space' disrupts what Sadao (2003) called biculturalism, or the need to move between two cultures and often where women of color are forced to accommodate themselves in the dominant culture resulting in being further marginalized.

WOMEN OF COLOR ONTOLOGIES AND EPISTEMOLOGIES

We were brought together due to active research agendas related to gender and race. Early in this project we perceived that we shared culturally rich ontologies from our own experiences and a commitment to education. Through this collaboration, we generate a deeper reflection about the rationale behind our social justice research agendas. In developing this work, we realize that as women scholars of color, we are an integral part of the research. The contextual interaction with the research participants characterizes the very nature of qualitative research—which is different from hypothetical assumptions in quantitative research. Women of color ontologies and epistemologies reflect the spirit of their communities. For example, in the Latina/o community, a spirit of *Latinidad* is noticeable as reported in Latina/o critical race theory (Alemán et al. 2013; Ladson-Billings 1999; Valdes 1997; Yosso 2005). Black feminism thought in the African-American community is similarly shared in critical social theory (e.g., Collins 2000).

The generation of critical research knowledge means confronting hegemonic absolutes we have been subjected to when growing up, including patriarchy, White supremacy, and racialized or gendered spaces. From a global view, we recognize that not all societies are patriarchal. In the Tongan culture, Wolfgramm-Foliaki (2009) shared that women come from an unbroken lineage of female chiefly descendants of Pulotu, connecting Tongan mythology of life, death, immortality, and abundance (Filihia 2001). In western societies, critical inquiry challenges Eurocentric thinkers (Collins 2000) in relation to the position of women of color. Western absolutes in relation to women of color had to be revisited in order to generate new knowledge and research paradigms that are inclusive.

FEMALE SCHOLARS OF COLOR GENERATING KNOWLEDGE IN SOCIAL JUSTICE LEADERSHIP

Educational research about women leaders of color seems to be generally focused on: (1) revealing norms and social conditions that restrain the full participation of women in education (Méndez-Morse 2003; Murakami-Ramalho 2008; Shakeshaft 1989; Smulyan 2000; Tyack and Hansot 1982); (2) strengthening our understanding of women's professional roles when improving community health and well-being (Elenes and Delgado Bernal 2010; Gutierrez 1990; Yosso 2005); and (3) confirming leadership characteristics conducive to the promotion of successful academic environments (Jean-Marie and Martinez 2007; Horsford and Grosland 2013).

An example of research revealing norms and social conditions restraining the participation of women in educational leadership includes, for example, Shakeshaft's (1998) analysis of the impact of affirmative action for women in school administration. Shakeshaft as well as Tyack and Hansot (1982) revealed how a 'conspiracy of silence' is still current. They indicate that even though affirmative action had been ruled, databases continued to be silent of reporting gender- and race-specific numbers for women school leaders. These scholars indicated that in the era of high statistical reporting, such absence is not unintentional. Méndez-Morse (2003) adds to this conspiracy, indicating that even though unreported for their contributions, within school districts women leaders of color endure extra scrutiny due to race and gender. Moreover, Murakami-Ramalho (2008) indicated that even at home, women of color's career plans are devalued by spouses or family members who think they should be home tending to children and their husbands. Smulyan's (2000) observation is a stark reminder about the effects of this conspiracy of silence, when she recognized that these same women carry this silence forward by not even wanting to talk about gender issues at work.

Challenges in school and community relations for women school leaders of color include their role as cultural translator for the community needs, especially when higher administrators are removed from connecting with these families' needs (by not possessing experiences amidst the struggles of populations of color, for example). Yosso (2005) defines the importance of community cultural wealth, as 'the knowledge, skills, abilities, and contacts possessed by socially marginalized groups that often go unrecognized and unacknowledged' (p. 69). For the purpose of this cross-country study, we draw upon the lessons provided by these scholars to reflect on our research agendas.

METHODS

In her work related to communities of color, Shakeshaft (1998) argued that research is a political and ideological act. Denzin (2003) confirms this notion recognizing that studies based on critical race-consciousness strongly relates to cultural politics, often addressing troubled spaces in search for social justice. Denzin elucidated:

> Performance [auto] ethnography is the future of ethnography, and ethnography's future is the seventh moment. In the seventh moment the dividing line between [auto] ethnography and ethnography disappears. The reflexive ethnographer becomes the guiding presence in the ethnographic text. In the seventh moment critical social science comes of age and becomes a force to be reckoned with in political and cultural arenas. (p. 259)

In this chapter, we bring about performance ethnography as illuminating how as scholars, our research carries moral and political connections to world problems. We briefly share our work related to ways and conditions in which cross-cultural women of color embody and enact leadership for social justice in four contextual spaces: two in the United States, one in Canada, and one in New Zealand while providing the context for the relationship between the researcher and the researched.

In order to exemplify the empirical research we produced with this focus, we used QSA (Gladstone et al. 2007; Heaton 1998). QSA is defined as using existing data collected from prior studies to pursue a new research question or utilize alternative theoretical perspectives. While utilizing quantitative data in secondary analyses is quite common, using qualitative data across continents or countries is an emerging phenomenon (Barbour and Eley 2007; Heaton 1998; Witzel et al. 2008). Interest in the use of QSA for this current cross-country study stemmed from conversations about our similar research on women of color, leadership, and social justice which led to ongoing discussions about the knowledge of women leaders in each context especially when co-creating findings with multiple ways of knowing. We reexamined primary data (i.e., interviews, observational and field notes, documents analysis, and our own experiences doing research on women of color in diverse) to consider two new empirical questions (e.g., How do women school leaders of color engage in advocacy and leadership for community uplift to create change in diverse contexts? In what ways do women researchers of color connect to the experiences of their participants within the intersection of race, gender, and advancing social justice?). Since we were either the lead or solo researcher, we were well positioned as secondary analysts to access and reanalyze tapes, interview transcripts, and field notes from each other's research. Since published reports are available on these studies, the findings share the analysis process among the scholars as to not infringe into copyright issues.

WOMEN OF COLOR RESEARCHERS AND THEIR CONNECTION TO THE EXPERIENCES OF RESEARCH PARTICIPANTS

In this section the narratives of each woman researcher of color shares the connection between their experiences and the research they develop. Reference to their research includes the selection of participants, purpose of their studies, and brief description of their findings. We begin with scholars in the United States.

Latinas and African-American Women Leaders in the United States

Two scholars currently develop their work in the United States. The context of US research can be found most often reporting on public school districts, charter schools, and independent schools due to the immediate availability of data produced by the National Center for Education Statistics (Bitterman et al. 2013). The aforementioned report informs that in 2011–2012, 52 % of 89,810 public school principals were female. The majority of women (64 %) worked in primary schools, followed by 30 % of women working in high schools, and 40 % in combined schools (like upper school combining middle and high school, for example). The report does not disaggregate males and females in reporting race. They report that among public school principals, 80 % of the overall principals are white, 10 % were African American, and 7 % were Hispanic or Latina/o. African American and Latina/o principals are in most part serving inner-city schools where poverty and societal problems influence the work of principals.

Latina Principals in South Texas

After obtaining her doctoral degree at Michigan State University, Elizabeth Murakami immersed herself in the investigation of Latina school principals in South Texas as professor of educational leadership at Texas A&M-San Antonio. The study of Latina school leaders has been receiving attention since school administrators in Texas are overseeing 5,000,000 children in K-12 schools, of which 52 % of students are Hispanic (Texas Education Agency 2014). Reflecting on her preparation and background, she shares:

> I had the fortune of being trained with one of the strongest culturally-relevant scholars in graduate school. Under her guidance while at Michigan State University, I served in projects involving the activities of American Indian communities. This experience made me aware about a divide between traditional and evolving epistemological and ontological thought in communities conflicted by colonization. I was able to transfer this knowledge in the analysis of traditional Mexican families who inquire whether the *border crossed them,* since they have been part of this community long before settlers defined the U.S. borders.
>
> Gender studies are a relevant part of my research because I am a woman of color, but also because I have had the chance to prepare Latina school leaders. For example, in a study entitled *La reina de la casa quiere democracia: Latina executive leaders and the intersection of home and the workforce* (Murakami-Ramalho 2008), I report the increasing number of Latinas in school leadership preparation programs, who continue to have less chances of landing on a job. Cultural factors rooted in the Latina/o community expectations influence this inequality. Especially in dual-earning couples, the queen of the house, *or la reina de la casa*, no longer expects 'fairy-tale versions of life or wants to live in terms of sovereignty or subjugation. Women executive leaders want democratic participation in their homes, in the same way they are preparing students for a democratic future' (p. 199). I point to the need for an ontological renewal, transforming deficient models of inequitable cultural negotiations between dual-earning Latina/o couples, and point to a lack for recognition for women executives carrying double duties at home and at work.
>
> Having the chance to observe the power of community as influencing leadership in schools, I often take a socio-political stance in developing research. My goal is to develop robust research that other groups would be interested in reading, such as women leadership studies that male counterparts would want to read, or Latina/o research that other groups would like to learn from. Based on my training of employing community indigenous knowledge, I develop research that informs and empowers Latina/o communities, often focusing on sharing findings about school leaders that can promote the success of first-generation students. I often revisit the importance of sociopolitical consciousness and the variability of lenses within this work to inform research. Latina/o students and their families are often immersed in high-need schools, and underserved geographical areas. They are also misrepresented and unrecognized for their indigenous knowledge and roots.

Currently, with a national team of Latina/o scholars reaching out to the U.S. Midwest, East, and Southwest, we report on the success of Latina/o principals. Based on a national survey of 233 practicing Latina Principals and Assistant Principals in K-12 schools (Murakami et al. 2015), Principals in the larger study were selected based on their (a) demonstrated commitment to improving student achievement; (b) demonstrated commitment to social justice, and (c) demonstrated commitment to enhancing school-community partnerships for the Latina/o community. Using a LatCrit framework and a phenomenological research approach, the findings share the importance of one's racial identity as fueling leadership practices geared towards social justice.

One case from the data focused on gender reports on a Latina principal's professional identity (Hernandez et al. 2014). Using a phenomenological approach (Moustakas 1994), we examined motivations and actions of Latina principals as moral and social justice advocates. The participant in this case study was an exemplar—a principal who demonstrated a larger number of attributes (Murakami et al. 2015). The data collection involved two additional in-depth phenomenological interviews (beyond the survey questions). The sociocultural and historical implications of how race, class, and gender were identified in the identity of this Latina leader through: (a) growing up living and understanding students' experiences; (b) understanding the Latino family and advocating for community engagement; (c) having high expectations for students of color by creating bridges between White teachers and students of color, as well as between families of color and White teachers; and, (d) having high expectations for students and an acute awareness of discriminatory practices in education.

Research on Latina school leaders under Murakami's scholarship brought lessons related to improving the conditions of students of color. A social justice focus in her research included principals reflecting on values, beliefs, and practices and exploring how these positively influence their work with students, families, and communities.

African American Leaders in Southwestern United States

Gaetane Jean-Marie is the incoming College of Education Dean and Richard O. Jacobson Endowed Chair of Leadership in Education at the University of Northern Iowa. She graduated from University of North Carolina, Greensboro and Rutgers, The State University. Her research focuses on women and leadership in P-20 systems, leadership development and preparation in a global context, and educational equity in K-12 schools. Gaetane shares:

> My experience as a woman scholar of color (i.e., Haitian-American descent) depicts the struggle women from underrepresented communities encounter and the pervasive racist and sexist attitudes that continue to limit opportunities for women of color (Cuadraz 2010; Hune 1998; Turner 2008). Over eighteen years ago, my interest and research on women of color and leadership were influenced by my multiple roles as an administrator and adjunct faculty in higher education, and doctoral student in cultural studies and educational leadership while simultaneously pursuing a post-baccalaureate certificate in women's studies. These joint pursuits provided an opportunity to examine the intersection of race, gender and class evoked from feminist theories, critical race theory, and leadership theories.

> In my doctoral program, professors encouraged me to develop my intellectual acumen as I grappled with an 'outsider-within' status as an emerging Black female scholar (Jean-Marie 2009). Reflecting on this graduate school experiences, the more I engaged texts critically in the multiple disciplines I pursued (e.g., cultural studies, educational leadership and women's studies), I became more acutely aware of the limited research on women of color:

>> The absence of women, in particular the experiences of Black women in mainstream literature was a void I wanted to fill in the research literature. My exposure to Anna Julia Cooper, Septima Clark, and Mary Church Terrell as teacher activists working for social justice documented in the work of Collins, Giddings, Guy-Sheftall, and Hine broadened my landscapes of learning...I yearned to learn about leadership for social justice through the voices and experiences of women of color, past and present.

In the early 2000s, the culmination of my experiences as a graduate student, an adjunct faculty, and an administrator in higher education caused me to reflect on the subtlety of racism and sexism. Since completing my doctoral studies, I continued my research strand on women and educational leadership. One of my studies related to formal and informal leadership of women examined issues of diversity, race, and gender:

This study about the professional experiences (formal and informal leadership preparation; leadership and management practices; and issues of diversity, race, and gender) included 11 female high school principals (i.e., seven Caucasians, two African-Americans, one Native American, and one Lebanese-American) in one southwestern state. Three major findings in this study reported that the principals highlighted the importance of engaging in collaborative efforts that cultivated leadership for improved student learning through consensus building efforts. These efforts represented relational dimensions of leadership practices where openness and trust were fostered. Second, another common element of relationship building was their approach to leadership. Specifically, principals connected their spiritual beliefs and values as having a direct influence on how they led their schools (i.e. articulated their beliefs and spiritual commitment about furnishing help and being of service to teachers, students, and the community). Finally, the leadership styles of the principals indicated an understanding of diversity and leadership for social justice (i.e. addressing the needs of the least 'voiced' in their schools such as marginalized students, students on drugs, teen pregnancy, low SES students, students who have incarcerated parents, students who live alternative lifestyles, students who are involved with juvenile justice system, and those who are sexually abused.).

I am reminded of the metaphor, the personal is political; so my research on the interlocking systems of race, gender, and leadership resonates personally and professionally. I subscribe to what Turner (2008) postulates as the 'unfinished agenda' on women of color in higher education but also in K-12 context: (1) without adequate pools of women of color as candidates for academic [and administrative] positions, [schools], colleges and university departments lose out on the perspectives they bring to the learning process; and (2) the lack of women of color in high academic [and administrative] positions sends a message that women of color cannot succeed in these positions and, most unfortunately, that our institutions cannot benefit from their participation. (p. 231)

Jean-Marie's research showed that gender and race play a significant role in the leadership of principals. Women in her research expressed that in order to be successful as females, they needed to be assertive and have more male-like qualities than female-like qualities. While issues of gender permeated the discussion, race was also significant. There was an assumption by several women in her studies that race did not matter when it was in fact present in much of their discussion.

Black Women Leaders in Southern Ontario, Canada

Ann Lopez is assistant professor, Teaching Stream at the University of Toronto's Ontario Institute for Studies in Education. Ann was born and raised in Jamaica and later migrated to Canada and is a member of the large Jamaican and Caribbean Diaspora in Canada. Ann's experience as a secondary school administrator formed part of the catalyst for her research with school leaders and teachers in diverse contexts (Lopez 2011, 2015). Ann writes:

> I was moved to conduct research with educational leaders who work in diverse contexts to bring their voices and experiences to the center of the conversation. As a Black woman who was in leadership in secondary schools and currently in leadership at the university level, through connection with my participants I am better able to understand my own contexts, pain, struggle and celebrations. I do this work to disrupt, inform, and transform.
>
> In Canada where the population is becoming increasingly diverse, the numbers of educators of color have not kept pace with the phenomenal growth in the numbers of students of color (Ryan et al. 2007). Ethno-racial minority group members (people of color) make up over 13 % of Canada's population; by the year 2017, this number will rise to 20 %; by the year 2017, more than half of Toronto's population will be people of color (Colour of Poverty Fact Sheet 2007). By 2031, it is projected that between 25 % and 28 % of the population could be foreign born and between 20 % and 32 % of the population could belong to a visible minority group (Statistics Canada 2010).
>
> Blackmore (2006) suggests that there continues to be a lack of diverse representation in system leadership and speaks to the work that needs to be done in educational administration. While women have made tremendous strides in labor participation the proportion of women in the higher echelons of educational leadership remains a cause for concern. As a social justice educator I am challenged to think about and research ways that schools can be reimagined to meet the needs of diverse students.
>
> I was born and raised in Jamaica with a history of slavery and colonization where a small percentage of the population owns the majority of the resources. My work and research has revolved around culturally responsive practices and leadership that empower students that are marginalized and excluded from the teaching and learning process (Lopez 2011, 2014). As woman of color with an accent and different experiences and values, I often experience the challenges of navigating academic spaces and contexts while at the same time advocating for meaningful change. Like my participants I use my work to find new epistemologies and ways of knowing.
>
> My positionality in the research is not neutral as I advocate for more culturally responsive and socially just approaches to leadership that is critical. By explicating the possibilities and tensions of culturally responsive leaders, I seek to posit ways that culturally responsive leadership approaches and strategies can be implemented and practitioners supported. In many ways

I see this as creating the praxis that so many school leaders and practitioners continue to call for and answer the following question: How and why do educational leaders embark on a journey of culturally responsive leadership? What practices do culturally responsive leaders engage in and why? What challenges and tensions do culturally responsive leaders face?

In my analysis of the data, I utilized tenets of culturally responsive leadership (Beachum 2011) that calls for: a) the development of emancipatory consciousness that focuses on educators' awareness of the history and detrimental impact of societal inequities; b) equitable insights that focus on the development of attitudes that promote inclusion throughout the school community; and c) engagement in reflexive practices whereby educators critically examine the work that they do. The school leaders in the research felt that an important aspect of their role as school leaders is to advocate for marginalized students and to be purposeful in their practice. They took risks as school leaders, reached out beyond their comfort zone and contexts and challenged resistance.

The leaders of color in Lopez's research saw the community outside and inside the school as an important part of their work. Their role as leaders did not immunize them from the realities of their own multiple sites of marginalization as women leaders of color. Her research adds new insights on the importance of culturally responsive leadership and how women leaders of color can be supported to continue their work on behalf of diverse and marginalized students.

New Zealand: Māori and Non-Māori Women Leaders Working with Māori

Lorri Santamaría is associate professor of educational leadership and Head of School at the University of Auckland in New Zealand. Lorri received her PhD from the University of Arizona in the area of Bilingual and Multicultural Special Education, Rehabilitation, and School Psychology. A Spanish-born American citizen, she is African American and Oklahoma Choctaw. Lorri shared her commitment to education:

I perceive my professional work as an educational leader, educationalist, researcher, and scholar of color to be an extension and evolution of a human essentially becoming herself in a world resistant to change. The act and practice of educational leadership is not as much choice as necessity for me. There are three parts of me involved in this process: my political, social, and scientific self. These co-exist within me, have existed since I was born, and are as tightly woven together as the plaits my mother lovingly placed on my childhood head. Two lines of inquiry have emerged as a result of being trained in a research-intensive institution with academics who saw potential past my gender, skin color, first generation university student status, and low socio-economic reality.

The first research platform extended that of my Supervisors. They were gracious teachers and academics who shared the technicalities of research performativity including impeccable research design, clean data collection, objective analysis and reporting (see Santamaría 2014; Santamaría et al. 2014). Over time, my political and social selves, the ones that embody intersectionality and dynamically birth my hopes and dreams, have given rise to a second research and educational leadership platform. This iteration would not have come to be without the first. In this second space, I am free to self-decolonize, know, forget, and act upon my intentions while drawing strength from the positive aspects of my identity. In this space I enter with humility. I also enter bearing meaningful reciprocity in mind.

My educational leadership practice and scholarship comes from two distinct orientations. One is informed by the history and philosophical context of the greater world around me. The realities that power and struggle are part of restoration, reclamation and rejuvenation of something that is amiss in education today. Some call this work multicultural education; others call it social justice or culturally-responsive practices or critical leadership (Santamaría and Santamaría 2012, 2016). I call it my life.

Currently, I develop work about Māori knowledge. New Zealand (NZ) has been governed by a bicultural (Māori /British) treaty since 1840. This agreement, which ensures the health, educational and political participation and well-being of all members of society including Indigenous Māori is the countries founding document (Orange 2011). Today, Māori constitute 30 % of the NZ population but are grossly underrepresented in education and educational leadership (MoE 2010).

I developed a study of leadership practices with more than 25 Māori and non-Māori women leaders in Aotearoa where Māori-based best practices were employed to benefit systemically underserved students (e.g., children in poverty, Pasifika [i.e., Samoan, Fijian, Cook Island, Tongan] descent). This study examined applied critical leadership (ACL), a U.S. based approach to leadership where educational leaders leverage aspects of their identities to improve educational inequities (Santamaría and Santamaría 2012). This inquiry emerged from an invitation to engage research in parity with members of Te Ara Hou or The Māori Achievement Collaboratives (MACs) community. The findings aimed to challenge status quo leadership practices resulting in persistent inequitable educational outcomes for Māori learners.

I argue that when Indigenous women express leadership in Indigenous contexts, these are more pronounced and appropriate for their particular contexts (Asuga et al. 2015; Santamaría et al. 2014). Women leaders in MACs demonstrated leadership that mirrored leadership practices suggested in ACL research.

Qualitative stories from women leaders in Lorri's research provided exemplars of authentic and appropriate pathways for implementing effective socially just leadership practices while aimed at promoting whānau (family), iwi (tribal), and hapū (subtribe) engagement, context-specific pedagogy, tikanga (cultural protocols), and whanaungatanga (relationships). These findings affirmed the benefit of critical, culturally appropriate, and socially just and equitable research.

In summary, each of us found meaning in developing research validating women of color leaders in different communities around the world. Even though the communities studied were not our birthplace, the struggles and needs for those communities spoke to the mission of social justice carried. Further, we expand on the importance of developing strong correlations between scholarship and practice.

DISCUSSION

In this chapter, women leaders of color in different contexts reimagined a scholarly discourse toward social, political, and scientific rejuvenation and reclamation. We do this by looking inward and outward, realizing that the manifestation of leadership practice is irreconcilably intertwined with our social, political, and scientific identities. The individual and collective stances are on the cutting edge of scholarship in educational leadership, arguably pushing beyond what is known and practiced. At the core of these women scholars and leaders' vulnerable selves is a dynamism and energy that expertly toggles within social, scientific, and political realms. This multifaceted reality enables them to consider a future for educational leadership, promoting social justice and educational equity that is open and can reveal new possibilities.

Commonalities in this research showed that the engagement of scholars called for the same justice, by revealing instances of oppression and a need for community uplift in order to create impactful change. The shared reflections about their studies demonstrated the transformative potential to uplift a broader educational community. In conducting QSA, all the women of color in this research demonstrated agency, reflection, and determination to transform. These qualities were evident as they sought out spaces to act boldly on behalf of marginalized peoples.

The leaders' experiences in education, agency, and creativity relate to the *new materialism* referred by Dolphijn and Van Der Tuin (2012). They connect to what '*may be*' in regard to theories and practice in the present and at the same time into the unknown future. Evolving educational leadership work of this nature may be likened to the shifting theory into the future for a changing world in response to known crises without fully understanding which practices are optimal for addressing challenges in the present (Anderson 2009). *New Materialists* suggest that the kind of educational leadership the scholars featured involves "a movement of becoming 'more and becoming other,' which comprises the orientation to the creation of the new, to an unknown future, what is no longer recognizable in terms of the present" (p. 7).

The leadership practices featured here invokes a distinct, fertile, and rejuvenating space wherein leaders' most vulnerable selves evolve and reside. Figure 3.1 illustrates relationships between each author's social, political, and scientific self. It is important to understand the emergence of this kind of leadership as a valid, substantiated, and untapped infinite human resource.

The scholars' personal accounts and research revealed the manner and conditions under which cross-cultural women of color embodied and enacted

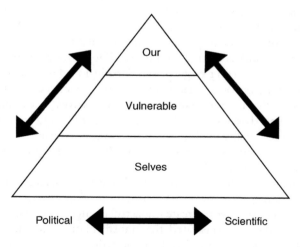

Fig. 3.1   Relationship aspects of social, political and scientific to scholars' selves

leadership for social justice in the United States, Canada, and New Zealand. Regardless of international geographic location and individual ethnic, linguistic, or cultural identity, the scholars engaged in theoretical frameworks that were intricately and purposefully tied to notions of improving conditions for systemically underserved learners. Collectively, the scholars offered evidence of the following aspects regarding their leadership worthy of further research:

- Research and leadership practices engaged on culturally responsive and socially just ideas
- Critical and moral imperatives in research
- Disparities and inequities as persistent in moral and ethical crises in education
- Shared belief that educational crises are prone to individual resolve
- Leaders and scholars are contributing players in the resolve of educational leadership challenges and issues
- Perceived diversity as opportunity
- Leadership practice and scholarship challenge existing educational leadership theoretical and practice canons
- Scholars' ontologies, epistemologies, and research methods among women of color ensure they are not replicating or upholding status quo practices.

The authors highlight community uplift to create change in diverse contexts in a myriad of different ways, depending on the specific context. There is no silver bullet or a one-size-fits-all approach. The scholars were original and culturally appropriate in documenting ways of working, while being consistent in their quests for social justice. They each connected to their participants' experiences by tapping into positive aspects of their identities. These scholars are continuously forging new territory in the social, political, and scientific areas of educational leadership. They model and reflect on their constituents' challenges and tensions. These women of color's unique and generative dual processes provide fuel for future educational fires in every corner of the world.

REFERENCES

Acker, S. (1995). Carry on caring: the work of women teachers. *British Journal of Sociology, 16,* 21–36.
Adair, J. E. (1989). *Great leaders.* Guildford, England: Talbot Adair Press.

Alemán, E. J., Delgado Bernal, D., & Mendoza, S. (2013). Critical race methodological tensions: Nepantla in our community-based praxis. In M. Lynn & A. Dixson (Eds.), *Handbook of critical race theory in education* (pp. 325–338). New York: Routledge.

Anderson, G. (2009). *Advocacy leadership: toward a post-reform agenda in education*. New York: Routledge Madison.

Asuga, G., Eacott, S., & Scevak, J. (2015). School leadership preparation and development in Kenya: evaluating performance impact and return on leadership development investment. *International Journal of Educational Management, 29*(3), 355–367.

Barbour, R.S., & Eley, S. (Eds.) (2007). Refereed special section: reusing qualitative data. *Sociological Research Online. 12*(3). http://www.socresonline.org.uk/12/3/contents.html. Accessed 30 June 2016.

Beachum, F. (2011). Culturally relevant leadership for complex 21st century school contexts. In F. English (Ed.), *The Sage handbook of educational leadership* (4th ed, pp. 27–35), Thousand Oaks, CA: Sage.

Bitterman, A., Goldring, R., & Gray, L. (2013). Characteristics of public and private elementary and secondary school principals in the United States: results from the 2011–12 schools and staffing survey (NCES 2013-313), U.S. Department of Education. Washington, DC: National Center for Education Statistics. http://nces.ed.gov/pubsearch. Retrieved 12 January 2016.

Blackmore, J. (1999). *Troubling women: feminism, leadership and educational change*. Buckingham, UK: Open University Press

Blackmore, J. (2006). Social justice and the study and practice of leadership in education: A feminist history. *Journal of Educational Administration and History, 38*(2), 185–200.

Bordas, J. (2007). *Salsa, soul and spirit: leadership for a multicultural age*. Oakland, CA: Berrett-Koehler Publishers.

Coleman, M. (2001). Achievement against the odds: the female secondary headteachers in England and Wales. *School Leadership and Management, 21*(1), 75–100.

Coleman, M. (2005). Gender and secondary school leadership. *International Studies in Educational Administration, 33*(2), 3–20.

Collins, P. H. (2000). *Black feminist thought: knowledge, consciousness, and the politics of empowerment*. New York: Routledge.

Colour of Poverty Fact Sheet. (2007). Understanding the racialization of poverty in Ontario. http://www.learningandviolence.net/lrnteach/material/PovertyFactSheets-aug07.pdf. Accessed 13 June 2016.

Connelly, F. M., & Clandinin, D. J. (2006). Narrative inquiry. In J. L. Green, G. Camilli, & P. Elmore (Eds.), *Handbook of complementary methods in education research* (3rd edn., pp. 477–487). Mahwah, NJ: Erlbaum.

Crevani, L., Lindgren, M., & Packendorff, J. (2007). Shared leadership: a post-heroic perspective on leadership as a collective construction. *International Journal of Leadership Studies*, 3(1), 40–67.

Cuadraz, G. H. (2010). From 'Shattering the silences to the politics of purpose: reflections on the culture of the academy. In R. G. Johnson III & G. L. A. Harris (Eds.), *Women of color in leadership: taking their rightful place* (pp. 176–195). San Diego, CA: Birkdale Publishers.

Denzin, N. K. (2003). Performing [auto]ethnography politically. *The Journal of Education Pedagogy and Cultural Studies*, 25(3), 257–278.

Dolphijn, R., & Van Der Tuin, I. (2012). New materialism: interview s and cartographies. Open access download from the University of Utrecht at Downloads/ Dolphijn%20and%20van%20der%20Tuin-%20New%20Materialism.pdf. Accessed 26 March 2016.

Elenes, C. A., & Delgado Bernal, D. (2010). Latina/o education and the reciprocal relationship between theory and practice: Four theories informed by the experiential knowledge of marginalized communities. In E. G. Murrillo, S. A. Villenas, R. T. Galván, J. S. Muñoz, C. Martínez, & M. Machado-Casas (Eds.), *Handbook of Latinos and Education: Theory, Research, & Practice* (pp. 63–89). New York: Routledge.

Filihia, M. (2001). Men are from MaAma, women are from Pulotu: female status in Tongan society. *The Journal of the Polynesian Society*, 110(4), 337–390.

Furman, G. (2012). Social justice leadership as praxis: developing capacities through preparation programs. *Educational Administration Quarterly*, 48(2), 191–229.

Gladstone, B. M., Volpe, T., & Boydell, K. M. (2007). Issues encountered in a qualitative secondary analysis of help-seeking in the prodrome to psychosis. *Journal of Behavioral Health Service Research*, 34(4), 431–442.

Grogan, M. (2010). Women around the world reshaping leadership for education. *Journal of Educational Administration*, 48(6), 782–786.

Gutierrez, L. (1990). Working with women of color: an empowerment perspective. *Social Work*, 90(2), 149–153.

Heaton, J. (1998). Secondary analysis of qualitative data. *Social Research Update*. No. 22, University of Surrey.

Hernandez, F., Murakami, E., & Quijada-Cerecer, P. (2014). A Latina principal leading for social justice: The influences of racial and gender identity. *Journal of School Leadership*, 24, 568–598.

Horsford, S. D., & Grosland, T. (2013). Badges of inferiority: the racialization of achievement in U.S. education. In M. Lynn & A. Dixson (Eds.) *The handbook of critical race theory in education* (pp. 153–166). New York: Routledge.

Hune, S. 1998, Asian Pacific American Women in higher education: claiming visibility and voice. A Report written for The Association of American

Colleges and Universities Program on the Status and Education of Women. Washington, DC: Association of American Colleges and Universities.

Jean-Marie, G. (2009). 'Fire in the belly': igniting a social justice discourse in learning environments of leadership preparation. In A. Tooms & C. Boske (Eds.), *Building bridges, connecting educational leadership and social justice to improve schools* (pp. 97–119). Book series: Educational Leadership for Social Justice. North Carolina: Information Age Publishing.

Jean-Marie, G., & Martinez, A. (2007). Race, gender, & leadership: perspectives of female secondary leaders. In S. M. Nielsen & M. S. Plakhotnik (Eds.), *Proceedings of the sixth annual college of education research conference: urban and international education section* (pp. 43–48). Miami: Florida International University. http://coeweb.fiu.edu/research_conference/. Accessed 20 December 2015.

Jean-Marie, G., & Normore, A. H. (2010). The impact of relational leadership, social justice, and spirituality among female secondary school leaders. *International Journal of Urban Educational Leadership*, 4(1), 22–43.

Jean-Marie, G., Normore, A. H., & Brooks, J. (2009). Leadership for social justice: preparing 21st century school leaders for a new social order. *Journal of Research on Leadership and Education*, 4(1), 1–31.

Krüger, M. L., Van Eck, E., & Vermeulen, A. (2005). Why principals leave: risk factors for premature departure in the Netherlands compared for women and men. *School Leadership and Management*, 25(3), 241–261.

Ladson-Billings, G. (1999). Just what is critical race theory, and what's it doing in a nice field like education? In L. Parker, D. Dehyl, & S. Villenas (Eds.), *Race is… race isn't* (pp. 7–30). Boulder, CO: Westview Press.

Lopez, A. E. (2011). Culturally relevant pedagogy and critical literacy in diverse English classrooms: case study of a secondary English teacher's activism and agency. *English Teaching: Practice and Critique*, 10(4), 75–93.

Lopez, A. E. (2014). Reconceptualising teacher leadership through curriculum inquiry in pursuit of social justice: case study from the Canadian context. In I. Bogotch & C. Shields (Eds.), *International handbook of educational leadership and social (In)justice* (pp. 465–484). New York, NY: Springer.

Lopez, A. E. (2015). Navigating cultural borders in diverse contexts: building capacity through culturally responsive leadership and critical praxis. *Multicultural Education Review*, 7(3), 171–184. Doi: 10.1080/2005615X.2015.1072080.

Méndez-Morse, S. (2003). Chicana feminism and educational leadership. In M. Young and L. Skrla (Eds.), *Reconsidering feminist perspectives in educational leadership* (pp. 162–177). New York, NY: SUNY Press.

Méndez-Morse, S., Murakami, E., Byrne-Jimenez, M., & Hernandez, F. (2015). Mujeres in the office: Latina school leaders. *Journal of Latinos and Education*, 14(3), 171–187, doi: 10.1080/15348431.2014.973566.

Moustakas, C. (1994). *Phenomenological research methods.* Thousand Oaks, CA: Sage.

Murakami-Ramalho, E. (2008). La reina de la casa quiere democracia: Latina executive leaders and the intersection of home and the workforce. In D. M. Beaty, W. H. Sherman, A. J. Muñoz, S. J. Mills, & A. M. Pankake (Eds.), *Women as school executives: celebrating diversity* (pp. 192–202). Austin, TX: The Texas Council of Women School Executives.

Murakami, E., Hernandez, F., Mendez-Morse, S., & Byrne-Jimenez, M. (2015). Latina/o school principals: Identity, leadership, and advocacy. *International Journal of Leadership in Education: Theory and Practice.* http://www.tandfonline.com/doi/abs/10.1080/13603124.2015.1025854. Doi: 10.1080/13603124.2015.102585. Accessed 14 June 2016.

MoE (Ministry of Education). (2010). Tu rangatira: Māori medium educational leadership. http://www.educational-leaders.govt.nz/Leadership-development. Retrieved 1 January 2016.

Orange, C. (2011). *The treaty of Waitangi.* Wellington, New Zealand: Bridget Williams Books.

Ryan, J., Pollock, K., & Antonelli, F. (2007). Teacher and administrator diversity in Canada: Leaky pipelines, bottlenecks and glass ceilings. Paper presented the annual conference of the Society for the Study of Education, Saskatoon. http://home.oise.utoronto.ca/~jryan/pub_files/Art.April09.numbers.pdf. Accessed 18 January 2016.

Sadao, K. (2003). Living in two worlds: success and the bicultural faculty of color. *Review of Higher Education, 26,* 397–418.

Santamaría, L. J. (2014). Critical change for the greater good: multicultural dimensions of educational leadership toward social justice and educational equity. *Education Administration Quarterly (EAQ), 50*(3), 347–391, doi: 10.1177/0013161X13505287.

Santamaría, L. J., & Jean-Marie, G. (2014). Cross-cultural dimensions of applied, critical, and transformational leadership: women principals advancing social justice and educational equity. *Cambridge Journal of Education, 44*(3), 333–360.

Santamaría, L. J., Jean-Marie, G., & Grant, C. O. (Eds.) (2014). *Cross cultural women scholars in academe: intergenerational voices.* New York: Routledge.

Santamaría, L. J., & Santamaría, A. P. (Eds.) (2012). *Applied critical leadership: choosing change.* New York: Routledge.

Santamaría, L. J., & Santamaría, A. P. (2016). *Culturally responsive leadership in higher education: praxis promoting access, equity and improvement.* New York: Routledge.

Shakeshaft, C. (1998). Wild patience and bad fit: assessing the impact of affirmative action on women in school administration. *Educational Researcher, 27*(9), 10–12.

Shakeshaft, C. (1989). *Women in educational administration*. Newbury Park, CA: Corwin Press.

Smulyan, L. (2000). Feminist cases of nonfeminist subjects: case studies of women principals. *Qualitative Studies in Education, 13*(6), 589–609.

Statistics Canada. (2010). Ethnic diversity and immigration. http://www41.stat can.gc.ca/2009/30000/cybac30000_000-eng.htm. Accessed 20 June 2016.

Texas Education Agency. (2014). Texas academic performance report. https://rptsvr1.tea.texas.gov/perfreport/tapr/2015/state.pdf. Accessed 20 January 2015.

Turner, C. S. (2008), Women of color in academe: experiences of the often invisible. In J. Glazer-Raymo (Ed.), *Unfinished agendas: new and continuing gender challenges in higher education* (pp. 230–252). Baltimore, MD: The John Hopkins University Press.

Tyack, D., & Hansot, E. (1982). *Managers of virtue: public school leadership in America, 1820–1980*. New York: Basic Books.

Valdes, F. (1997). LatCrit Consciousness, community, and theory. *California Law Review*. No. 1087, 1093–1094.

Witzel, A, Medjedović, I, & Kretzer, S. (2008). Secondary analysis of qualitative data /Sekundäranalyse qualitativer Daten. *Historical Social Research, 33*(3), 10–32.

Wolfgramm-Foliaki, E. A. (2009, December 3–6). *Pikipiki hama kae vaevae a manava-*. Paper presented at SIU'ALAIMOANA: Voyaging through the oceans of Tongan theories and practices, San Francisco, CA: Berkely University.

Young, M., & López, G. (2005). The nature of inquiry in educational leadership. In F. English (Ed.), *The SAGE handbook of educational leadership: advances in theory, research, and practice* (pp. 337–362). Thousand Oaks, CA: SAGE.

Yosso, T. (2005). Whose culture has capital? A critical race theory discussion of community cultural wealth. *Race, Ethnicity and Education, 8*(1), 69–91.

Elizabeth T. Murakami, PhD, is a professor and director of programmes in Educational Leadership in the College of Education and Human Development at Texas A&M University, San Antonio, USA. She holds her Master's and PhD from Michigan State University, USA. Her research focuses on successful school leadership and social justice at both national and international levels, including research on leadership dynamics and identity, gender, race and the academic success of Latin@ populations from P-20 to advanced professions in education. She has published in prestigious journals such as *Journal of School Leadership, Educational Management Administration and Leadership, Journal of School Administration, Academe, Journal of Studies in Higher Education* and *International Journal of Qualitative Studies in Education*. Her latest co-edited books are *Brown-Eyed Leaders of the Sun: A Portrait of Latina/o Educational leaders* (IAP, 2016) and *Abriendo puertas, cerrando heridas: Latinas/os Finding Work-Life Balance in Academia* (IAP, 2015).

Gaëtane Jean-Marie, PhD, is Dean of the College of Education and Richard O. Jacobson Endowed Chair of Leadership in Education at the University of Northern Iowa, USA. Prior to that, she was chair and professor of educational leadership in the Department of Educational Leadership, Evaluation, and Organizational Development at the University of Louisville, USA. Her research focuses on women and leadership in P-20 system, leadership development and preparation in a global context, and educational equity in K-12 schools. To date, she has over 80 publications which include books, book chapters, and academic articles in peer-reviewed journals. She is the editor of the *Journal of School Leadership* and serves on the editorial board. She is also a reviewer for several journals. She is a former president of the Leadership for Social Justice AERA/SIG and co-founder of Advancing Women of Color in the Academy (AWOCA), an international scholarly network of women of colour.

Lorri J. Santamaría, PhD, is an associate professor and Head of School in the Faculty of Education and Social Work at the University of Auckland, New Zealand. Her research interests include transmuting diversity as resource as well as culturally responsive and sustainable educational, leadership and research practices. These are reflected in selected publications: *Culturally Responsive Leadership in Higher Education: Praxis Promoting Access, Equity and Improvement* (Routledge Books, 2016); "Counteracting Racism with Applied Critical Leadership: Culturally Responsive Practices Promoting Sustainable Change" in *International Journal Multicultural Education* (2015); "Culturally Responsive Leadership in Cross-Cultural International Contexts" in *Cross-Cultural Collaboration and Leadership in Modern Organizations* (IGI Global, 2015); and "Critical Change for the Greater Good: Multicultural Dimensions of Educational Leadership Toward Social Justice and Educational Equity" in *Education Administration Quarterly* (2014).

Ann E. Lopez, PhD, is a faculty member in the Department of Leadership, Higher and Adult Education, Ontario Institute for Studies in Education, University of Toronto, Canada. Over the last 23 years Ann has held several positions in public education in Canada. She is a former secondary teacher and school administrator, and most recently was the Academic Director of Initial Teacher Education at the University of Toronto. Ann's research and teaching focus on culturally responsive leadership in diverse contexts, equity and diversity in teacher education. Recently, she was elected President-Elect of the National Association for Multicultural Education, USA.

CHAPTER 4

A Comparative Analysis of Intersections of Gender and Race Among Black Female School Leaders in South Africa, United Kingdom and the United States

Pontso Moorosi, Kay Fuller, and Elizabeth C. Reilly

INTRODUCTION

The underrepresentation of women in educational leadership is a long-standing problem, which has received attention for over four decades globally (Shakeshaft 1987; Blackmore 1999; Coleman 2002; Moorosi 2010; Fuller 2013). Although feminist in character many of the earlier studies focused largely on white middle-class women, whose experiences do not represent the majority of women. As a result, black women's experiences of subjugation and

P. Moorosi (✉)
University of Warwick, Warwick, United Kingdom
e-mail: P.C.Moorosi@warwick.ac.uk

K. Fuller
University of Nottingham, Nottingham, United Kingdom
e-mail: Kay.Fuller@nottingham.ac.uk

E.C. Reilly
Loyola Marymount University, San Antonio, United States
e-mail: elizabeth.reilly@lmu.edu

© The Author(s) 2017
P. Miller (ed.), *Cultures of Educational Leadership*, Intercultural
Studies in Education, DOI 10.1057/978-1-137-58567-7_4

success have remained on the periphery even in contexts where they are in the majority. This omission of black female leadership narratives 'along with an adequate analysis of the contexts in which leadership has worked, limits our ability to develop ways to improve schools and communities for children who live in poverty and children of color' (Murtadha and Watts 2005, p. 591). Intersectionality theory (see Crenshaw 1991), therefore, helps address this gap by focusing on the ignored experiences of black women in leadership and how their gender and blackness influence those experiences. As Essed (1991) claimed, despite their attainment of leadership positions, black women continue to struggle against 'gendered racism'. This is even more significant in contexts that have the historical baggage of racism and colonialism, such as the United States with its legacy of slavery and racial segregation; the United Kingdom with its legacy of colonialism and contemporary racism; and South Africa as a victim of colonialism and later plagued by apartheid.

Discrimination against women in leadership is well noted in the South African context and despite policy intervention (Moorosi 2010) women continue to be underrepresented and marginalized and face challenges when they are hired in positions of leadership (Schmidt and Mestry 2014). More studies in South Africa are increasingly showing black women principals' experiences in schools that suffer from multiple deprivations (Faulkner 2015; Lumby 2015), highlighting not only the gendered constraints, but the inherent complexities of colonialism and racism that make the lives of black women principals even more difficult. In England, women in general make up 37% of secondary head teachers in state secondary schools and black minority ethnic women below 4% (DfE 2015). To date, bespoke training programmes (Campbell-Stephens 2009; Johnson and Campbell-Stephens 2010, 2013; Ogunbawo 2012) have not secured black women's proportionate representation in headship or in teaching as a profession. Indeed, black women head teachers in England have recounted their experiences of discrimination (Brady 2014), unfair dismissal (Barling 2011), bullying and isolation (Grant 2015). The United States pioneered the research in women in educational leadership (e.g. Schmuck 1980; Shakeshaft 1981) and continued to interrogate issues of discrimination including the conceptualisation of intersectionality (Crenshaw 1991; Collins 2000) at the realization of the neglect of black women's experiences. Although a great deal of work has gone into the subject, and some significant achievements have been made, recent work (Newcomb and Niemeyer 2015) shows African American women's continued disproportionate representation in school leadership and struggle in marginalized and deprived communities. The sense we make from these studies is that black women are still underrepresented and discriminated against and this discrimination can be 'subtle and nuanced or blatant and harsh' (Schmidt and Mestry 2014, p. 8).

The political commitment to changing this position of women is therefore universal. From a research point of view, our approach is to adopt multiple conceptions of feminism that enable the interrogation of the multi-layered experiences of women in leadership in globalized multicultural societies. This perspective reflects women's own personal experiences of subjugation as shaped by the interaction of multiple identities, including gender and race. In this regard, we find Crenshaw's (1991) conception of 'intersectionality' that explains the interaction of gender and race a helpful lens in providing an understanding of the pervasive disproportionate representation and discrimination of black women in leadership positions. But more significantly, it helps us understand how women across different cultures negotiate multiple oppressive behaviours to become successful leaders. A cross-cultural comparative analysis is therefore not only timely, but long overdue, given the complexity of the phenomenon. Since Crenshaw's study (1991), many have used 'intersectionality' to explain women's experiences in leadership; however, such studies have largely focused on small context-specific case studies (Richardson and Loubier 2008; Jean-Marie et al. 2009; Schmidt and Mestry 2014) that do not offer much for cross-cultural understanding.

In this chapter we examine the experiences of three black women school leaders in the three different contexts (England, South Africa and the United States), thereby creating an opportunity for cross-cultural comparative analysis. The aim is to understand how women leaders achieve success against complex multiple oppressions and how these experiences impact on headship in different contexts. We address, in particular, the question of what has led to black women's success in achieving school leadership as constructed from their gendered and raced life experiences. After this brief introduction we present a methodological overview, which is followed by an analysis of the three women's stories followed by comparative discussion and conclusions.

METHODOLOGY

This study was designed as a collaborative initiative that consists of different national studies of successful female school leaders. To facilitate sampling, success was defined as the achievement of top leadership positions (e.g. school principalship/headship) within the school context. Using a life-history methodology, the black women leaders were interviewed using a set of topics that informed the interviews, but also allowed some flexibility to follow up interesting unexpected contextual patterns that enhance the data on women leaders' experiences. Our aim was to contribute to knowledge on cross-cultural understandings of intersectional leadership by recognizing the uniqueness of each national study in our comparative analysis.

The three countries involved in the study are England, South Africa and the United States, chosen purely on the basis of the different research collaborators' locations or interests. We were aware of the vast differences in geographical, economic, socio-political and cultural terms amongst the three selected countries, but such comparative analysis as premised on a shared legacy of contemporary racism in the post-colonial and post-apartheid eras, was deemed necessary and long overdue. This scholarship is believed to advance black women's ways of knowing and has significant implications for policy in the respective contexts. We acknowledge further, the differences in the conception of 'blackness' in the countries participating; black is African in the South African context; black and global majority/black and minority ethnicity (BGM/BME) in England; and African American in the United States. We provide the flexibility for these differences to accommodate Blackness as used and understood in the particular contexts.

Further, we acknowledge the 'problematic' nature of our own positions as researchers. Firstly, all authors are university-based researchers, and none of us share any form of commonality with the practitioner experiences of the black women in our study. Secondly, whilst all authors are women, two of them are white women whose racial background and profile bears no similarity to those of the participants. We are grateful that the women shared their stories with us, and whilst we established familiarity and rapport with these women, we would not want to take their accommodation of our outsider status for granted. We hope we have been sensitive to our participants. At least one of us engaged in self-disclosure in an effort to answer spoken and unspoken questions from interviewees that implied the desire to know 'Who are you?' and 'Why should I talk to you?' (Dunbar et al. 2002). By way of analysis, interviews were transcribed and each transcript coded with emerging themes. Each of the three stories was written up using pseudonyms in reporting on the stories of the women principals, but their stories remain actual constructions of what they shared with us. Each researcher followed the ethical approval protocols of their own institution.

ENGLAND: 'THE TRIPLE WHAMMY'—YOUNG, FEMALE AND BLACK

Nicola was a first-generation black British woman of Caribbean heritage. In her late 30s, married and with a child of school-going age, she was leading a mixed secondary school in an urban setting. Eighty percent of the school population was of BGM/BME heritage. Fifty percent of children spoke English as an additional language and only 20 % claimed Free School Meals. The stigma associated with claiming state benefits meant levels of disadvantage were probably higher than that suggested.

Nicola described 'the triple whammy' of her identity in being young, female and black. The intersection of 'race', sex and age, as well as a working-class family background, was multiple sites of oppression that played out as racism and sexism by way of unconscious bias, prejudice based on stereotypes, and overt and covert discrimination. She was 'a very lonely figure' at head teacher meetings. Determined to express her opinion she noticed people 'shifting' when she spoke, suggesting 'maybe I shouldn't really be speaking, but that won't ever stop me'. Nicola's identity as a black female head teacher is 'self-defined and self-determining within intersecting oppressions' (Collins 2000, p. 273).

Nicola achieved headship against the odds (Coleman 2001). She was one of a small number of head teachers of ethnic minority heritage making up 4 % of women secondary head teachers in England (DfE 2015). Nicola's parents emigrated from the Caribbean in the late 1950s or early 1960s. Her older siblings experienced racist attitudes from children and teachers in a white working-class area. Nicola was removed from her first primary school because teachers' expectations were too low (see Rollock et al. 2015 for a discussion of black, middle-class experiences of education). At 9 or 10 years old, a Jewish female teacher, Nicola's advocate, enabled her to teach a lesson about apartheid. Later, during a time of unrest, her secondary school was closed for the day due to a march by the British National Party (a far-right political party). Nicola left school as one of 13 pupils gaining five good General Certificate of Secondary Education passes (GCSE). She decided to attend college away from non-aspirational influences. These college years were a time of conscientization (Freire 1970) when she 'locksed' her hair wanting,

> to feel happy in my own skin and that's part of me being a Black female and I don't have to conform to ideas about what my hair is [laughter] and how that translates to me and so I'm going to own that.

- Post 1—*Newly qualified teacher* in *School 1* in urban setting
- Post 2—*African-Caribbean support teacher* in non-metropolitan district (1 term)
- Post 3—Returned to *School 1* in urban setting (3–4 years)
- Post 4—*School Improvement Officer* for ethnic minority achievement (Local Authority) (2 years)
- Post 5—Residency via Future Leaders' Trust and *Assistant Headteacher* in *School 2* in urban setting (80% BGM/BME pupils) (3 years)
- *Career gap*—Child and parent care (18 months)
- Post 6—*Vice Principal* in *School 3* in non-metropolitan district (initially in special measures and raised attainment from 33% to 45% of children gaining 5 A*-C GCSE grades) (1 year)
- Post 7—*Deputy Headteacher* in current *School 4* (2 years)
- Post 8—*Headteacher* in current *School 4* (1 year ongoing)

Fig. 4.1 Nicola's career pathway

Higher Education continued the process of identity formation with 'me emerging and knowing what I really wanted from my life'.

Despite deciding to teach at a very young age, Nicola's career pathway was non-linear (see Fig. 4.1).

It demonstrates her commitment to working with BGM/BME pupils. Nicola encountered a number of barriers such as working in a local authority where the values 'did not meet mine in any way, shape or form'; a selection process at which she was asked (by a white, male governor) how she would take care of her child; and refusal (by a white, male head teacher) of a request to reduce her hours so she could balance family commitments with work. In each case, Nicola exercised agency. In her own mind, she dismissed the interview question about childcare as 'ridiculous'. The refusal of part-time hours was turned to,

> Well if you're not going to allow me to, I'm going to take control of it. I'm not going to allow you to have that power. So if you're saying 'no' I can't go to four days, I'm not going to allow you to make me work five days [laughs] when I don't want to work five days because actually I have family who I need to deal with right now and that's more important to me. And therefore I'm just going to take time out and I'm going to make the best of taking my time out.

Despite setbacks, Nicola constructed her career pathway as 'being incredibly lucky'. Senior leaders had mentored her; one black woman planted the idea of headship helping her to imagine herself into the post (see Fuller

2015). Nicola agreed that her positive mind-set and exercise of agency had been influential. Her critical consciousness ensured values of justice and equality were at the forefront of her leadership. Language, policies, structures and practices were questioned with respect to fairness, openness and helping others by breaking down barriers. Nicola was concerned about the acquisition of privilege through her words and actions, 'If we do this for this person, how can I justify it in my own conscience that it's okay to not do it for somebody else?'

Everyday racism occurred in the professional setting at meetings (described previously) and in dialogue with some staff. Following a white male, middle-aged head teacher Nicola identified herself, 'I've got the triple-whammy, you know, I'm young and I'm female and I'm Black'. The microaggressions of racism (Delgado and Stefanic 2001) were present in non-verbal expression or 'shifting'. One illustration was a white, middle-aged man's disagreement with Nicola's decision on a personal matter. She reported the conversation,

> You're really annoyed with me. You've gone and spoken to other members of staff about it before you've actually come back to me and spoken to me about it. I don't really think that's fair. You haven't given me an opportunity to right that with you and I think you've been actually really quite selfish in your behaviour.

This was not necessarily typical,

> he's older, white male and I think that can sometimes be difficult for some. Not all, because there are other members of staff who seem to rub along with me really well from all kinds of backgrounds: same faith, no faith, different faith.

Nicola constructed her embodiment of diversity (see Ahmed 2009) as disconcerting for those whose bodies are privileged in leadership as white and male. She was acutely aware of disrupting leadership 'embodiment in gendered and raced forms and its emotional evocations [that] are often not confronted' (Christie and Limerick 2004, p. 3).

South Africa: Always Aware of Blackness

Molly was a grandmother, a mother and a wife in her early 60s and about to retire. She grew up in the Northern Cape province in the heart of apartheid South Africa, brought up by her maternal grandparents who originally came from Lesotho. As a child she would frequently visit her paternal grand-parents in Botswana and she remembers fondly how her maternal grand-mother would always ask them to go and 'wash their mouths' (so they could speak proper Sesotho) because she did not want to be confused by the mixture of Setswana and Sesotho as two closely related languages. Growing up in a predominantly Afrikaans-speaking community in the Northern Cape, Molly's outlook to life has been shaped immensely by her exposure to this 'mosaic' of cultures and languages—she was fluent in four languages at a very young age. Although she grew up during the times of Bantu Education (which meant that black people received an inferior quality of education) in the middle of apartheid South Africa, she was educated within a private Catholic education school run by German nuns. Her other great influence was, therefore, the Catholic values of discipline, hard work and responsibility, as well as those of caring and respect instilled from home. She became an ambassador and travelled all over South Africa representing her school. She said, 'I thank God for the sisters because they made us strong. . . we were not stopped from saying our minds giving our opinions and taking decisions.' And that has been Molly's way of leading: she is assertive, hard-working and an absolute perfectionist.

Growing up in the heart of apartheid South Africa, Molly was always aware and conscious of her blackness. She had to contend with racist and other prejudiced attitudes, albeit to varying degrees. As a child of the migrant labour system, her mother worked for a white family as a domestic helper and so she practically grew up with the white children from that family. However, due to the laws of the land at the time that did not allow mixed-race interactions, their intercommunication was confined to the yard. When they met outside the yard they behaved like strangers. She acknowledges that it only made sense much later in life, but her father would spend nights in the police van for no apparent reason or come back home because he forgot a 'pass'.

Molly's first career love was medicine, which she could not do in South Africa due to apartheid laws. Although the nuns had made arrangements for her to study in Germany, it would mean leaving South Africa illegally and she would not be able to come back. Her family, and most particu-larly, her then ailing father could not deal with that prospect. After staying home for 2 years, she ended up in a teacher training college, where she qualified as a maths and science teacher. Her hard work and good results earned her first promotion into principalship in a secondary school during her eighth year of teaching.

Although Molly achieved her first headship very early in her teaching career, her experiences were not free from prejudice. She, however, considered herself very fortunate to have had the opportunity to become a principal at such a young age. Her first headship was in a rural community where people in the area had never had a woman as a principal, let alone a young, small-statured woman in her late 20s. Molly had to relocate to this community to follow her husband who was working in the area. This part of her story resonates with other women's lives both in the West and in the Global South as seen in Coleman's (2002) work. However, her lack of initial acceptance placed her in the same category as many of the women of her time in South Africa (see Moorosi 2010) and elsewhere. She stated that the local chief of the area was very angry that the Department of Education was 'not serious' to be sending such a 'young girl' to their area as a school principal. In the whole area, which had 20 high schools it was only herself and a Catholic nun who were women principals of high schools. Molly recounted 'life was not easy in the man's world'. She was viewed as a 'distraction'—'the old men I found in the field looked at me suspiciously and because of cultural values, I found it difficult to approach them when they had made a mistake'. Others would tell her outright that they did not want to be 'led by a small girl'. Molly acknowledged she was very lean—'I looked (to them) like a small girl who doesn't know what she is doing. So I had to work double to please these people'. And that is exactly what she did—worked extra hard to earn her acceptance in that community, by ensuring improved school performance through a great deal of parental and community involvement.

As a school teacher and later a school leader working in rural areas that were predominantly black minimized her exposure to racist experiences, even though as a norm the system limited her chances of getting employment elsewhere. It was only when she moved to the bigger town to upgrade her studies in a former homeland with no apartheid rules that she experienced being treated as an outsider, not on racial grounds, but because she was from 'the farms', which was regarded a lower form of social existence. Molly says coming from rural areas, people were always 'suspicious' of her for being the 'other' person, and she struggled to even get a teaching post after many years of experience as a school principal. This however did not put her off, with a new university degree, she started from the beginning and at the time of the interview, Molly was in her third headship leading a large urban secondary school in a socially deprived area devastated by substance abuse in a largely black mono-ethnic area. She fully acknowledged the challenges of heading a low socio-economic status school with less educated parents. But Molly's strategy was to get parents involved in education one way or another. For her, 'where there are children, books and parents, I don't have a problem'.

AFRICAN AMERICAN: SURROUNDED BY GOOD COMPANY

Kay is an African American woman who served as elementary principal (grades K-8) in a large urban school system in the greater Los Angeles region of California. Noteworthy is that the Los Angeles area is home to the second largest school system in the United States. The demographics of the district in which the principal worked included 75 % of the children eligible for free or reduced lunch, which indicates a high poverty community, and 62 % of the children having a non-English-speaking background. Over 79 % of the children identified as Latino and 19 % as black or African American. Certificated staff (teachers and administrators) were 45 % African American, 26 % Latino, 10 % Asian and 10 % White. Kay was between the age of 40 and 50 years old and had served in her role for over 10 years.

Kay described herself as a foster child whose mother was unfit to care for her and her brother due to drug abuse/misuse. Her father was incarcerated for many years in the California State prison system. In early elementary school, a foster family took in Kay and her brother and subsequently adopted them. She attended high poverty schools throughout Southern California but noted that even with the disruption of losing her mother and moving into foster care, it did not affect her drive to excel in school or her accomplishments. Kay, who considered her adopted family to be the one with whom she is most close, maintained relationships with her birth mother and father (who was no longer incarcerated). She took pride in the fact that she was the first in her biological and adopted family to earn a bachelor's degree, then a master's degree and finally a doctoral degree.

One individual, who influenced Kay's early childhood and led to her reflections on her work as an educational leader, was her first grade teacher, Mrs Crawford (a pseudonym), who influenced her profoundly through her caring from when Kay was only 6 years old:

> She understood some things about my mother and she helped me to understand that excuses were barriers. If I would show up to class without my homework at all, she'd say, 'Where is it?' She wanted to have a conversation with me because she knew there was a story. [I told her] my

mother wasn't there, she came home late, she was with her boyfriend, and I think she was smoking something that made her act funny. She'd say, 'What does that have to do with you? I asked you to do the homework. I didn't ask your mother. You're my student; she is not'.

These formative, recurring conversations with Mrs. Crawford helped Kay to cultivate, out-of-the-box thinking—looking for alternatives—because that is what she began teaching her. She said, 'So, I carry that with me in my career. When things are tough at work, I know how to surround myself with, in the words of my mother, good company.'

As a woman principal, Kay experienced attitudes from her colleagues that she believed were not experienced by men. In advocating for maintenance or repairs at her school, for example, staff would say,

'What does the princess want for her school?' and I often wonder when male principals ask for something, do the staff say, 'What does the little prince want?' Why is it that I am not being viewed just as an advocate for kids or as a principal who is continually looking for opportunities to improve the instructional programs at her school?

Whilst Kay reflected that she should probably have challenged their behaviour and characterization of her, she said that to this point she had used humour to deflect the comments.

Kay believed that being a woman had a positive impact on her leadership as she served as a role model for girls and women. Kay offered, 'I am the only professional woman my students see. We've evolved from nurses and teachers, nannies and housekeepers. It's important that girls see us in positions of power.' She described principally the differential treatment she experienced in terms of what was an acceptable leadership style for women versus men and the way assertiveness is viewed. To some degree, the staff's views were incongruent: laissez-faire women principals were considered weak but assertive principals who advocated for their schools were behaving in a manner that suggested they were entitled.

As an African American woman, Kay's story suggested the history of slavery in the United States and subsequent and ongoing racism has had a pervasive impact on black women's ability to lead—and that to this day no form of national reconciliation with and widespread healing from the past has happened with African Americans. This leads to what she characterized as a generational curse. She specifically identified that to her surprise,

African American women in the school system have been the greatest detractors. Whilst she also was quick to say that many African American women have served as guides and mentors, she was categorical in her view that her greatest detractors are those who are most similar to her in gender and race. 'It felt like the mission of Black women was to see me fail. Not Latinos, Whites, Black men, Filipinos, Blacks from Africa—but African American women,' Kay reported. Kay further explained,

> When one African American woman sees another who is self-confident, courageous, and believes in herself, she does not see it as motivated and so on, but instead she thinks I believe I am better than she is.

She sees this as an attempt to destroy and diminish, akin to the use of fear, psychological abuse and class differences amongst slaves (e.g. house slaves versus field slaves) that led to the lack of self-esteem amongst slaves.

DISCUSSION

Early Influences

Growing up on three continents, Nicola, Molly and Kay were raised under very different socio-economic and political circumstances. With entirely different familial experiences, some commonality was shared in how these experiences shaped the type of women leaders that they became. Their stories explain the sources of their courage, values and inspiration (Adler 2008) deeply rooted in their cultural and familial histories and that become the early influences of leadership. Adler (2008) classifies these early influences in three categories: historical, cultural and societal.

Nicola's immigrant parents had little formal education themselves but valued education to the point of educating all their children and ensuring teachers' expectations of Nicola were sufficiently high. Their immigrant experiences subjected them to a great deal of 'racism' and 'unrest' and Nicola's sense of being 'first generation British' conscientized her to social justice and equality. Nicola's critical consciousness ensured she led with values of justice and equality. The work of the school was questioned with respect to fairness and openness. She sought to help other black women and girls by breaking down barriers. However, Nicola was also concerned about the acquisition of privilege her words and actions enabled. That is the type of leader Nicola has become, one influenced strongly by virtues of social justice and equality. Her close-knit familial ties suggest a strong sense of community and it is perhaps not surprising that she views successful leadership in terms of teamwork.

Although Molly's parents were also not educated, the influence she got from her mother and grandparents was particularly powerful. As a child of the migrant labour system descending from grandparents who landed in South Africa for economic reasons, she used the richness of her diverse cultural background to her advantage. These experiences made her an adaptable and assertive woman leader who would land on her feet after being thrown in the deep end of rural patriarchy. Her assertiveness and hard-working nature stem strongly from the values instilled at school by her 'colonial' school, which carried her and influenced greatly the type of woman leader she became. Her early exposure to racism through white friends who would become strangers in the street, parents who would be arrested for no apparent reason, conditioned her to difference and she became alert. Molly says, rejection in the rural village and in the city did not scare her. It made her resilient. She had her own 'black box' that she opened when things got difficult.

Even with great deprivation through her early years, and little parental oversight, Kay believed that were it not for the experience of poverty and severely dysfunctional parents, she would not have embraced at such an early age and with such clarity that a different and better life were hers to choose. She chose a life different from her parents, to break down the barriers of structural inequalities, and embraced different ways of understanding and responding to her situation as presented to her by her teacher.

The role of school in shaping Kay's and the other two women's leadership is significant. Whilst Kay's greatest early influences trace to a caring teacher and foster mother who adopted her, Nicola's inspiration also came from a teacher who enabled her to teach about apartheid, whilst Molly's greatest influence also stemmed from her interaction with the nuns and their values of hard work, responsibility and discipline.

Thus, common to the three women is how they cite the influence of those formative years on who they are as leaders today. The opportunity to move beyond the small world of their birth to the broader universe of the perspectives of caring parents, grandparents and teachers paved the way for the possibility to imagine, to dream and to realize who they could become. What is apparent from these stories is that significant, formative events early on impelled them to seek lives of service to children who have also been deprived. They worked in poor areas, affected by various social ills and with children mostly from less privileged backgrounds. Could this be what possibly inspired them to be good leaders? The women display strong resilience to all challenges that come their way and persistence to confront obstacles. Not only have they broken the generational curse, but they strive to ensure that their charges likewise have a choice of paths on the journey. The three women understand their roots and how these have shaped who they are as women and as leaders. Indeed as Adler (2008, p. 13) says, 'the more clearly we understand the roots of our identity and humanity, the more able we will be to use our strengths and core values to achieve the vision we have for ourselves and the world around us': these women are rooted in their history and culture.

Resistance, Agency and Strength

What also becomes evident in the stories of these three women is their construction of powerful enactments of resistance, agency and strength. Each found ways to resist the hegemonic discourse of white, male leadership and female sabotage by continuing to speak up in public, by doing leadership, by engaging in dialogue or by ignoring as ridiculous their experiences of overtly discriminatory attitudes. By crossing boundaries, including breaking out of the powerful structures of inequalities such as poverty, racism and sexism, to succeed in education and by breaking out of the powerful discriminatory attitudes in education to succeed in educational leadership these women demonstrated their exercise of agency. The stories are of powerful women who self-define and self-determine. Mirza (1997, p. 270) frames their success in the system(s) as 'subversive and transformative'. It should not be read as 'colluding with the mainstream' but as 'collectively opening up transformative possibilities for their community' by 'the power of education to transform and change the hegemonic discourse' (Mirza 1997, p. 276). Further analysis of these stories and others is likely to shed light on how they might have 'evolved a strategic rationalization which has its own logic, values and codes' (Mirza 1997, p. 276).

CONCLUSION

Whilst we framed and limited the study to gender and race intersections, other intersecting aspects of identity (such as age, class, ethnicity, culture) emerged, suggesting the need to open up parameters of the intersectional analysis. We were, however, satisfied with the level of analysis and although we are cautious in our conclusion given the size of our sample of the narrative research, we do suggest that there is merit in looking to make these stories uniquely contextual as well as cross-culturally shared. As this sample is presently small and the issues have not been sufficiently explored, we caution against drawing any broad conclusions regarding, for example, what Kay reports as internal sabotage from fellow African American women in the United States; the sabotage from fellow African American women requires much more work to expand the number of voices of African American women who share their stories and are courageous enough to examine its relationship to slavery and racism in the United States. In the same vein, we treat with caution Molly's and Nicola's simultaneous interplay of multiple identities that include age, culture, ethnicity and class and their relationship to colonialism, apartheid and contemporary racism. We acknowledge that in these three contexts, the role of gender and race in leadership is exceedingly complex and needs to be understood within the context of other identities. Whilst the role of family in shaping identities has been established in previous research, the role school plays may need close interrogation in all three contexts.

REFERENCES

Adler, N. (2008). I am my mother's daughter: early developmental influences on leadership. *European Journal of International Management, 2*(1), 6–21.

Ahmed, S. (2009). Embodying diversity: problems and paradoxes for Black feminists. *Race Ethnicity and Education, 12*(1), 41–52.

Barling, K. (2011, December 23). Headteacher of London faith school wins dismissal case. *BBC London News.* http://www.bbc.co.uk/news/uk-england-16322994. Accessed 21 January 2016.

Blackmore, J. (1999). *Troubling women: feminism, leadership and educational change.* Buckingham: Open University Press.

Brady, P. (2014, April 6). Headteachers reveal their struggle. *The Voice* [online]. http://www.voice-online.co.uk/article/headteachers-reveal-their-struggle. Accessed 21 January 2016.

Bush, T., Glover, D., Sood, K., & Cardno, C. (2006). Black and minority ethnic leaders in England: a portrait. *School Leadership and Management, 26*(3), 289–305.

Campbell-Stephens, R. (2009). Investing in diversity: Changing the face (and heart) of educational leadership. *School Leadership and Management, 29*(3), 321–331.

Christie, P., & Limerick, B. (2004). Editorial overview. *Discourse: Studies in the Cultural Politics of Education, 25*(1), 3–6.

Coleman, M. (2001). Achievement against the odds: the female secondary headteachers in England and Wales. *School Leadership and Management, 21*(1), 75–100.

Coleman, M. (2002). *Women as headteachers: striking the balance.* Stoke on Trent: Trentham Books.

Coleman, M., & Campbell-Stevens, R. (2010). Perceptions of career progress: the experience of Black and minority ethnic school leaders. *School Leadership and Management, 30*(1), 35–49.

Collins, P. H. (2000). *Black feminist thought* (2nd edn). New York: Routledge.

Crenshaw, K. (1991). Mapping the margins: intersectionality, identity politics, and violence against women of color. *Stanford Law Review, 43*(6), 1241–1299.

Delgado, R., & Stefanic, J. (2001). *Critical race theory: an introduction.* New York: New York University Press.

Department for Education. (2014) Talent management: developing new leaders in schools. https://www.gov.uk/guidance/talent-management-developing-new-leaders-in-schools. Accessed 21 January 2016.

Department for Education. (2015) School workforce in England: November 2014. https://www.gov.uk/government/statistics/school-workforce-in-eng land-november-2014. Accessed 4 January 2016.

Dunbar, C., Rodriguez, D., & Parker, L. (2002). Race, subjectivity, and the interview process. In J. Gubrium & J. Holstein (Eds.), *Handbook of interview research* (pp. 279–298). Thousand Oaks, CA: Sage.

Essed, P. (1991). *Understanding everyday racism: an interdisciplinary theory.* Newbury Park, CA: Sage.

Faulkner, C. (2015). Women's experiences of principalship in two South Africa high schools in multiply deprived rural areas: a life history approach. *Educational Management Administration & Leadership, 43*(3), 418–432.

Freire, P. (1970). Cultural action and conscientization. *Harvard Educational Review, 40*(3), 452–477.

Fuller, K. (2013). *Gender, identity and educational leadership.* London: Bloomsbury.

Fuller, K. (2015). Headteacher preparation: an account of one woman headteacher's supportive practices. In K. Fuller & J. Harford (Eds.), *Gender and leadership: women achieving against the odds* (pp. 115–146). Oxford: Peter Lang.

Garner, R. (2015, April 5). Headteachers urged to recruit more black and ethnic minority teachers. *Independent* [online]. http://www.independent.co.uk/news/education/education-news/headteachers-urged-to-recruit-more-black-and-ethnic-minority-teachers-10157044.html. Accessed 21 January 2016.

Grant, V. (2015, February 3). Isolation, stress and tears...the truth about being a headteacher. *The Guardian.* http://www.theguardian.com/education/2015/feb/03/headteacher-how-deal-with-stress-isolation-tips. Accessed 21 January 2016.

Jean-Marie, G., Williams, V. A., & Sherman, S. L. (2009). Black women's leadership experiences: examining the intersectionality of race and gender. *Advances in Developing Human Resources, 11*(5), 562–581.

Johnson, L., & Campbell-Stephens, R. (2010). Investing in diversity in London schools: leadership preparation for Black and global majority educators. *Urban Education, 45*(6), 840–870.

Johnson, L., & Campbell-Stephens, R. (2013). Developing the next generation of black and global majority leaders for London schools. *Journal of Educational Administration, 51*(1), 24–39.

Lumby, J. (2015). Leading schools in communities of multiple deprivation: women principals in South African. *Educational Management Administration & Leadership, 43*(3), 400–417.

Mirza, H. (Ed.) (1997). Black women in education: a collective movement for social change. In *Black British feminism*. London: Routledge.

Moorosi, P. (2010). South African female principals' career paths: understanding the gender gap in secondary school management. *Educational Management Administration and Leadership, 38*(5), 547–562.

Murtadha, K., & Watts, D. M. (2005). Linking the struggle for education and social justice: historical perspectives of African American leadership in schools. *Educational Administration Quarterly, 41*, 591–608.

McKenley, J., & Gordon, G. (2002). *Challenge plus: the experience of Black and Minority Ethnic school leaders.* Nottingham: National College for School Leadership.

McNamara, O., Howson, J., Gunter, H., & Fryers, A. (2009). *The leadership aspirations and careers of Black and minority ethnic teachers.* Birmingham: NASUWT.

Newcomb, W. S., & Niemeyer, A. (2015). African American women principals: heeding the call to serve as conduits for transforming urban school communities. *International Journal of Qualitative Studies in Education, 28*(7), 786–799.

National Union of Teachers. (2002). Black and minority ethnic teachers in senior management: an NUT survey: pushed to prove themselves more. teachers.org. uk/files/nut-survey.sg_.doc Accessed 21 January 2016.

Ogunbawo, D. (2012). Developing Black and minority ethnic leaders: the case for customized programmes. *Educational Management Administration and Leadership, 40*(2), 158–174.

Richardson, A., & Loubier, C. (2008). Intersectionality and leadership. *International Journal of Leadership Studies, 3*(2), 142–161.

Rollock, N., Gillborn, D., Vincent, C., & Ball, S. (2015). *The colour of class.* Abingdon: Routledge.

Schmidt, M., & Mestry, R. (2014). South African principalship, agency and intersectionality theory. *Comparative and International Education/Éducation Comparée et Internationale, 43*(1), 6.

Schmuck, P. (1980). *Sex equity in educational leadership: the Oregon story.* Newton, MA: Education Development Corporation.

Shakeshaft, C. (1981). Women in educational administration: a descriptive analysis of dissertation research and paradigm for future research. In P. Schmuck, W.

Charters, & R. Carlson (Eds.), *Educational policy and management: sex differentials.* New York: Academic Press.

Shakeshaft, C. (1987). *Women in educational administration.* Newbury Park, CA: Sage.

Welham, H. (2015, March 15). Self-esteem is key to improving diversity among UK headteachers. *The Guardian* [online]. http://www.theguardian.com/teacher-network/2015/mar/15/diversity-gap-headteachers-schools. Accessed 21 January 2016.

Pontso Moorosi, PhD, is Associate Professor of Educational Leadership and Management at the Centre for Education Studies, University of Warwick, UK. She has formerly taught at universities in South Africa, Canada and England. She has served on the editorial board of *Educational Management Administration & Leadership* and currently serves on the Agenda Feminist Media's editorial board. Her areas of research interests are gender in educational leadership and educational leadership development. She is leading on the cross-cultural intersections of gender and race in educational leadership (in England, South Africa and the United States) on which the chapter in this book is based.

Kay Fuller, EdD, is Associate Professor of Educational Leadership and Management at the University of Nottingham, UK. Her research interests are centred in gender in educational leadership, and she is a member of the International Women Leading Education Network. Kay is also an elected member of the British Educational Leadership, Management and Administration Society (BELMAS) and co-convenor of the Gender and Leadership Research Interest Group. She is a former English teacher, a deputy head teacher of mixed comprehensive schools, a former Initial Teacher Educator and currently leads the MA in Educational Leadership and Management at the University of Nottingham.

Elizabeth C. Reilly, PhD, is Professor and Department Chair of Educational Leadership in the School of Education, Loyola Marymount University, Los Angeles, California, USA. In the years preceding her appointments in higher education, Dr Reilly served as a classroom teacher and educational leader in K-12 school districts. A recognized international scholar investigating women in educational leadership, with graduate students and fellow scholars, she presents and researches globally on leadership, organizational culture and change, and women in leadership. She works with leaders of multinationals, government, non-governmental organizations and education on five continents.

CHAPTER 5

The Challenge of Leadership: Ethnicity and Gender Among School Leaders in England, Malaysia and Pakistan

Victoria Showunmi and Maria Kaparou

INTRODUCTION

Do you know how many people walk into my school after four years and go to my secretary or one of the PAs to be the head teacher? People turn up at my door and actually walk away or assume I am the secretary.... (African Caribbean Leader 1)

Leadership, as a contested notion within the 'male dominated hierarchy of schools' (Blackmore 1999, p. 2), may be conceptualised differently within and across countries. The discrepancy in leadership discourses may be linked to the way leadership is shaped by contextualised experiences and policy agendas. As Coleman (2003, p. 37) argues, 'Leadership is a very "gendered" concept [while] in a wide variety of cultural contexts, leadership continues to

V. Showunmi (✉)
UCL Institute of Education, 20 Bedford Way, London, United Kingdom
e-mail: V.Showunmi@ioe.ac.uk

M. Kaparou
University of Southampton, Southampton, United Kingdom
e-mail: M.Kaparou@soton.ac.uk

© The Author(s) 2017
P. Miller (ed.), *Cultures of Educational Leadership*, Intercultural Studies in Education, DOI 10.1057/978-1-137-58567-7_5

95

be identified with the male.' However, theoretical and empirical studies on women's leadership in the field of education have been predominantly evident in the literature of English-speaking countries—the United Kingdom (e.g. Coleman 2001, 2007), the United States (e.g. Shakeshaft 1987), Australia (e.g. Blackmore 1999, 2006) and New Zealand (e.g. Strachan 1999)—where the knowledge base reflects practices within English-speaking cultural contexts. Attention to how this area has been contextually conceptualised in South Africa (e.g. Bush and Moloi 2006; Moorosi 2010), Asia (e.g. Morriss et al. 1999; Shah 2010) and European countries (e.g. Kaparou and Bush 2007) is not commensurate with the importance of inclusion of women in leadership positions. Although black and minority ethnic women hold leadership positions in professional organisations (e.g. schools, higher education institutions, government, business), little attention has been paid to the experiences of women—other than middle- or upper-class white females—in leadership positions (Collins 2000), exceptions being the seminal works of Sobehart (2009), Lyman, Strachan and Lazaridou (2012) and Reilly and Bauer (2015), which portray multiple accounts of women performing leadership roles in the continents of the world.

The current study provides a valuable contribution to the contemporary debates about intersectionality and leadership by exploring, through narrative inquiries, the leadership experiences of women from black and other ethnic minority groups in England and Malaysia and Muslim women principals in Pakistan, in order to:

- shed light on their experiences and provide nuanced understandings of their leadership career path and the challenges they encounter;
- examine whether and how ethnicity and gender influence women's leadership practices.

Despite the progress which has been made in theoretical postcolonial literature, research about women from black and other ethnic minority and religious groups may remain partially 'theoretically erased' (Crenshaw, 1989: 58) since it may be unevenly researched and spread. Therefore, the findings of this empirical study offer an insight into how gender and race influence women's career paths and leadership practices, whilst contributing to the growing literature and theories of identity and leadership at schools in different international contexts.

This chapter has woven together the stories related to the leadership experiences of nine women principals from Muslim, black and other ethnic minority groups, working in the Anglophone and non-Anglophone world. In the literature review, we present a theoretical and empirical review derived from international scholars' work in leadership and intersectionality, whilst the next section sets the methodological context of this comparative study. The analysis of the findings is presented as narratives drawn from different contexts. A discussion of empirical literature is integrated in the section in order to provide an understanding of participants' reality in the researched countries and the wider world. In the next section, findings are interwoven to develop an understanding of the subject of research in three different contexts. The conclusion presents an overview of the discussions in this chapter, and offers recommendations for future research, policy and practice.

Literature Review

In reviewing the theoretical and empirical literature related to leadership and intersectionality, this section establishes the knowledge base underpinning the research purpose, with a particular focus on gender, ethnicity and leadership within different cultures.

The Conceptual Basis of the Study

The conceptual framework that informs this research is based on the study of leadership in education, intersectionality and the role of societal culture in leadership enactment. As Dimmock and Walker (2002, pp. 70–71) argue, '[Culture] exerts a considerable influence on how and why school leaders think and act as they do.' Despite the debate regarding the concepts underpinning management and leadership (e.g. Bush 2008) and the contested conceptualisations of leadership (e.g. Collinson and Collinson 2005), the discussion in this chapter is grounded in educational leadership as an organisational activity which 'initiate[s] change', whilst management is linked with 'maintaining efficiently and effectively current organizational arrangements' (Cuban 1988, p. xx). The principal's role is multidimensional and remains an important lever for determining school improvement (e.g. Robinson et al. 2008) whilst Kaparou and Bush (2015) study also echoes Hallinger's (2003) view that 'a leadership perspective on the role of the principal does not diminish the principal's managerial roles'. A conceptualisation of leadership as a notion which 'remains white, middle-class, heterosexual and male' (Blackmore 1999, p. 6) has reinforced Showunmi et al.'s (Showunmi et al. 2015) argument that 'traditionally, leadership theory [...] suppressed and neutralised "difference", including considerations of how gender and race/ethnic dimensions may impact leadership (Parker, 2005)'.

The Relationship of Leadership, Gender and Race

'Issues of identity have been examined in relation to intersectionalities of difference, such as "race", class and gender' (Bhopal and Danaher 2013, p. 21), whilst the examination of identity requires an understanding of the notion of culture and ethnicity. The term intersectionality is often attributed to Kimberlé Crenshaw (1991), who drew attention to the invisibility of black women's experiences in research that privileged white women's voices in gender studies and black men's voices in race studies. Since then, researchers have adopted intersectionality as a useful lens for considering how multiple identity dimensions such as religion, sexual orientation, social class and nationality influence women's experiences across the globe (e.g. Essers and Benschop 2009; Hite 2007). One of the most commonly critiqued aspects of Islam is the status and the role of Muslim women, which is a target of multiple contending positions and politicised discourses. 'Popular discourses contradict the emphasis on human equality texts and contextual-based practices from different Muslim societies are used as evidence to support the claim that Islam is in conflict with liberal thought and equal rights, particularly with regard to gender' (Shah 2016, p. 67).

Evidence from the international literature on gender and education (e.g. Blackmore 2006; Coleman 2001) has predominantly focused on the under-representation of women in leadership positions, as women may be perceived as 'outsiders', given that leadership has been identified with men (Moorosi 2010; Schein 2001). The discourse about gender and leadership also highlights the overt and covert barriers to their progress (Coleman 2007; Kaparou and Bush 2007), whilst there are common internal and external barriers that lead to their marginalisation in their careers (Shakeshaft 1981).

The experience and tension that white women face in leadership positions has been widely documented (Collins 2000). Whilst some progress has been made in relation to examining the leadership of black and other ethnic minority women, there remains work to be done to achieve true gender equality at the very top of organisations, given the recognised 'covert' gender discrimination and the implications of 'double jeopardy' for black women in leadership positions (Jean-Marie et al. 2009). Showunmi et al. (2015) showed the interplay of identities within the leadership experiences of a diverse group of women leaders—CEOs, business owners, local politicians, senior public sector workers—in private and public organisations.

Much of the literature on gender and leadership has focused on the extent to which gender differences exist in leadership styles. The increased appreciation of stereotypically feminine attributes in leadership (collaboration, cooperation, mentoring) suggests an increased value in women's role in leadership, and an 'easier' acceptance of the privilege accorded to women in these positions (Ely and Meyerson 2000). Some styles of leadership (e.g. feminist or transformational leadership) may be more advantageous to women. Lyman et al. (2012, p. 169) state that 'transformation and transformative leadership are often mentioned in the literature on advancing social justice outcomes'. Batliwala (2011) confirms that the 'transformational nature of feminist leadership undermines power inequalities, as its agenda is political and is used to fight injustice and oppression whenever it results from discrimination due to people's gender, race, ethnicity, class and/or privilege'. Feminist leaders will collectively and individually 'transform themselves to use their power resources, strength and skills to mobilise others around a shared agenda of social, cultural, economic and political transformation for equality and the realisation of human rights for all' (Gray and Schubert 2016, p. 114). In this chapter, feminist leadership is described as leadership that focuses not only on expanding access but also on changing and interrupting the formal and informal rules and norms which are at the heart of discrimination globally.

METHODOLOGY

Given the exploratory nature of this study—exploring women's leadership experiences in schools and the challenges that occur in relation to intersectionality—the interpretivist paradigm is prominent in the methodology as it is appropriate for the understanding of different 'socially constructed realities' (Blaikie 2000, p. 25), which are influenced by participants' experiences and values. Women principals' stories and experiences of identity and leadership were explored through narrative inquiry. Riessman (2008) explains that, although narratives as stories have been linked with human beings since time immemorial, the development of narrative as a way of inquiry seems to be a relatively new phenomenon. It follows a constructivist approach to social research which posits that an individual's experience of the social world is constructed through social interaction and that researching it should consider not just the individual but also the socio-cultural milieu within which it happens. Interviews were undertaken in three different countries over a 6-month period (2014–2015).

Nine participants, aged between 25 and 60, came from a culturally diverse group of women with 5–34 years of work experience within the education sector. The six women in England comprised two African-Caribbean, one African, two South Asian and one who identifies as BME (black minority ethnic), whilst the one principal in Malaysia had a Chinese background and the two Pakistani participants were Muslims of South Asian ethnicity.

Throughout this chapter the term BME is used to describe the African, African-Caribbean or South Asian women that participated in the research.

More specifically, for the data collected in England, the research participants were approached through the Race for Opportunity (RfO) Champion Network, which funded the research in this country. Thirty participants were recruited through snowball sampling, having heard about the study through friends or colleagues. We followed a non-probability sampling strategy for the Malaysian and Pakistani participants, using convenience sampling (Robson 2009), owing to the difficulty in accessing potential research participants in these contexts. We do recognise the limitations of this sampling strategy, mainly in relation to a non-representative sample, but the research benefitted from a targeted convenience sample which was readily accessible to participate in the research.

Semi-structured interviews gave an opportunity to the research participants to provide insights into their subjective interpretation (Ribbins 2007) of leadership enactment at their schools. The interview guides comprised a set of open questions based on the areas of theoretical interest. Specifically, participants were asked questions around three key areas: (1) their personal definitions of leadership, (2) the relationship between their social identities (gender/minority-ethnic/cultural/religious) and identities as leaders and (3) their career journey into leadership, including when they first saw themselves as leaders, and factors that may have hindered this journey.

This research adhered to all the ethical guidelines laid down by a university in England, including the voluntary nature of participation and treating interview responses as confidential, and followed the British Educational Research Association guidance (BERA 2011). The two researchers alone have access to this data and it will be securely stored for 6 years.

Analysis

Data-derived from the analysis of narratives- were analysed themati-
cally, as the researchers sought to make explicit the structures and
meanings the participants embodied in their responses (Gooty et al.
2009). Coding and analysis were conducted in an iterative, constant
comparative process (Neck et al. 1999). During analysis, both authors
adopted intersectional sensibilities (Crenshaw 1991). This meant noti-
cing when and how gender and ethnic identities became salient in
respondents' experiences of leadership. The final stage of data analysis
was to synthesise the data derived from each country and create themes
reflecting homogeneity and heterogeneity, and then compare and contrast data from the narrative inquiries of women educational leaders in
three different contexts.

The next section synthesises the evidence from women leaders' narratives, whilst empirical literature is integrated in the discussion. We present
the stories of women principals in depth in order to theorise about their
experiences in education.

FINDINGS AND DISCUSSION

The findings are presented in the context of England, Malaysia and
Pakistan. The United Kingdom consists of England, Wales, Scotland and
Northern Ireland. The United Kingdom is ethnically diverse, partly from
the legacy of the British Empire. Malaysia, which was subject to the British
Empire, is a multi-ethnic country comprising Malays (defined as Muslims
in the constitution) and non-Malays (Chinese minority and Tamils).
Pakistan is an Islamic country where Islam is practised by the majority of
Pakistanis and governs the country's personal, political, economic and
legal lives.

Narratives drawn from England

In this chapter, data are drawn from six school principals' narratives which
form part of a larger study of 130 women practitioners in the state and
private sectors in London. The women from England, as previously
described, had been or were currently principals of a primary or secondary
school. Both of the African-Caribbean women were in their second leadership position. Each of the women had achieved the required national

standard for headship. The two South Asian women leaders were born outside the country and arrived in England when they were in primary school. The woman who identified as BME and the two African-Caribbean women were born and schooled in the United Kingdom. The African woman leader was not born in the United Kingdom.

The participants' experience as a leader in a school ranged from 3 to 12 years. The women were not asked about their personal lives; however, three of the women mentioned that they had received support from their families whilst becoming leaders. The other three discussed and were thankful for the acknowledgement from the community and their network of friends.

The women that took part in the study spoke about leading diverse groups of women and how that influenced what they saw as leadership. Interestingly, some of the BME women in the wider study were reluctant to define themselves as leaders and referred to the Western concept of leadership to assist them in denying that they were leaders. The Asian leader 2 had a clear understanding of what she considered leadership to be:

> I think 'leadership' [means] you have to lead people and management is managing systems and that's the way I have simplified it for myself. Trying to manage people is a total different concept than trying to lead people. Leadership is hard to define but you know when you have got it right.

Challenges in Asserting One's Position as a Leader from a Minority Background

All of the women interviewed identified challenges that they faced on their journey to becoming a leader. Some of the women felt that their leadership style was being questioned by others who held stereotyped and prejudiced views on how women from BME backgrounds should lead. Some expressed concern that high-level leadership positions were being indirectly denied to leaders with childcare responsibilities. Many of the BME women faced being stereotyped as single parents who struggled to secure childcare arrangements, which then deterred them from being considered as leaders. The BME women also commented on having to face others' doubts about their ability to lead.

> Some people don't think that ethnic minority women can lead as they [Asian women] may appear to have less confidence or assertiveness as they may not express their views as forcefully as maybe their white counterparts. (Asian leader 2)

BME leaders have articulated their concern about barriers to women gaining and exercising leadership, fuelled by stereotypes related to gender and ethnicity. Similarly, Bush, Glover and Sood (2006) stressed the invisible criteria for selection and career advancement, while McNamara et al. (2009) showed that discrimination against BME teachers was a barrier to gaining a leadership post.

Impact of Identity on Leadership Style

Many interpreted their identity as giving them a social responsibility for others coming up through the system. Most of the women believed that their own identity had influenced the way they lead teams within their organisations.

> I came here when I was two, so I grew up here and so cultural identity is probably a bit mixed actually. [Cultural identity] impacts on how you are as an individual because you are more sensitive to those issues. Whereas a lot of people don't have to deal with those sorts of issues, so in terms of how it impacts your leadership you are particularly sensitive to issues around race, around sex, around minority groups. (BME leader 1)

Others grappled with the whole idea of identity and what it meant in their context.

> As a Pakistani woman—then yes. I would say that my leadership skill is based more towards my ethnicity of my parents, which is the hard work ethic. (Asian leader 2)

Another woman stated:

> I think it is inevitable. Part of my identity is also my experience of life, it makes me who I am, not just my colour, not just my gender, and so I would put that on an equal par as being women, being black and my experiences. (African Caribbean leader 2)

Interestingly, the women from BME backgrounds were able to identify with the question as it was something that they had considered whilst on their leadership journey. Understanding their own identity contributes to knowing who they are and where they belong. Moreover, the women from BME backgrounds are used to being asked 'Where are you from?'—meaning 'Where are your parents from?' Other BME women would be told that they speak extremely nicely—'How did you learn English so well?'

Cultural Stereotyping in Leadership

As previously mentioned, there are two competing models of leadership that have been fully advanced, based almost exclusively on studies of white women and men but presented as racially and culturally neutral: masculine instrumentality and feminine collaboration (Parker and Ogilvie, 1996). In general, masculine and feminine models of leadership based on Western (white middle- and upper-class) gendered identities exclude the experiences of other groups and render them non-legitimate or unimportant in the production of knowledge. When some of the senior women were appointed to their current position, the challenge was breaking down the preconceived stereotype that their team members held. The issues that arose focused on the BME leader instead of the need for the team to develop in its understanding of diversity. Therefore, the BME leader was not seen as competent for the position. One participant reflected:

> I think you are prepared, as a Black person, if you are managing White people to come across a couple of issues. I think what is...interesting is Black people weren't receptive to me leading them either. That came as a bit of a surprise. (African-Caribbean leader 2)

As revealed by Johnson and Campbell-Stephens (2013, p. 31) in their study on BME school leaders in London, discrimination from other teachers and governors is a barrier in the career path of BME leaders. These findings support the view that some people do not 'see [BME leaders'] leadership potential' and 'promotions to middle-level leadership positions were not based on merit' (Johnson and Campbell-Stephens 2013, p. 31).

The following quote describes the way the woman leader believes BME leaders are stigmatised:

People try to box you in, and if you are a white leader I would imagine, I don't know I'm not one, or if you are a male leader you don't have to be defined by this very strict box, you can be whoever you want to be. You are allowed to be diverse and yet ironically we are the people who are supposed to be the diverse leadership. (Asian leader 1)

Narrative drawn from Malaysia

The Malaysian participant is a middle-class Malaysian Chinese married woman who had experienced principalship in two secondary schools (Form 1–6) in Malaysia, during 2006–2012, without having received any kind of formal training. Her post-principalship career includes a lectureship at a university in Malaysia. Prior to holding a senior leadership position, she acted as a head of department for 13.5 years out of her 34 years of teaching experience in Malaysian schools.

Leadership Path

In her narrative, the Malaysian leader discussed her leadership career path, and the challenges and opportunities that she faced as a woman from a minority ethnic group. She explained that the career trajectory for a school principal in Malaysia is quite long, since the expectation is that a teacher should be in the teaching profession 'for at least 14 years before being appointed to a senior management role'. She explained:

> I was appointed by the Ministry of Education to head the school [...] and I was sent to a different district . . . to defuse a political situation. The board had their own candidate (someone whom they could control), the different racial political parties had their own candidates and the school was in the constituency of the opposition party.

Gender and race discrimination underpinned the school board's disapproval. The fact that 'the board had their own candidate' reveals the power of politics and of cultural communities during the selection stage. As in Pakistan, school boards—all of whose members are men—are very powerful (Kirk 2004). The Malaysian leader stated:

> I was not the board's choice, nor the community's choice. When I arrived, I was an unknown person. I did not go through the career trajectories.

I was Head of Department and straight promoted to Principal of this A grade school.

Similarly to Moorosi's (2010) study, evidence of discrimination in recruitment can be seen in the selection committee phase.

Obstacles to Leadership

Drawing from her experience as a school principal, the Malaysian leader recognised the marginalisation of a woman with an ethnic minority background, whilst she referred to direct and covert discrimination within the Malaysian context. She stated:

I did not expect to rise to the level of principal as I was disadvantaged by several factors:

1. A female (predominately principals were male)
2. Non-Malay (limited schools for non-Malay females)
3. Do not have 'O' Level Chinese language so that means not qualified for Chinese schools despite [being] able to converse and understand the language
4. Not Methodist although the approval of the Methodist Council Board is required.

As her narrative illustrates, there is evidence of workplace discrimination that a woman may encounter, where gender (see comment 1 in the previous list) and ethnicity (see comment 2 in the previous list) may affect whether somebody will embark on a leadership position. It seems that the Malaysian leader has 'confronted the double jeopardy of race and gender bias' (Jean-Marie et al. 2009, p. 571). This prejudice may be perceived as representing 'the glass ceiling' (Coleman 2001; Wirth 2001) which hinders women's progression up the career ladder. She also mentioned:

I also suspect that the Chinese community preferred male, as male teachers could easily fit in and socialise with the members of the board,...and be better in their role.

She recognised leadership as 'highly gendered' (Coleman 2007, p. 385) whilst she expressed her concern about 'essentialist stereotypes' (2007, p. 386) embedded in the Chinese community's mind set. This stereotypical mentality 'that women are less likely to be good leaders than men' (2007, p. 386) has been identified as a factor of discrimination against women which may lead to women's under-representation. The conservative and hierarchical norms of the Chinese community may reinforce the acceptance of a stereotypical male leadership style. Unsurprisingly, 'the patriarchal notion of leadership and its moral dimension in China draws its power from the social ideology based on Confucianism, and functions within that value system (Tung, 2003; Wong, 2001)' (Shah 2010, p. 30).

In addition to sex discrimination there was a reference to the cultural and linguistic discrimination encountered by the Malaysian participant. A possible barrier to the career advancement of a woman may be related to cultural values. As Hallinger and Leithwood (1996, p. 105) suggest, 'from a micro-organizational perspective . . . organizations (and the institutional systems in which they operate) have their own cultures. These cultures can be inferred from the values, norms, expectations and traditions that describe human interaction with the system.' In fact, the Malaysian participant identified herself as the 'person in this [Chinese Malaysian school] population [who is] perceived to be distant in characteristics [in this case, in terms of language and background] from the usually unstated norm of the dominant group' (Lumby and Morrison 2010, p. 4).

In addition, the Malaysian leader emphasised culture and the implications of her Westernised mentality when exercising leadership. It could be argued that the Malaysian participant's British colonial education equipped her with a 'colonial mentality' (Whitehead 1995) which may have influenced her performance as leader. This viewpoint receives support from the literature, whilst Hallinger and Leithwood (1996, p. 101) state that 'the tendency for Western knowledge to overshadow the intellectual traditions of other cultures has become even more acute in recent decades'.

The Malaysian leader also recognised the difficulties for women leaders to combine their careers and family, but 'working a double shift' (Acker 1994, p. 183) was not the case for her, since 'my children were grown [at that point] and therefore I was free to do my own thing'. In contrast to other studies (e.g. Coleman (2007) for England and Shah (2010) for Pakistan) which acknowledged geographical factors as a potential obstacle for women with families in rural communities, the Malaysian participant was geographically mobile.

Challenges in Leadership Enactment

The Malaysian leader commented that she had not experienced any racial tension in asserting her role as a school leader. However, she was aware of other cases where ethnic minority women face discrimination in Malaysian schools, 'except for schools that have a strong board of governors who could demand their own candidates'.

Leadership Styles

Given that both schools she has led were 'in a terrible state in terms of both performance and infrastructure', the Malaysian leader admitted that she had 'no other choice but to be autocratic' and adopt a task-oriented leadership style in order to make sure that students' performance and teachers' professional attitude would improve. She also described her leadership enactment as creating a vision to guide teachers characterised by low performance and absenteeism to a culture of professional commitment to school. Her narrative suggests that her management-related foci were driven by her determination 'to turn the whole school around', which she did by improving students' results, using data to make decisions, building a shared vision, 'making myself visible' and changing the school culture in terms of ethical approaches. Therefore, she perceived herself as a problem-solver and an agent of school improvement. This is in line with findings from the literature (e.g. Restine 1993), suggesting that women in educational leadership positions act as problem-solvers and set high expectations for the purpose of school improvement. Within this framework, the Malaysian leader identified transformational leadership as the most logical first step for running two low-performing schools (at different times) with the vision of raising their level of performance. She said that:

> When things improved, I played less of an autocratic leader and became more democratic, [and tried to make them communicate with each other]...I also made sure that they knew that I care for them.

Encouraging participation and communication, having a caring role and sharing power entail a feminine leadership style, as identified in the literature (e.g. Morriss et al. 1999). However, Grogan (1999, p. 528) argues that 'the fact that many women bring traditionally approved feminine qualities to leadership is often seen to reinforce a less than desirable stereotype—one that can also suggest race and class as well as gender'.

As the data suggest, amongst the Malaysian interviewee's leadership practices were the encouragement of thinking outside the box and strengthening teamwork and consensus at school. Jean-Marie et al. (2009, p. 573) suggest that 'in many ways, the participants' transcendence of racial and gender stereotypes became the impetus for developing a leadership style that is inclusive, builds consensus, and [is] collaborative'. Another leadership style that the researched Malaysian leader believes she had adopted was a participatory style, 'in the sense that I allowed teachers to participate in policy-making, especially the senior leadership team'. But, as Coleman's (1996) study highlights, the final word lies with the principal, and as a result the level and extent of teacher participation become debatable. The Malaysian leader said that she was an advocate of distributing her power when things were at a point of running the school smoothly and she enacted a distributed perspective on leadership (Harris 2008). She said: 'I did not distribute power to people who [felt that changes would have] threatened their comfort zone.'

Challenging Practices

The Malaysian participant's comments on challenging practices highlight that culture and politics are at the heart of the 'discrimination problem' within the Malaysian education system. Since 'cultures can change and adapt at any given time and at any given place' (Bhopal and Danaher 2013, p. 28), the Malaysian leader 'tried hard' to shape the school culture through establishing common values, influencing staff interactions and changing the *status quo*:

> When implementing change and new programmes, teachers who resist change and parents who are in league with these teachers will use racial tension and racially sensitive issues to give problems to the principal. It is very politicised, and sensitive issues like the rights of the Bumiputera (Malays) [or] religious matters can be issues that can get a principal transferred out in 24 hours.

It seems that there are complexities associated with the notion of 'Malay' identity compared to 'Malaysian Chinese' which may entail identity oppression and have political implications.

Narratives drawn from Pakistan

This deals with the experiences of two Pakistani women aged 36 and 48 who started their careers in school as teachers, progressed to school principal, then decided to complete a doctorate and were now in senior leadership positions in higher education. Both women had always wanted to become teachers and felt that teaching was a natural career to follow as women in Pakistan. Being in education enabled these women to be in control of both their personal and their professional lives. Furthermore, working in the field of education meant that they could structure holidays around their children's holidays.

Leadership Pathway and Obstacles to Leadership

In Pakistan, spaces for women leaders are being produced through media awareness, appropriate legislation about human rights in favour of women, policies about workplace harassment (Shah 2016). The stories of these two Pakistani women revealed that women in a Muslim society generally face pressures from family and society, and that they have to fight against pre-conceived gender discrimination, where male dominance is a powerful image (Shah 2015).

In contrast to the prevailing patriarchal culture (Shah 2015) and their culturally constructed role as Muslim women, both Pakistani interviewees referred to the support of their family as a positive factor in their career progression. The following quote supports this:

> My family never creates any hurdle in my career and in my job. I have always been doing challenging things because of the support of my father and brother. (Pakistani leader 1)

Bernas and Major (2000, p. 176) state that 'supportive home and work environment are directly associated with reduced stress and indirectly linked to diminished work–family conflict'. As stated, their traditional role as women in a Muslim society has not vanished because of their leadership responsibilities. Their domestic responsibilities and motherhood remain central in their lives, since the Quran states that the family is the main responsibility for a woman. One of the Pakistani participants mentioned that:

A female has to perform the dual functions of a male and a female as well. She is earning for a family like a male and she is serving her family like a female. (Pakistani leader 2)

Data from this study show that the women believe that they have to sacrifice more than men as a prerequisite for leadership positions. Many successful female role models are childless (Eisenbeiss 2012). As Shah (2010, p. 34) states, 'The roles of female [...] heads were discursively constructed through historically inscribed discourses of what it was to be a Muslim, a woman, and in the "domestic/public", according to given interpretations of religion in that culture.'

Leadership Style

It is thought that success as a leader in education needs masculine characteristics of courage, aggression and boldness. Both participants explained that they have to be more courageous and face challenges on their own.

I have needed to be determined and enthusiastic in the role as a leader so that I am able to push against what is expected as a school leader. I find that I have become more mature as I have a much broader vision and I know how to make decisions and I have started to believe in myself as a leader. (Pakistani leader 2)

The qualities that are desirable for men are taken as negative for women: for example, being too bold and strong is taken as being contrary to femininity. 'However, these stereotypical limitations can actually benefit women by inspiring them to increase their courage quotient by acknowledging and honouring their individual courageous behaviours' (Alharbi 2012).

Their leadership practices underpinned their religious beliefs. Pakistani leader 2 said:

My religion is important to me as it shapes who I am as a Muslim woman. I lead through experience and with the spiritual guidance of my belief.

Both women discussed their spiritual approach to leadership: how they worked very hard and left everything else to God. Pakistani leader 1 said that she was satisfied with her leadership and that her full faith sustains her; furthermore, she said, 'Satisfaction lies in the efforts not in the attainment. Full effort is victory to God.'

One of the participants also mentioned the concept of *Izzat*, 'a powerful discourse that determines women leaders' professional practices and roles in Pakistan' (Shah 2010, p. 38). Pakistani leader 2 confirmed the expectation that as a Muslim woman she will 'uphold the honour of the family community', protecting her *Izzat* (2010, p. 38), despite her 'radical attitude' of opposition to some norms accepted in her culture, as explained in the following:

> As a woman leader I have multiple responsibilities . . . I have to support my family and members in the community and there are times when I am seen as somebody that is going against what I should be doing as a Muslim woman. I find [I am] doing more and more so that people accept me as a leader. (Pakistani leader 2)

Conclusion

Given that prevailing literature on women in leadership focuses on gender difference and white women's leadership, this research contributes to the discourse about racial and ethnic diversity in leadership, through exploring BEM and Muslim women leaders in three different contexts. This study also adds to international explorations of leadership within a 'cross-cultural [comparative study] of school leaders in different societies' (Dimmock and Walker 2002, p. 72). Our work has the potential to fill in the knowledge gap in the female leadership domain from a cross-cultural context. As explained later in this section, the benefits of this research lie within the insights gained from the educational settings in the study, since leadership is not perceived as a monopolised notion.

Whilst leadership has been perceived by most of the English participants as an activity to facilitate change through leading and nurturing people, the Malaysian interviewee explained that her leadership styles formed a blended approach (autocratic, transformational, distributed), subject to the school's needs. The women leaders from Pakistan viewed leadership through the lens of Islam, which shaped the way in which they led and interacted with teams. Despite the different focus on leadership styles, participants' narratives showed a tendency to adopt stereotypically male attributes (e.g. target driven, authoritative), especially at the beginning of their career and in their attempt to establish their leadership reputation in their school contexts. Many of the women were unable to be their authentic selves as they appeared to be confined to a particular box. The black and other ethnic minority leaders in England stated that their leadership style was being questioned by others who held stereotyped and prejudiced views on how women from BME backgrounds should lead. As the data show, in a Muslim society such as Pakistan, women principals prefer to adopt masculine characteristics of courage, aggression and boldness in their practices. This may be the corollary of a patriarchal society which accepts masculine attributes. Similarly, Blackmore (1995), Coleman (2011), Hall (1996) and Shakeshaft (2010) (cited in Shah 2015) have identified in their studies that 'predominantly masculine' characteristics and behaviours of leadership originate from a contextual, societal and cultural background where position and power are conceptually gender specific.

As indicated by the findings, all women in England and Malaysia clearly stated that they were facing challenges as minority leaders due to gender and ethnicity. The perception that 'men are favoured while women are discriminated' has been experienced by the Malaysian and Pakistani woman leaders, and this is an example of covert discrimination (Coleman 2007). As in international studies exploring women, leadership and gender (e.g. Coleman 1996; Kaparou and Bush 2007; Bush and Moloi 2006), gender stereotyping was one of the most important barriers for women to overcome in order to progress to leadership positions. It seems that this issue is exacerbated for BME and other ethnic minority principals in London, since they encounter 'double bind' racism which is tied to oppression based on gender and colour discrimination. The Malaysian participant's reflection on ethnicity as a barrier to leadership advancement poses a question that highlights the political implications which may influence the recruitment process in Malaysia. Similar views have emerged from the comments of BME and other ethnic minority women principals in England, since they have to 'prove themselves as leaders' (Coleman 2007). These leaders perceived themselves as distinctive, in that they have succeeded professionally 'against the odds' (Coleman 2001). Women principals' progress has been inhibited by a culturally constructed notion of the preferred male-gendered leadership. As a result, prevailing prejudice and covert discrimination against women are still problematising the discourse of gender and leadership.

The findings from this research show that there are commonalities amongst the participants' experiences and that these are related to cultural dimensions of leadership (e.g. the role of women in different societies, and

BME leadership perceptions). All the women recognised the difficulties for women leaders in combining career and family, whilst the Pakistani women leaders highlighted cultural stereotypes related to their role in family care and motherhood. The findings from this research are in line with Acker's (1994, p. 183) argument that women principals are likely to work a 'double shift'. School leaders in England claim that senior leadership positions were being indirectly denied to leaders with childcare responsibilities.

Despite the limitations of our research, there is evidence to suggest potential recommendations. Progress has been made in a number of areas, but there is still more to be done in research and in practice. Although some research participants mentioned class as a leadership challenge in their narrative, this theme is not developed in this chapter, but should be more widely explored in research on intersectionality. Nevertheless, BME and Muslim women must be included in research studies concerned with the development of women. For instance, if women of colour continue to be left out of the data, then the findings may be questioned over the representativeness of the sample. Influenced by the study by Johnson and Campbell-Stephens (2013) about 'Investing in Diversity'—a Black-led programme that addresses the under-representation of BME leaders in London schools—we argue for the urgency of customised leadership programmes. Developing black women and those from minority ethnic groups on the basis of their cultural needs will help them 'bring who they are to their leadership' (Johnson and Campbell-Stephens 2013, p. 24). As Fuller (2010) suggests, a leader's multiple identities are shaped by what it means to belong to a group. Our work recognises school leaders' multiple identities that may be perceived as stigmatised identities, occasionally linked to negative stereotypes. Although participants have experienced discrimination concerning their identities, they overcame the challenge of the intersection of gender and race in order to progress in a leadership position. The narrative inquiries of women participants in this study show that the intersected identities can challenge the status quo, and give an insight about leadership enactment beyond the eyes of whiteness. Can insights from this study be used to inform policy? Clearly, gender discrimination and racism may remain a problem in the leadership discourse unless there is a wider acceptance of women leaders—from BME and other ethnic groups—in policy discourse and practice within organisations. More actions are required to facilitate access to leadership positions in education, given that the notion of gender and leadership may be intersecting with religion, ethnicity or language. Since leadership practice enacted by female principals may be influenced by the cultural forces and societal norms in 'contrasting' contexts (England may be characterised as a modern society in contrast to the conservative nature of Malaysian and Pakistani society), more empirical evidence is required in order to gain a deeper understanding about whether and to what extent women's leadership is culturally contingent.

REFERENCES

Acker, S. (1994). *Gendered education*. Buckingham: Open University Press.

Alharbi, M. F. (2012). *The moderating effect of organizational culture on the relationship between leadership styles and quality management practices in public hospitals in Saudi Arabia*. Doctoral dissertation. University Utara Malaysia.

Batliwala, S. (2011). *Feminist leadership for social transformation clearing the conceptual cloud*. New Delhi: CREA. http://web.creaworld.org/files/f1.pdf. Accessed 15 April 2012.

Bernas, K. H., & Major, D. A. (2000). Contributors to stress resistance: testing a model of women's work-family conflict. *Psychology of Women Quarterly, 24*(2), 170–178.

Bhopal, K., & Danaher, P. A. (2013). *Identity and pedagogy in higher education: international comparisons*. London: Bloomsbury.

Blackmore, G. (1995). Educational leadership: A feminist critique and reconstruction. In J. Smyth (Ed.), *Critical discourses on teacher development* (pp. 93–129). London: Cassell.

Blackmore, J. (1999). *Troubling women: feminism, leadership and educational change*. Buckingham: Open University Press.

Blackmore, J. (2006). Deconstructing diversity discourses in the field of educational management and leadership. *Educational Management Administration & Leadership, 34*(2), 181–199.

Blaikie, N. (2000). *Designing social research: the logic of anticipation*. Cambridge: Polity Press.

British Educational Research Association (BERA). (2011). *Ethical guidelines for educational research* (online). https://www.bera.ac.uk/wp-content/uploads/2014/02/BERAEthical-Guidelines-2011.pdf?noredirect=1. Accessed 25 October 2012.

Bush, T. (2008). From management to leadership semantic or meaningful change? *Educational Management Administration Leadership, 36*(2), 271–288.

Bush, T., Glover, D., & Sood, K. (2006). Black and minority ethnic leaders in England: a portrait. *School Leadership and Management, 26*, 289–305.

Bush, T., & Moloi, K. (2006). *Race, racism and discrimination in school leadership: evidence from England and South Africa*. Paper presented to the CCEAM Conference, Cyprus.

Coleman, M. (1996). Barriers to career progress for women in education: the perceptions of female headteachers. *Educational Research*, *38*(3), 317–332.

Coleman, M. (2001). Achievement against the odds: the female secondary head-teachers in England and Wales. *School Leadership and Management*, *21*(1), 75–100.

Coleman, M. (2003). Gender in educational leadership. In M. Brundrett, N. Burton, R. Smith (Eds.), *Leadership in education* (pp. 36–51). London: Sage.

Coleman, M. (2007). Gender and educational leadership in England: a comparison of secondary headteachers' views over time. *School Leadership & Management*, *27*(4), 383–399.

Coleman, M. (2011). *Women at top: Challenges, choices and change*. Palgrave Macmillan.

Collins, P. H. (2000). *Black feminist thought: knowledge, consciousness, and the politics of empowerment*. New York: Routledge.

Collinson, D., & Collinson, M. (2005). *'Blended leadership': employee perspectives on effective leadership in the U.K F.E. sector*. Lancaster: Centre for Excellence in Leadership.

Crenshaw, K. (1989). Demarginalizing the intersection of race and sex: a Black feminist critique of antidiscrimination doctrine, feminist theory, and antiracist politics. University of Chicago Legal Forum, pp. 57–80.

Crenshaw, K. (1991). Mapping the margins: intersectionality, identity politics, and violence against women of color. *Stanford Law Review*, *43*(6), 1241–1299.

Cuban, L. (1988). *The managerial imperative and the practice of leadership in schools*. Albany, NY: State University of New York Press.

Dimmock, C., & Walker, A. (2002). School leadership in context-societal and organisational cultures. In T. Bush and L. Bell (Eds.), *The principles and practice of educational management* (pp. 70–85). London: Sage.

Ely, R. J., & Meyerson, D. E. (2000). Advancing gender equity in organizations: the challenge and importance of maintaining a gender narrative. *Organization*, *7*(4), 589–608.

Eisenbeiss, S. A. (2012). Re-thinking ethical leadership: an interdisciplinary integrative approach. *The Leadership Quarterly*, *23*(5), 791–808.

Essers, C., & Benschop, Y. (2009). Muslim businesswomen doing boundary work: the negotiation of Islam, gender and ethnicity within entrepreneurial contexts. *Human Relations*, *62*, 403–423.

Fuller, K. (2010). Talking about gendered headship: how do women and men working in schools conceive and articulate notions of gender? *Journal of Educational Administration and History*, *42*(4), 363–382.

Gooty, J., Gavin, M., Johnson, P., Frazier, M., & Snow., D. (2009). In the eyes of the beholder. *Journal of Leadership & Organizational Studies*, *15*(4), 353–367.

Gray, M., & Schubert, L. (2016). Do something, change something. In S. Wendt & N. Moulding (Eds.), *Contemporary feminisms in social work practice* (pp. 113–118). Abingdon: Routledge.

Grogan, M. (1999). Equity/equality issues of gender, race, and class. *Educational Administration Quarterly*, *35*(4), 518–536.

Hall, V. (1996). *Dancing on the ceiling: A Study of women managers in education*. London: Paul Chapman Publishing.

Hallinger, P. (2003). The emergence of school leadership development in an era of globalisation: 1980–2002. In P. Hallinger (Ed.), *Reshaping the landscape of school leadership development: a global perspective*. Lisse: Sewts and Zeitlinger.

Hallinger, P., & Leithwood, K. (1996). Culture and educational administration. *Journal of Educational Administration*, *34*(5), 98–116.

Harris, A. (2008). Distributed leadership: according to the evidence. *Journal of Educational Administration*, *46*(2), 172–188.

Hite, L. M. (2007). Hispanic women managers and professionals: reflections on life and work. *Gender, Work & Organization*, *14*, 20–36.

Jean-Marie, G., Williams, V. A., & Sherman, S. L. (2009). Black women's leadership experiences: examining the intersectionality of race and gender. *Advances in Developing Human Resources*, *11*(5), 562–581.

Johnson, L., & Campbell-Stephens, R. (2013). Developing the next generation of black and global majority leaders for London schools. *Journal of Educational Administration*, *51*(1), 24–39.

Kaparou, M., & Bush, T. (2007). Invisible barriers: The career progress of women secondary school principals in Greece. *Compare: A Journal of Comparative and International Education*, *37*(2), 221–237.

Kaparou, M., & Bush, T. (2015). Instructional leadership in centralised systems: evidence from Greek high performing secondary schools. *School Leadership & Management*, *35*(3), 321–345.

Kirk, J. (2004). Impossible fictions: the lived experiences of women teachers in Karachi. *Comparative Education Review*, *48*(4), 374–395.

Lumby, J., & Morrison, M. (2010). Leadership and diversity: Theory and research. *School Leadership & Management*, *30*(1), 3–17.

Lyman, L. L., Strachan, J., & Lazaridou, A. (2012). *Shaping social justice leadership: insights of women educators worldwide*. Plymouth, UK: Rowman and Littlefield Education.

McNamara, O., Howson, J., Gunter, H., & Fryers, A. (2009). *The leadership aspirations and careers of Black and minority ethnic teachers*. Nottingham, UK: National College of School Leadership.

Moorosi, P. (2010). South African female principals' career paths: understanding the gender gap in secondary school management. *Educational Management Administration & Leadership*, *38*(5), 547–562.

Morriss, S. B., Tin, L. G., & Coleman, M. (1999). Leadership stereotypes and styles of female Singaporean principals. *Compare: A Journal of Comparative and International Education*, *29*(2), 191–202.

Neck, C. P., Neck, H. M., Manz, C. C., & Godwin, J. (1999). 'I think I can; I think I can': a self-leadership perspective toward enhancing entrepreneur thought patterns, self-efficacy, and performance. *Journal of Managerial Psychology, 14*(6), 477–501.

Parker, P. S., & Ogilvie, D. (1996). Gender, culture, and leadership: toward a culturally distinct model of African-American women executives' leadership strategies. *The Leadership Quarterly, 7*(2), 189–214.

Parker, P. (2005). *Race, gender, and leadership: Re-envisioning organizational leadership from the perspectives of African American women executives.* Mahwah, NJ: Lawrence Erlbaum Associates.

Reilly, E. C., & Bauer, Q. J. (2015). *Women leading education across the continents: overcoming the barriers.* London: Rowman and Littlefield.

Restine, L. N. (1993). *Women in administration: facilitators for change.* Newbury Park, CA: Corwin Press.

Ribbins, P. (2007). Interviews in educational research: conversations with purpose. In A. Briggs and M. Coleman (Eds.), *Research methods in educational leadership and management* (2nd Ed.), (pp. 207–223). London: Sage.

Riessman, C. K. (2008). *Narrative methods for the human sciences.* London: Sage.

Robinson, V. M. J., Lloyd, C. A., & Rowe, K. J. (2008). The impact of leadership on student outcomes: An analysis of the different effects of leadership types. *Educational Administration Quarterly 44*(5), 635–674.

Robson, C. (2009). *Real world research: a resource for social scientists and practitioner-researchers.* Malden, MA: Blackwell.

Schein, V. E. (2001). A global look at psychological barriers to women's progress in management. *Journal of Social Issues, 67,* 675–688.

Shah, S. J. A. (2010). Re-thinking educational leadership: exploring the impact of cultural and belief systems. *International Journal of Leadership in Education, 13*(1), 27–44.

Shah, S. (2015). Where does the power lie? Gender, leadership, and positional power. In E. C. Reilly & Q. J. Bauer (Eds.), *Women Leading Education across the Continents: Overcoming the Barriers* (pp. 165–171). Plymouth: Rowman & Littlefield.

Shah, S. (2016). *Education, leadership and Islam: theories, discourses and practices from an Islamic perspective.* London and New York: Routledge; Taylor & Francis.

Shakeshaft, C. (1981). Women in educational administration: a descriptive analysis of dissertation research and a paradigm for future research. In P. A. Schmuck, W. W. Jr. Charters, R. O. Carlson (Eds.), *Educational policy and management: sex differentials.* London: Academic Press.

Shakeshaft, C. (1987). *Women in educational administration.* Newbury Park, CA: Sage.

Shakeshaft, C. (2010). Gender and educational change. In A. Hargreaves, A. Lieberman, M. Fullan and D. Hopkins (Eds.), *International handbook of educational change* (pp. 969–984). London: Springer.

Showunmi, V., Atewologun, D., & Bebbington, D. (2015). Ethnic, gender and class intersections in British women's leadership experiences. *Educational Management Administration & Leadership*, 1–19. doi:10.1177/1741143215587308.

Sobehart, H. C. (2009). *Women leading education across the continents: sharing the spirit, fanning the flame*. USA: Rowman & Littlefield Education.

Strachan, J. (1999). Feminist educational leadership in a New Zealand neo-liberal context. *Journal of Educational Administration, 37*(2), 121–138.

Tung, R. L. (2003). Managing in Asia: Cross-cultural dimensions. In M. Warner and P. Joynt (Eds.), *Managing across cultures: Issues and perspectives* (pp. 137–142). London: Thomson Learning.

Whitehead, C. (1995). The medium of instruction in British Colonial education: a case of cultural imperialism or enlightened paternalism? *History of Education, 24*(1), 1–15.

Wirth, L. (2001). *Breaking through the glass ceiling: women in management*. Geneva: International Labour Office.

Wong, K.-C. (2001). Chinese culture and leadership. *International Journal of Leadership in Education*, 4(4), 309–319.

Victoria Showunmi, EdD, is a lecturer in the Department of Education Society and practice at UCL Institute of Education, UK. Her research interests include Gender and Leadership in Education and, more recently, black girls and young black women well-being. She is an established academic that has conducted research in leadership which spans across different sectors and contexts. This includes working in Pakistan, Germany and the United States. She is a qualitative researcher that has conducted research in social justice, intersectionality and leadership which spans across different sectors and contexts.

Maria Kaparou, PhD, is a lecturer at Southampton Education School, UK, and is currently Assistant Director of the BSc (Hons.) Education programme. Maria has taught education programmes in secondary, further and higher education in England (University of Warwick), Greece and Asia (University of Nottingham Malaysia Campus, Sri Lanka). Maria holds a PhD in Educational Leadership from the University of Warwick, and she is the winner of the prestigious BELMAS Best Thesis Award 2015. Maria is an active early career researcher, while her main research interests include leadership and management, school improvement, gender and leadership, and comparative educational research.

CHAPTER 6

Gender and Leadership in Brazilian, Singaporean and Spanish Secondary Schools: An In-depth Analysis Based on the 2013 TALIS

Marina García-Carmona, Miren Fernández-de-Álava,
and Carla Quesada-Pallarès

INTRODUCTION

Principal leadership has been reviewed by countless authors and from multiple perspectives (Arias and Cantón 2006; Beycioglu and Pashiardis 2014; OECD 2014a), such as gender (Antonakis et al. 2003; Cáceres et al. 2012; Cuevas et al. 2014), students' academic achievement (Heck and Hallinguer 2010; Marks and Printy 2003) or work climate (Martín 2000; Martín et al. 2014).

M. García-Carmona (✉)
Universidad de Granada, Melilla, Spain
e-mail: marinagc@ugr.es

M. Fernández-de-Álava
Universidad de las Islas Baleares, Palma de Mallorca, Spain
e-mail: miren.fernandez@uib.es

C. Quesada-Pallarès
University of Leeds, Leeds, United Kingdom
e-mail: C.Quesada-Pallares@leeds.ac.uk

© The Author(s) 2017   121
P. Miller (ed.), *Cultures of Educational Leadership*, Intercultural
Studies in Education, DOI 10.1057/978-1-137-58567-7_6

However, there are very few studies aimed at helping our understanding of school leadership at a multiple country level.

This chapter provides an overview of leadership through an international lens by exploring (1) the leadership style of principals in Brazilian, Singaporean and Spanish Secondary Schools, according to the results of the Programme for International Student Assessment (PISA) 2012; (2) the gender's role on principal's leadership style; and (3) the impact of principal's leadership style and other profile variables on school's climate and principal's job satisfaction.

LEADERSHIP STYLES IN TALIS REPORT

In TALIS 2013 report (OECD 2014b) two leadership styles of school principals are analysed: distributed and instructional. Here, we offer a theoretical framework and some research outcomes for understanding their main characteristics.

Understanding Distributed Leadership

Distributed leadership is often identified with the improvement of learning outcomes (Harris 2009) and school (Hallinger and Heck 2010). Harris (2004) defines it as 'a form of collective agency incorporating the activities of many individuals in a school who work at mobilising and guiding other teachers in the process of instructional change' (p. 14). That is, distributed leadership focuses its attention on specific ways of action and provides a new conceptual framework for reconceptualising and reconfiguring the practice of leadership in schools (Harris 2004; Murillo 2006). It considers decision, information sharing and participative control of the process (Hallinger and Heck 2010; OECD 2013b; Spillane 2006) because it is based on interactions amongst teachers, principals, families and students. In fact, a distributed perspective on leadership goes beyond and gathers informal leaders amongst the community members (Spillane 2006; Spillane and Diamond 2007). For instance, some principals have tried to involve teachers in the sustained dialogue and the decision-making process (Darling-Hammond et al. 2010; Marks and Printy 2003), being associated with the 'teacher leadership' (Lieberman and Miller 2004).

Understanding Instructional Leadership

Instructional leadership encompasses those actions that promote student growth in the learning process (Flath 1989; OECD 2013b). It carries a 'transformative' task by altering school and classroom conditions in order to improve the education offered and the teaching practices (Murillo 2006; Printy et al. 2009). Instructional leadership tries to distribute the authority and supports teachers in the decision-making process (Leithwood 1994; Marks and Printy 2003) to improve the organisation. Thus, it provides an intellectual direction: innovation within the organisation (Sans et al. 2014).

Research conducted by Elmore (2000), King (2002) and Spillane et al. (2000) confirms that instructional leadership extends beyond the scope of the school principal to involve other leaders as well. Volante (2008) underlines that principals' instructional leadership positively influences the outstanding academic achievement and the expected learning outcomes.

According to Firas et al. (2011), most studies that examine policy pre-scriptions for distributed leadership against empirical evidence have been descriptive rather than analytical (Heck and Hallinger 2005; Leithwood et al. 2009). In TALIS 2013, distributed and instructional leadership styles appear as two different approaches even though they constitute the two extremes of a continuum of leadership. Therefore, successful school leaders must master both leading and learning environments and they must navi-gate and shape the school-level context in order to reform the teaching and learning context (Halverson and Clifford 2013).

This chapter analyses the liaison between distributed and instructional leadership styles in principals of secondary schools through a comparative and an international approach. We formulate the following hypothesis (H_{a1}): principals with statistically significantly higher levels of both leader-ship styles will represent successful secondary schools.

LEADERSHIP STYLES AND GENDER

Literature shows that there is never one way to approach gender in leadership roles. Kanter (1977) and Nieva and Gutek (1981) state that there are no gender differences in leadership aptitude or style; that is, women and male leaders behave similarly. On the contrary, many researchers who explored links between leadership styles and women and men's performance found few differences (Bartol and Martin 1986). Eagly and Johnson (1990) highlight that female leaders adopt democratic and/or participative styles, whereas male leaders adopt autocratic or directive styles. According to Loden (1985), female leaders opt for cooperativeness, collaboration, lower control, problem solving, empathy and rationality, which means that women, compared to men, adopt models characterised by friendship, agreeable feelings, interest in people, expression and sensitivity (Eagly 1987; Hall 1984).

Since the 1970s (Kanter 1977), the number of women who assume leadership roles has grown but they usually hold positions of little power or they are offered fewer opportunities for advancement. There are persons who do not want to be supervised by women on the assumption that (1) they are less qualified to be leaders; and (2) female leadership seems to have a negative impact on morale (Riger and Galligan 1980; Terborg 1977).

Cáceres et al. (2012) and Fansher and Buxton (1984) prove that the presence of women decreases during the transition from primary education to secondary education. This imbalance in schools can be linked to the glass ceiling: the barriers that women found to advance and to be leaders (Rose et al. 1998). In this sense, educational researchers focus their attention on different themes (Reynolds 2002), such as (1) invisibility of women as school leaders; (2) strategies for improving the participation of women leaders; (3) characterisation of roles held by women leaders; and (4) links between gender and power in school organisations.

Given that the vast majority of researchers demonstrate how women's practices in educational leadership differ from those of male's practices (Shakeshaft 1989), we formulate the following hypothesis (H_{a2}): principals' leadership style is statistically significantly different according to their gender.

The Impact of Leadership Styles on Climate and Job Satisfaction

The Impact of Leadership Styles on Climate

Aron and Milicic (1999), Martín et al. (2014) and Milicic (2001) indicate that school climate, if positive, facilitates (1) human learning, (2) a sense of well-being, (3) confidence in their own abilities, (4) belief in the relevance of what is learned or how it is taught, (5) identification with the institution, and (6) positive peer interaction. Nevertheless, some factors, such as the decisive role of principal's leadership, affect school climate, its effectiveness and its improvement. On the one hand, Tajasom and Ahmad (2011) show that instructional leadership has a positive effect on school climate's affiliation—also indicated by Oyetunji's (2006)—innovation, professional interest and resource adequacy. Grizzard (2007) states that effective schools have leaders who maintain and support an academic emphasis with a focus on instruction.

On the other hand, Grant (2011) underlines that distributive leadership components are related to leadership effectiveness in schools, which 'setting direction' is the strongest predictor of leadership effectiveness.

According to the literature, we formulate the following hypothesis (H_{a3}): both instructional and distributed leadership styles will have a positive effect on school climate.

The Impact of Leadership Styles on Job Satisfaction

The vast majority of studies are performed in worldwide financial organisations (Silverthorne 2004; Walumbwa et al. 2005); but their findings help to illustrate how important organisational culture is on job satisfaction and commitment. In fact, all those studies confirm that (1) bureaucratic cultures have lowest levels of job satisfaction and commitment; (2) the best organisational environment opts for an innovative culture; (3) innovative and supportive cultures, together with leadership style, have positive effects on managers' job satisfaction and commitment; and (4) instructional leaderships have positive and strongest effects on organisational commitment and job satisfaction.

In school settings, even though it has not been explored extensively, Bogler (2001) finds that those principals who are more focused on instructional leadership have an impact on teachers' satisfaction. In the same vein, Nguni et al. (2006) provide evidence that transformational leadership strongly affects not only job satisfaction and organisational commitment, but also organisational citizenship behaviour.

Thus, we formulate the last hypothesis (H_{a4}): both instructional and distributed leadership styles will have a positive effect on principals' job satisfaction.

METHODOLOGY

The literature review showed a lack of experiences centred on school principals from an international comparative; for this reason, this chapter presents (1) the analysis conducted from a cross-country perspective in Brazilian, Singaporean and Spanish Secondary Schools, via principals' leadership (distributed and instructional) and its impact on school climate and job satisfaction; and (2) the extent to which gender has an impact on principal's leadership style.

We followed a secondary data analysis which uses major data resources for a deeper exploitation in order to deliver high-quality and high-impact research (Vartanian 2011). In this section, we provide the specific information regarding the methodology followed in this study.

Empirical Setting

Many countries participated both in TALIS and PISA, allowing a general comparison of their academic performance results and their leadership styles. The reason for selecting Singapore, Brazil and Spain was their TALIS profile according to their results in PISA 2012: Singapore performed above the PISA average; Brazil performed below the PISA average; and Spain remained anchored below the PISA average (OECD 2014c).

Under the assumption that a best performance in PISA comprises school autonomy, collaboration, assessment and appraisal mechanisms (OECD 2012), in Table 6.1 we characterise Singaporean, Brazilian and Spanish educational systems according to these variables.

Sample

TALIS 2013 was the second round of the survey applied in 2008. The TALIS 2013 international population targeted principals and teachers from lower secondary schools (ISCED level 2), restricted to ordinary schools. Participating countries could also include primary and upper secondary teachers (OECD 2014b) even though they could make some changes to the TALIS population criteria 'choosing to restrict the coverage of their national implementation to parts of the country' (2014b p. 74). Nonetheless, the minimum sample size was established at 200 schools per country.

The national sampling method of TALIS 2013 was systematic random sampling with probability proportional to size within explicit strata, according to the national sampling plans (OECD 2014b). Considering selected countries, its specific school sample size was Brazil ($n = 1{,}142$), Singapore ($n = 197$) and Spain ($n = 200$); thus, we managed a final sample of $1{,}531$ respondents from secondary schools, with a greater presence of Brazil (68.8%).

Table 6.1   Main features of Singaporean, Brazilian and Spanish educational systems

	Brazil	Singapore	Spain
Results from PISA 2012	• Brazil performs below the OECD average (OECD 2014c) although there was an improvement, compared to results from PISA 2003. • This improvement in PISA performance is seen in students from lowest to upper-middle socio-economic status (OECD 2014c).	• Singapore has the highest number of top-performing students in problem solving (OECD 2014d). • There is a strong bond between education, economy and national development (OECD 2011; UNESCO 2011b).	• The public spending on education increased 35 %—a third more than in 2003, a similar increase to the other OECD countries. Nevertheless its performance in PISA remains anchored just below the OECD average (OECD 2012).
School autonomy	• Federal Government through the Ministry of Education (MoE). • The individual states are responsible for the administration of elementary and secondary education. • The Federal Constitution recognises different educational systems: the federal system, the state system and the federal district system, and the municipal system (UNESCO 2011a).	• The government, under the supervision of the MoE, aids public and private educational institutions (UNESCO 2011b). • The MoE, the National Institute of Education (NIE) and the schools are responsible for policy coherence and implementation consistency (OECD 2011).	• The MoE is responsible for the administration of public education. • The current schools structure shows little autonomy on curricula, regarding the content that must be taught and assessed, in comparison to other OECD countries (OECD 2012).

(continued)

Table 6.1 (continued)

	Brazil	Singapore	Spain
Principals, climate and appraisals	• Disciplinary climate improved in 2012 compared to 2003 (OECD 2014c). • Schools have been able to attract and retain qualified teachers (OECD 2014c). - Learning environment improved due to disciplinary climate (OECD 2014c). • Dropout rates are still large because the curriculum is not engaging students or they have the need or desire of working (OECD 2014c).	• The high-performing education system includes high-quality and strong principals, who have long-term visions and quality teachers (UNESCO 2011b). • Students will be provided with a Holistic Development Profile which will keep parents updated on their children's progress (UNESCO 2011b).	• School principals' views of how student behaviour affects learning are generally more positive than across OECD countries (OECD 2012). • Schools rarely reward teachers for their work. • Most of schools are using those student assessments for comparing school performance against regional or national benchmarks (OECD 2012).
Teachers collaboration	• The MoE wrote the National Curriculum Parameters for Secondary Education to support the work of classroom teachers (UNESCO 2011a).	• Teachers share and discuss students' development and needs (UNESCO 2011b). • Parents act as partners to prepare young people for the future (UNESCO 2011b).	• Collaboration among teachers is less frequent compared to other OECD countries (OECD 2012).

Data Collection

The survey collected data in 2013 on the role performed by principals: responsibilities, leadership, socio-demographic characteristics—including gender, formal education, previous experience, school climate, and job satisfaction. All factors detailed -following paragraphs- were measured using a 4-point Likert scale (strongly disagree; strongly agree); in these cases, the fourth factor indexes—both leadership styles, school climate and job satisfaction—were 'calculated to have a standard deviation of 2.0, and the mid-point of 10 to coincide with the mid-point of the scale' (OECD 2014b, p. 174); Appendix 6.1 provides the specific items. The rest of the variables were measured by different types of questions (dichotomous and multiple-choice answers).

Leadership was measured by two factors. The first one was 'instructional leadership' composed by three items about teachers' active role in school's development and management. The internal consistency and validation tests showed a high consistent factor in each of the three countries ($\alpha > 0.74$). The second factor was 'distributed leadership' formed by three items regarding the opportunities offered by the school to the various stakeholders who actively participate in school decisions. Its reliability was above 0.67, providing also a validated scale in each of the countries.

The school climate factor was formed by four items about a culture of mutual respect amongst staff. The scale had a high internal consistency ($\alpha > 0.70$) and was validated in each of the three countries.

The principal's job satisfaction factor was composed of two scales formed separately: satisfaction with current work environment—four items pertaining to the suitability of the school to work—and satisfaction with the profession—three items regarding the current job position as principal. Both scales had a medium-high internal consistency ($\alpha > 0.60$) and were validated.

Data Analysis

Data was analysed using SPSS v22 Inc. performing various statistics. First of all, descriptive and exploratory tests were conducted to check the normality of the scales. Results suggested that there were no normality so non-parametric inferential tests were performed. In this case, Mann–Whitney and Kruskall–Wallis tests and their effect size were calculated. Finally, multiple linear regression models by stepwise method were ran transforming categorical variables into dummy variables (gender, educational level, employment status as principal, school administration training, instructional leadership training, school's location, school's country, school's management type) besides ordinal variables (age, years of experience as principal in total, years of experience as principal in the surveyed school, years of experience in other managerial roles, distributed leadership degree, instructional leadership degree, school's climate of mutual respect and principal's job satisfaction level). Data results informed that none of the linear regression model assumptions were violated.

FINDINGS

Principals' Overview

Gathering the countries together, we analysed 1,531 principals, 54 % of them were women; however, gender distribution was different depending on the country: 70 % were Brazilian women, 62 % were Spanish men and 54 %were Singaporean women. Given that TALIS 2013 did not stratify the sample using gender as a criterion, we cannot ensure that gender distribution in each

Table 6.2 School description according to its country

		Brazil	Singapore	Spain	Total
Type of secondary school	Lower secondary school	100 %	50 %	100 %	89.9 %
	Upper secondary school	0 %	50 %	0 %	10.1 %
	Total (*n*)	1,070	318	192	1,050
School's location	Rural area (≤1,000 people)	15.3 %	0 %	1.6 %	10.7 %
	Village (1,001 to 3,000 people)	5.7 %	0 %	9.4 %	5.1 %
	Small town (3,001 to 15,000 people)	22.6 %	0 %	22.5 %	18.3 %
	Town (15,001 to 100,000 people)	25.2 %	0 %	29.8 %	21 %
	City (100,001 to 1,000,000)	18.1 %	0 %	29.3 %	16.1 %
	Large city (>1,000,000 people)	13.2 %	100 %	7.3 %	28.9 %
	Total (*n*)	1,040	289	191	1,520
School's management	Publicly managed	95.3 %	100 %	75.3 %	93.7 %
	Privately managed	4.7 %	0 %	24.7 %	6.3 %
	Total (*n*)	1,053	287	190	1,530

country actually represents principals' gender distribution in secondary schools. Table 6.2 provides a description of the schools, observing that most of the schools are lower secondary schools (89.9 %), which include 12 to 15-year-old students; schools are mostly located in large cities (28.9 %) and towns (21 %); and schools are predominately publicly managed (93.7 %). Table 6.2 also shows schools' profile by country.

Analysing other profile variables, we noted that principals' average age was 48 years old; the Spanish principals were the oldest (51 years old). More than 93 % of the principals have a master's degree which indicates a high educational level. In general, principals have 7.30 years of experience in their actual occupation, and they also have 5.87 years of experience in other managerial roles. However, Brazilian and Singaporean principals have more experience in this role in other schools than their Spanish counterparts, which suggests that Spanish principals do no tend to gain this type of experience in other schools.

When principals' roles are examined in detail, we observe that Singaporean principals focus more on managerial instead of teaching tasks. Table 6.3 shows that Spanish principals are less educated in school administration and instructional leadership whilst more than 90 % of Singaporeans have attended at least one course of each, mostly before they became school principals.

Leadership Styles and Gender

Analyses regarding both leadership styles were performed for the complete sample and for the three sub-samples (by country). Brazilian and Spanish

Table 6.3 Formal education on school administration and instructional leadership

		Brazil	*Singapore*	*Spain*
Formal education on school administration or principal	Before	28 %	66 %	23 %
	After	38 %	5 %	38 %
	Before and after	22 %	22 %	24 %
	Never	13 %	7 %	15 %
Formal education on instructional leadership	Before	25 %	49 %	13 %
	After	27 %	5 %	35 %
	Before and after	26 %	37 %	12 %
	Never	22 %	9 %	41 %

principals predominantly used a distributed leadership style as opposed to their Singaporeans counterparts who employed more instructional style (see Table 6.4).

From a gender perspective (see Table 6.4), we observe that females have a higher level of both distributed and instructional leadership styles than males; however, non-parametric tests (see Table 6.6) inform that only the distributed leadership is significantly higher in females than males ($p = 0.004$) with a small size of the effect ($r = -0.074$).

After a more in-depth analysis between gender and country, findings suggest different patterns in both leadership styles; however, these patterns are not statistically significant.[1]

School Climate, Job Satisfaction and Gender

When considering school climate and job satisfaction variables (see Table 6.4), principals think that their secondary school has a good climate of mutual respect (13.54) even though their job satisfaction is slightly lower (13.00).

Kruskall–Wallis test confirms that school climate and job satisfaction are significantly different in each country: school climate [$H(2) = 81.29, p < 0.05, r = 0.05$] and job satisfaction [$H(2) = 105.72, p < 0.05, r = 0.07$] (see Table 6.5). Then, Singaporean principals perceive a higher job satisfaction and a better school climate in comparison with Brazilian and Spanish.

On the contrary of leadership styles, females tend to assess school climate more positively and job satisfaction more negatively; however, only job satisfaction is significantly different (see Table 6.6) which means that males are actually more satisfied with their role as principal than females ($p = 0.013$), with a small size effect ($r = 0.064$).

Looking for gender trends, we observe that Brazilian females are generally more positive about the school climate and principal's job satisfaction (see Table 6.4). This situation reverses when Spanish and Singaporean principals are males; a deeper analysis indicates that these country differences are not supported by further analyses; that is, no significant differences were found amongst males and females within the countries.[2]

The Connection Among School Climate, Job Satisfaction, Leadership Styles and Other Profile Variables

Once the different variables have been analysed, the question about what factors determine each leadership style as well as school's climate and

Table 6.4 Descriptive statistics of leadership styles, school climate, job satisfaction and gender amongst countries. Inferential tests confirm previous results; Kruskall–Wallis test informs that both principals' leadership styles are significantly different in each country: distributed leadership [$H(2) = 212.02$, $p < 0.05$, $r = 0.14$] and instructional leadership [$H(2) = 103.20$, $p < 0.05$, $r = 0.07$]

		Distributed leadership		Instructional leadership		School climate		Job satisfaction	
		M	SD	M	SD	M	SD	M	SD
Brazil	Female	13.57	2.03	11.51	1.93	13.53	2.01	12.75	1.75
	Male	13.49	2.25	11.56	1.79	13.30	1.91	12.62	1.94
	Both	13.55	2.10	11.52	1.89	13.46	1.98	12.71	1.80
Singapore	Female	12.07	1.56	12.05	1.89	13.99	1.92	13.68	1.72
	Male	11.83	1.36	12.13	1.88	14.20	1.79	13.98	1.80
	Both	11.95	1.47	12.06	1.89	14.05	1.91	13.81	1.77
Spain	Female	13.04	2.37	10.32	1.98	13.12	1.90	13.23	1.74
	Male	13.37	2.39	10.40	2.20	13.33	1.98	13.49	1.74
	Both	13.24	2.37	10.37	2.11	13.25	1.94	13.39	1.73
Total	Female	13.29	2.06	11.50	1.96	13.57	2.00	12.93	1.77
	Male	13.07	2.22	11.45	1.99	13.52	1.93	13.12	1.95
	Both	13.21	2.13	11.47	1.97	13.54	1.98	13.00	1.84

Note: M = Mean; SD = Standard deviation.

Table 6.5 Inferential tests for leadership styles, school climate, job satisfaction depending on country

		Brazil—Singapore	Brazil—Spain	Singapore—Spain
Distributed	U	420.604	148.531	272.072
leadership	z	14.457	4.336	6.683
	p	0.000	0.000	0.000
Instructional	U	−150.803	263.491	−414.295
leadership	z	−5.156	7.672	−10.137
	p	0.000	0.000	0.000
School climate	U	−224.038	111.117	−335.154
	z	−7.690	3.240	−8.217
	p	0.000	0.001	0.000
Job satisfaction	U	−286.829	−170.484	−116.345
	z	−9.769	−4.931	−2.831
	p	0.000	0.000	0.005

Table 6.6 U Mann-Whitney tests for leadership styles, school climate and job satisfaction depending on gender

	Distributed leadership	Instructional leadership	School climate	Job satisfaction
U	238,585.500	257,921	260,932.500	281,765
z	−2.882	−0.468	−0.094	2.484
p	0.004	0.640	0.925	0.013
r	−0.074	–	–	0.064

principal's job satisfaction arises. Four multiple linear regression models were conducted using the stepwise method to give clarity on the results.[3]

The first model we ran used distributed leadership as the dependent variable whereas the other variables were used as factors or independent variables. After three steps, the model emerged was formed by three factors (schools located in Singapore, schools being publicly managed and the attendance of instructional leadership courses) which explain the 11.8% of the distributed leadership degree. Given its goodness of fit (adjusted $R^2 = 0.118$), the model does not explain what factors determine the most of the distributed leadership in school because the 88.2% of the model is explained by other factors not considered in it.

The second model we ran used instructional leadership as the dependent variable. Six steps were needed to obtain a model formed by six factors that explain the 9.6 % of the dependent variable (i.e., attendance of instructional leadership courses, schools located in Spain, principals' dedicated to full-time without teaching obligations, schools located in rural areas, schools located in small towns and principals' years of experience as principal in total). The low goodness of fit of the model suggests that 90.4 % of the instructional leadership is explained by other factors not included in the model.

The next two models are more complex than the previous two; indeed, a second layer was added including both leadership styles as factors, and a third layer was added swapping the factor that formed it between the principal's job satisfaction and school's climate of mutual respect. Thus, a third model was tested using school's climate of mutual respect as the outcome and principal's job satisfaction as the third layer (as independent variable or factor). The model emerged after six steps and factors explaining the 25.4 % of the school's climate (Appendix 6.2); the final model is formulated as follows:

School's climate of mutual respect = 4.613 + (0.366 × Job satisfaction) + (0.270 × School located in a large city) − (0.267 × Not attended instructional leadership courses) + (0.172 × Distributed leadership) + (0.146 × Instructional leadership) + (0.027 × Years working as principal)

The fourth and final model was based on principal's job satisfaction as the outcome and school's climate of mutual respect as the factor of the third layer. The model emerged with nine factors—after nine steps—that explain the 25.2 % of principal's job satisfaction (Appendix 6.3); the model is formulated as follows:

Principal's job satisfaction level = 7.249 − (0.722 × School located in Brazil) + (0.321 × Climate of mutual respect) + (0.067 × Distributed leadership) + (0.036 × Years working as principal at the analysed school)

DISCUSSION

This chapter reports a secondary analysis of data from OECD's TALIS 2013 that widens the outcomes found by Sans-Martín et al. (2015) in European countries. What makes the difference between both studies, even though they used the same data, is the selection of the sample. In our study, we considered the country results in PISA 2012 to three countries (OECD 2014c): one developing country (Brazil) which performed below the PISA average; and two countries from two different continents (Singapore, which performed best in PISA; and Spain, which remained anchored the PISA average).

This study covered all the hypotheses providing analysis on 1,531 principals involved in this study. A surprising result on principals' background is that Singaporean principals fully dedicate their workload to managerial tasks, which allow them to be focused on leadership underpinned in specific training in school management. So, is there any connection between the focus on leadership and better academic performance in Singapore?

Examining our hypotheses, results inform that H_{a1} is partially refuted. As previously noted (see Gronn 2009; Halverson and Clifford 2013; Marks and Printy 2003) distributed and instructional leadership styles must work together. Nevertheless, our study finds that in Brazilian, Singaporean and Spanish secondary schools both leadership styles are not the two extremes of a continuum. According to inferential data, Brazil is the country with the highest distributed leadership degree whereas Singapore—the country with the most successful students' academic achievement—shows the highest instructional leadership degree.

School principals play an important role in the design and identification of school leadership (Mulford 2003). Successful school leaders must master the leading and the learning environments and they must navigate and shape the school-level context in order to reform the teaching and learning context. For that reason, principals should be trained in distributed and instructional leadership styles before they hold this post. Considering that Singaporean principals are more trained in school administration and instructional leadership, their involvement in student growth (Flath 1989; OECD 2013b), pedagogical issues and teachers' autonomy is more probable.

On the other hand, we come across that Brazil and Spain, countries with lower outcomes in PISA 2012, show higher levels in distributed leadership. The OECD (2014c) suggests that Brazilian principals may opt for this leadership due to the high dropout rates, the socio-economic context and the students who repeat a year, which implies a higher dedication to work with low-performing students.

The H_{a2} is also partially confirmed. Specifically, inferential data indicates that distributed leadership is significantly higher in females than males. It is surprising that even though women adopt a style characterised by decision, information sharing, appraisal mechanisms and participative control of the process (Eagly et al. 2003; Hallinger and Heck 2010; OECD 2013b; Spillane 2006), which has a strong and positive effect on individual, group and organisational level (Bass and Avolio 1994), there are still barriers that hinder their efforts to hold leader positions. In fact, less than 5 % of directorships are held by women (ibid). Furthermore, the fact that distributed leadership is the most widespread leadership approach used amongst women confirms the idea that female leaders opt for cooperativeness and collaboration and adopt models that show friendship and interest in people (Cuevas et al. 2014; Eagly 1987).

The H_{a3} is confirmed. The regression model emerged with six factors explaining the 25.4 % of its variance; amongst these factors, coefficients show that both leadership styles have a positive effect on school climate: in order to have a good school climate, both distributed and instructional leadership styles are necessary to lead effectively. In this sense, research shows that creating a positive school climate increases school effectiveness (Raczynski and Muñoz 2005) and educational outcomes (Revees 2010).

Furthermore, principals in TALIS 2013 value their secondary school with a good climate of mutual respect, but again Singapore scores higher in that aspect. In this line, the high-performing education system of Singapore includes high-quality and strong principals, who have long-term visions, and quality teachers (UNESCO 2011b) who influence the school climate.

The H_{a4} is partially confirmed. The model emerges with four factors that explain the 25.2 % of its variance; however, only the distributed leadership acts as a significant factor in this model which means that it has a positive effect on principal's job satisfaction. School leaders are in charge of improving schools; for that reason, those who opt for encouraging a collaborative culture, for empowering staff or for encouraging distributed leadership (Barker 2007; Daly 2009) are promoting less traditional or rigid organisational cultures. Without doubt, high levels of participative practices (Kim 2002) increase job satisfaction that, simultaneously, has an impact on a shared aim: the school progress. In this model, it is surprising that Brazil has a negative effect on principal's job satisfaction; in fact, the model suggests that considering the other factors in it, Brazilian schools will have the lower principal's job satisfaction as compared to the other two countries. Brazil may consider the possibility of rewarding teachers for their work such as new professional development opportunities, promotions, public recognition or a new role in school improvement (OECD 2012) and the use of participative strategic planning processes (Kim 2002).

In summary, this study achieved the goals established but only one of the four hypotheses was totally confirmed. Results suggest that there are several gaps in the literature that could help us to understand how leadership in these countries, and others, impacts on other school variables.

Implications for Practice

Several lessons are learned from this study, but two important ideas can be translated into a more practised context. On the one hand, women show a tendency to lead in schools through a distributed leadership which is a disadvantage if we consider that they should master both instructional and distributed leadership styles.

On the other hand, both male and female school principals need to attend training activities that help them to understand both leadership styles and to apply them in their specific context. This training could be formally implemented—continuous professional development courses—or informally promoted—communities of practice amongst principals. A better understanding of this topic will impact on a high self-confidence on principals' job and therefore on their job satisfaction and school climate.

Limitations of the Study and Further Researches

The main limitation of this study is the amount of countries selected to be analysed. Even though the three countries were chosen according to their performance in PISA 2012, the addition of more countries that participated in both PISA 2012 and TALIS 2013 would help us to achieve a better understanding of the problem studied. Furthermore, TALIS 2013 provides information about other variables that could explain some of the results; in this respect, our study has a limited range in understanding and explaining leadership styles' impact on school variables.

Aligned with this, another limitation is the fact that TALIS 2013 only measures two types of leadership styles and even though these are the most powerful to guarantee school quality, there are other leadership styles such as democratic and/or participative, transformational or transactional that could help us to understand the topic a bit more.

Furthermore, more countries participating in PISA and TALIS surveys could be analysed in order to compare their results and to understand their academic performance in terms of leadership styles. Primary schools could be also studied if TALIS would include them in their database. Finally, qualitative research could be conducted with the countries and schools analysed in this study in order to deepen the outcomes and establish specific strategies to promote a more distributed and instructional leadership irrespective of their gender, and enhance a more positive school climate and a higher principals' and possibly teachers' job satisfaction.

APPENDIX 6.1. ITEM WORDINGS OF THE FOUR TALIS SCALES USED IN THIS STUDY

Scale	Items
Distributed leadership	This school provides staff with opportunities to actively participate in school decisions. This school provides parents or guardians with opportunities to actively participate in school decisions. This school provides students with opportunities to actively participate in school decisions.
Instructional leadership	I took actions to support cooperation amongst teachers to develop new teaching practices. I took actions to ensure that teachers take responsibility for improving their teaching skills. I took actions to ensure that teachers feel responsible for their students' learning outcomes.
School climate of mutual respect	School staff have an open discussion about difficulties. There is mutual respect for colleagues' ideas. There is a culture of sharing success. The relationships between teachers and students are good.

(*continued*)

(continued)

Scale	Items
Principal job satisfaction— Satisfaction with current work environment	I enjoy working at this school. I would recommend my school as a good place to work. I am satisfied with my performance in this school. All in all, I am satisfied with my job.
Principal job satisfaction— Satisfaction with profession	The advantages of this profession clearly outweighs the disadvantages. If I could decide again, I would still choose this job/position. I regret that I decided to become a principal.

APPENDIX 6.2. MULTIPLE REGRESSIONS ON SCHOOLS' CLIMATE OF MUTUAL RESPECT

	B	SE B	β
Step 1			
Constant	13.161	0.088	
Year(s) working as a principal in total	0.056	0.010	0.165*
Step 2			
Constant	13.317	0.095	
Year(s) working as a principal in total	0.051	0.010	0.152*
Principals did not attend instructional leadership courses	−0.583	0.138	−0.122*
Step 3			
Constant	13.186	0.101	
Year(s) working as a principal in total	0.050	0.010	0.147*
Principals did not attend instructional leadership courses	−0.525	0.139	−0.109*
School located in large city	0.451	0.126	0.103*
Step 4			
Constant	13.177	0.101	
Year(s) working as a principal in total	0.050	0.010	0.149*
Principals did not attend instructional leadership courses	−0.557	0.139	−0.116*
School located in large city	0.402	0.126	0.092**
Having a master degree or more	1.110	0.372	0.086**

(*continued*)

(continued)

	B	SE B	β
Step 5			
Constant	8.193	0.444	
Year(s) working as a principal in total	0.049	0.009	0.146*
Principals did not attend instructional leadership courses	−0.338	0.134	−0.070**
School located in large city	0.543	0.124	0.124*
Having a master degree or more	0.902	0.353	0.070**
Degree of distributed leadership in school	0.216	0.026	0.232*
Degree of instructional leadership in school	0.179	0.028	0.179*
Step 6			
Constant	4.613	0.504	
Year(s) working as a principal in total	0.027	0.009	0.079**
Principals did not attend instructional leadership courses	−0.267	0.126	−0.056**
School located in large city	0.270	0.118	0.062**
Degree of distributed leadership in school	0.172	0.025	0.185*
Degree of instructional leadership in school	0.146	0.027	0.146*
Principals' job satisfaction level	0.366	0.029	0.341*

Note: $R^2 = 0.026$ for Step 1, $\Delta R^2 = 0.01$ for Step 2 ($p < 0.001$), $\Delta R^2 = 0.01$ for Step 3 ($p < 0.001$), $\Delta R^2 = 0.01$ for Step 4 ($p < 0.05$), $\Delta R^2 = 0.10$ for Step 5 ($p < 0.001$), $\Delta R^2 = 0.10$ for Step 6 ($p < 0.001$). SE = standard error; * $p < 0.001$; ** $p < 0.05$.

APPENDIX 6.3. MULTIPLE REGRESSIONS ON PRINCIPALS' JOB SATISFACTION

	B	SE B	β
Step 1			
Constant	13.623	0.092	
Brazil	−0.916	0.112	−0.233*
Step 2			
Constant	13.158	0.114	
Brazil	−0.832	0.111	−0.211*
Year(s) working as a principal in total	0.059	0.009	0.189*
Step 3			
Constant	12.904	0.140	
Brazil	−0.630	0.128	−0.160*
Year(s) working as a principal in total	0.059	0.009	0.189*
School located in large city	0.406	0.132	0.100**

(*continued*)

(continued)

	B	SE B	β
Step 4			
Constant	12.696	0.161	
Brazil	−0.660	0.129	−0.168*
Year(s) working as a principal in total	0.057	0.009	0.181*
School located in large city	0.355	0.133	0.087**
Principals attended instructional leadership courses	0.334	0.126	0.075**
Step 5			
Constant	12.656	0.161	
Brazil	−0.654	0.128	−0.166*
Year(s) working as a principal in total	0.057	0.009	0.182*
School located in large city	0.317	0.133	0.078**
Principals attended instructional leadership courses	0.360	0.126	0.081**
Having a master degree or more	0.947	0.337	0.079**
Step 6			
Constant	12.600	0.162	
Brazil	−0.650	0.128	−0.165*
Year(s) working as a principal in total	0.036	0.012	0.113**
School located in large city	0.386	0.136	0.095**
Principals attended instructional leadership courses	0.353	0.126	0.079**
Having a master degree or more	0.962	0.336	0.080**
Year(s) working as a principal at this school	0.038	0.015	0.099**
Step 7			
Constant	12.617	0.162	
Brazil	−0.627	0.128	−0.159*
Year(s) working as a principal in total	0.036	0.012	0.114**
School located in large city	0.378	0.135	0.093**
Principals attended instructional leadership courses	0.344	0.126	0.077**
Having a master degree or more	0.961	0.336	0.080**
Year(s) working as a principal at this school	0.037	0.015	0.097**
Principal's role is part-time without teaching obligations	−0.533	0.259	−0.057**
Step 8			
Constant	9.792	0.406	
Brazil	−0.792	0.127	−0.201*
Year(s) working as a principal in total	0.034	0.012	0.108**
School located in large city	0.387	0.135	0.095**
Having a master degree or more	0.823	0.329	0.068**
Year(s) working as a principal at this school	0.038	0.015	0.098**
Principal's role is part-time without teaching obligations	−0.509	0.253	−0.055**

(*continued*)

(continued)

	B	SE B	β
Degree of distributed leadership in school	0.138	0.025	0.160*
Degree of instructional leadership in school	0.106	0.027	0.113*
Step 9			
Constant	7.249	0.432	
Brazil	−0.722	0.120	−0.183*
Year(s) working as a principal at this school	0.036	0.014	0.093**
Degree of distributed leadership in school	0.067	0.024	0.078**
School climate of mutual respect	0.321	0.026	0.345**

Note: $R^2 = 0.053$ for Step 1, $\Delta R^2 = 0.03$ for Step 2 ($p < 0.001$), $\Delta R^2 = 0.01$ for Step 3 ($p < 0.05$), $\Delta R^2 = 0.00$ for Step 4 ($p < 0.05$), $\Delta R^2 = 0.01$ for Step 5 ($p < 0.05$), $\Delta R^2 = 0.00$ for Step 6 ($p < 0.05$), $\Delta R^2 = 0.00$ for Step 7 ($p < 0.05$), $\Delta R^2 = 0.04$ for Step 8 ($p < 0.05$), $\Delta R^2 = 0.10$ for Step 9 ($p < 0.05$). SE = standard error; * $p < 0.001$; ** $p < 0.05$.

NOTES

1. Mann–Whitney test was applied but no significant differences were found; therefore, no data is provided.
2. Mann–Whitney test was applied but no significant differences were found; therefore, no data is provided.
3. To review the regression model procedure applied, see the Data Analysis subsection within the Methodology section.

REFERENCES

Antonakis, J., Avolio, B. J., & Sivasubramaniam, N. (2003). Context and leadership: an examination of the nine-factor full-range leadership theory using the multifactor leadership questionnaire. *The Leadership Quarterly, 14*(3), 261–295.

Arias, A. R., & Cantón, I. (2006). *El liderazgo y la dirección de Centros Educativos.* Barcelona: Davinci Continental.

Aron, A. M., & Milicic, N. (1999). Climas sociales tóxicos y climas sociales nutritivos para el desarrollo personal en el contexto escolar. *Revista Psykhé, 2*(9), 117–123.

Barker, B. (2007). The leadership paradox: Can school leaders transform student outcomes? *School effectiveness and school improvement, 18*(1), 21–43.

Bartol, K. M., & Martin, D. C. (1986). Women and men in task groups. In R. D. Ashmore & F. K. Del Boca (Eds.), *The social psychology of female-male relations. A critical analysis of central concepts* (pp. 259–310). Orlando, FL: Academics Press.

Bass, B. M., & Avolio, B. J. (1994). Shatter the glass ceiling: women may make better managers. *Human Resource Management*, *33*(4), 549–560.

Beycioglu. K., & Pashiardis, P. (Eds.) (2014). *Multidimensional perspectives on principal leadership effectiveness.* Hersey: IGI Global.

Bogler, R. (2001). The influence of leadership style on teacher job satisfaction. *Educational Administration Quarterly*, *37*(5), 662–683.

Cáceres, M. P., Trujillo, J. M., Hinojo, F. J. Aznar, I., & García, M. (2012). Tendencias actuales de género y el liderazgo de la dirección en los diferentes niveles educativos. *Revista Educar*, *48*(1), 69–89.

Cuevas, M., García, M., & Leulmi, Y. (2014). Mujeres y Liderazgo: controversias en el ámbito educativo. *Journal of Educators, Teachers and Trainers*, *5*(3), 79–92.

Daly, A. J. (2009). Rigid response in an age of accountability: The potential of leadership and trust. *Educational Administration Quarterly*, *45*(2), 168–216.

Darling-Hammond, L., Meyerson, D., LaPointe, M., & Orr, M. (2010). *Preparing principals for a changing world: lessons from effective school leadership programs.* San Francisco: Jossey Bass.

Eagly, A. H. (1987). Reporting sex differences. *American Psychologist*, *42*(7), 756–757.

Eagly, A. H., & Johnson, B. T. (1990). Gender and leadership style: a meta-analysis. *Psychological Bulletin*, *108*(2), 233–256.

Eagly, A. H., Johannesen-Schmidt, M. C., & van Engen, M. L. (2003). Transformational, transactional, and laissez-faire leadership styles: a meta-analysis comparing women and men. *Psychological Bulletin*, *129*(4), 569–591.

Elmore, R. (2000). *Building a new structure for school leadership.* Washington, DC: The Albert Shanker Institute.

Fansher, T. A., & Buxton, T. H. (1984). A job satisfaction profile of the female secondary school principal in the United States. *NASSP Bulletin*, *68*(468), 32–29.

Firas, S., Jinan, I., & Paiman, M. (2011). Perceptions towards distributed leadership in school improvement. *International Journal of Business and Management*, *6*(10), 256–264.

Flath, B. (1989). The principal as instructional leader. *ATA Magazines*, *69*(3), 19–22.

Grant, C. P. (2011). *The Relationship between distributed leadership and principal's leadership effectiveness in North Carolina.* Ph.D. thesis, North Carolina State University.

Grizzard, T. (2007). *The impact of instructional leadership on school climate: a model for principal and teacher improvement.* Ph.D. thesis, Tennessee State University.

Gronn, P. (2009). From distributed to hybrid leadership practice. In A. Harris (Ed.), *Distributed leadership: different perspectives* (pp. 197–217). London: Springer.

Halverson, R., & Clifford, M. (2013). Distributed instructional leadership in high schools. *Journal of School Leadership*, *23*(2), 389–419.

Hall, C. S. (1984). A ubiquitous sex difference in dreams revisited. *Journal of Personality and Social Psychology*, *46*, 1109–1117.

Hallinger, P., & Heck, R. H. (2010). Collaborative leadership and school improvement: understanding the impact on school capacity and student learning. *School Leadership & Management: Formerly School Organization, 30*(2), 95–110.

Harris, A. (2004). Distributed leadership and school improvement. *Educational Management Administration & Leadership, 32*(1), 11–24.

Harris, A. (2009). *Distributed leadership in schools: developing leader tomorrow.* London: Routledge & Falmer Press.

Heck, R. H., & Hallinger, P. (2005). The study of educational leadership and management: where does the field stand today? *Educational Management, Administration & Leadership, 33*(2), 229–244.

Heck, R. H., & Hallinguer, P. (2010). Collaborative leadership effects on school improvement: integrating unidirectional—and reciprocal—effects models. *Elementary School Journal, 111*(2), 226–252.

Kanter, R. M. (1977). *Men and women of the corporation.* New York: Basic Books.

Kim, S. (2002). Participative management and job satisfaction: lessons for management leadership. *Public Administration Review, 62*(2), 231–241.

King, D. (2002). The changing shape of leadership. *Educational Leadership, 59*(8), 61–63.

Leithwood, K. (1994). Leadership for school restructuring. *Educational Administration Quarterly, 30*(4), 498–518.

Leithwood, K., Mascall, B., & Strauss, T. (2009). What we have learned, where we go from here. In: B. M. K. Leithwood & T. Strauss (Eds.), *Distributed leadership according to the evidence* (pp. 269–282). New York: Routledge.

Lieberman, A., & Miller, L. (2004). *Teacher leadership.* San Francisco, CA: Jossey Bass.

Loden, M. (1985). *Feminine leadership: How to succeed in business without being one of the boys.* New York: Crown.

Marks, H. M., & Printy, S. M. (2003). Principal leadership and school performance: an integration of transformational and instructional leadership. *Educational Administration Quarterly, 39*(3), 370–397.

Martín, M. (2000). Clima de trabajo y organizaciones que aprenden. *Revista Educar, 27*, 103–117.

Martín, M., García, M., Zahonero, A., Aguilera, V., & Alvear, L. H. (2014). Liderazgo y clima de trabajo en las organizaciones educativas. In A. Medina, C. Rodríguez, & D. A. Ansoleaga (Eds.), *Desarrollo de las instituciones y su incidencia en la innovación de la docencia* (pp. 365–380). Madrid: Universitas.

Martínez, M., Badia, J., & Jolonch, A. (Eds.) (2013). *Lideratge per a l'aprenentatge. Estudis de cas a Catalunya.* Barcelona: Fundación Jaume Bofill.

Milicic, N. (2001). *Creo en ti. La construcción de la autoestima en el contexto escolar.* Santiago: LOM Ediciones.

Mulford, B. (2003). *School leaders: challenging roles and impact on teacher and school effectiveness.* Tasmania: OECD, Leadership for Learning Research Group.

Murillo, F. J. (2006). Una dirección escolar para el cambio: del liderazgo transformacional al liderazgo distribuido. *Revista Electrónica Iberoamericana sobre Calidad, Eficacia y Cambio en Educación, 4,* 11–24.

Nguni, S., Sleegers, P., & Denessen, E. (2006). Transformational and transactional leadership effects on teachers' job satisfaction, organizational commitment, and organizational citizenship behaviour in primary schools: the Tanzanian case. *School effectiveness and school improvement, 17*(2), 145–177.

Nieva, V. F., & Gutek, B. A. (1981). *Women and work: a psychological perspective.* Santa Barbara, CA: Praeger Publishers.

OECD. (2009). *Creating effective teaching and learning environments: first results from TALIS.* [Online]. Paris: OECD Publishing. http://goo.gl/RBYfud. Accessed 10 September 2015.

OECD. (2011). *Lessons from PISA for the United States, strong performers and successful reformers in education.* [Online]. Paris: OECD Publishing. http://goo.gl/nRE4V7. Accessed 17 October 2015.

OECD. (2012). *Spain. Key findings. Results from PISA 2012.* [Online]. Paris: OECD Publishing. http://goo.gl/ZxjeQ5. Accessed 20 September 2015.

OECD. (2013a). Assessing higher education learning outcomes in Brazil. *Higher Education Management and Policy.* [Online]. Paris: OECD Publishing. http://dx.doi.org/10.1787/hemp-24-5k3w5pdwk6br. Accessed 28 September 2015.

OECD. (2013b). *Leadership for 21st century learning, educational research and innovation.* Paris: OECD Publishing.

OECD. (2014a). *PISA 2012 Results in focus. What 15-year-olds know and what they can do with what they know.* [Online]. Paris: OECD Publishing. http://goo.gl/fYx07r. Accessed 18 October 2015.

OECD. (2014b). *TALIS 2013 Technical report.* [Online]. Paris: OECD Publishing. http://goo.gl/x73HYw. Accessed 10 April 2015.

OECD. (2014c). *Brazil. Country note. Results from PISA 2012.* [Online]. Paris: OECD Publishing. http://goo.gl/yHrgjR. Accessed 10 September 2015.

OECD. (2014d). *Singapore. Country note. Results from PISA 2012 problem solving.* [Online]. Paris: OECD Publishing. http://goo.gl/frKA1C. Accessed 12 September 2015.

Oyetunji, M. O. (2006). *The relationship between leadership style and school climate in Botswana secondary schools.* Ph.D. thesis, University of South Africa.

Printy, S. M., Marks, H. M., & Bowers, A. J. (2009). Integrated leadership: how principals and teachers share transformational and instructional influence. *Journal of School Leadership, 19*(5), 504–532.

Raczinsky, D., & Muñoz, G. (2005). *Efectividad escolar y cambio educativo en condiciones de pobreza en Chile.* Santiago de Chile: Mineduc.

Revees, M. (2010). *Liderazgo directivo en escuelas de altos niveles de vulnerabilidad social.* Ph.D. thesis, University of Chile.

Reynolds, C. (Ed.) (2002). *Women and school leadership. International perspectives.* New York: State University of New York Press Albany.
Riger, S., & Galligan, P. (1980). Women in management: an exploration of competing paradigms. *American Psychologist, 35*(10), 902–910.
Rose, H., David, M., & Woodward, D. (1998). An accidental academic. In M. David and D. Woodward (Eds.), *Negotiating the glass ceiling: careers of senior women in the academic world* (pp. 101–113). London, Washington, DC: Routledge.
Sans-Martín, A., Guàrdia, J., & Triadó-Ivern, X. M. (2015). El liderazgo educativo en Europa: Una aproximación transcultural. *Revista de Educación, 371*, 83–106.
Sans, A., Guàrdia, J., Triadó X. M., & Cabrera, V. (2014). Las Europas de la educación. Semblanzas y diferencias en las características del liderazgo a partir del informe TALIS. In Instituto Nacional de Evaluación Educativa (Ed.), *TALIS 2013. Estudio Internacional de la Enseñanza y el Aprendizaje. Informe español. Análisis secundario* (pp. 211–228). Madrid: INEE.
Shakeshaft, C. (1989). *Women in educational administration.* California: Sage Publications.
Silverthorne, C. (2004). The impact of organizational culture and person-organization fit on organizational commitment and job satisfaction in Taiwan. *Leadership & Organization Development Journal, 25*(7), 592–599.
Spillane, J. P. (2006). *Distributed leadership.* San Francisco: Jossey-Bass.
Spillane, J., Halverson, R., & Diamond, J. (2000). *Toward a theory of leadership practice: a distributed perspective.* Evanston, IL: Institute for Policy Research.
Spillane, J. P., & Diamond, J. B. (Eds.) (2007). *Distributed leadership in practice.* New York: Teachers College Press.
Tajasom, A., & Ahmad, Z. (2011). Principals' leadership style and school climate: teachers' perspectives from Malaysia. *The International Journal of Leadership in Public Services, 7*(4), 314–333.
Terborg, J. R. (1977). Women in management: a research review. *Journal of Applied Psychology, 62*(6), 647.
UNESCO. (2011a). *World data on education. Brazil.* [Online]. (7th edn). Geneva: International Bureau of Education. http://goo.gl/tH68IM. Accessed 10 September 2015.
UNESCO. (2011b). World data on education. *Singapore.* [Online]. (7th edn). Geneva: International Bureau of Education. http://goo.gl/T98xnC. Accessed 18 September 2015.
Vartanian, T. P. (2011). *Secondary data analysis.* New York: Oxford University Press.
Volante, P. (2008). Influencia del liderazgo instruccional en resultados de aprendizaje. In Ó. Maueira (Ed.), *Perspectivas de gestión para la innovación y el cambio educativo* (pp. 185–214). Santiago: Ediciones Universidad Católica Cardenal Raúl Silva Henríquez.

Walumbwa, F. O., Orwa, B., Wang, P., & Lawler, J. J. (2005). Transformational leadership, organizational commitment, and job satisfaction: a comparative study of Kenyan and U.S. financial firms. *Human Resource Development Quarterly, 16*(2), 235–256.

Marina García-Carmona, PhD, a researcher and an assistant professor in the Department of Didactics and School Organization, Faculty of Education and Humanities, University of Granada, Spain. She graduated in Infant Education and Pedagogy at the University of Granada and holds a PhD in Education from the same university. She is a member of the research group "Analysis of the Andalusian Educational Reality." She has been a visiting researcher at different universities such as Fordham University (New York), National University of Cuyo (Mendoza, Argentina), National University of Salta (Argentina), among others. Her main research interests are educational leadership, intercultural education, inclusive school, family involvement in school, immigration and education, gender and education, international education, school organization and innovation in the field of education.

Miren Fernández-de-Álava, PhD, is a postdoctoral researcher in Education at the Universitat of Lleida, Spain, where she teaches subjects related to organizational development and training. Before her work at the Autonomous University of Barcelona, she worked in the Direction of Educational Innovation and Academic Quality at Escola Superior d'Administració i Direcció d'Empreses (ESADE), Barcelona, Spain. She holds a PhD in Education from the Autonomous University of Barcelona. She has been a visiting scholar at Teachers College, Columbia University, New York, and at the Universidad Complutense de Madrid, Spain. Her scholarly interests are organizational learning, informal workplace learning, educational leadership, continuing professional development, and training and women, among others.

Carla Quesada-Pallarès, PhD, is a postdoctoral researcher at Enterprise and Entrepreneurship Education Centre for Enterprise and Entrepreneurship Studies, University of Leeds, UK, since 2015. She holds a PhD in Education from the Universitat Autonoma de Barcelona, Spain, in 2014; a Master's in Education from UAB, in 2009; and a Master's in Methodology UNED, in 2014. She is currently doing research on enterprise and education in the United Kingdom with the involvement of other international universities. She is a member of the group EFI and the Research in Enterprise and Entrepreneurship Studies research team at the University of Leeds. Her research has focused on the evaluation of transfer of learning; further education; continuing professional development; work, training and women; university teacher training; and training and entrepreneurship, among others.

CHAPTER 7

Policy Leadership, School Improvement and Staff Development in England, Tanzania and South Africa: Schools Working Together

David Middlewood, Ian Abbott, Vhonani O. Netshandama, and Phil Whitehead

INTRODUCTION

If you want to go fast, go alone; if you want to go far, go together.
(African Proverb)

D. Middlewood (✉)
University of Warwick, Northampton, United Kingdom
e-mail: davidm38@outlook.com

I. Abbott
University of Warwick, leicester, United Kingdom
e-mail: i.d.abbott@warwick.ac.uk

V. O. Netshandama
University of Venda, Thohoyandon, South Africa
e-mail: Vhonani.Netshandama@univen.ac.za

P. Whitehead
University of Nottingham, Semenyih, Malaysia
e-mail: philip.whitehead@nottingham.edu.my

© The Author(s) 2017   149
P. Miller (ed.), *Cultures of Educational Leadership*, Intercultural
Studies in Education, DOI 10.1057/978-1-137-58567-7_7

With research evidence over a period of years indicating that cross-nation practice was erroneously based on the concept of successfully transposing lessons from one culture to another, especially Western culture onto Eastern culture (Stephens 2012), ideas are needed for practice which can have positive effects in a range of countries. It is necessary therefore to seek ideas about practices which are universal to the way people operate, and at the same time applicable to contexts in countries which may have widely different geographical, political and resource issues.

One of these, we suggest, is the practice of collaboration between people and organisations for increased effectiveness. Clearly, various models of collaborative practice exist but what all the most effective ones have in common is the capacity for those involved to learn from each other. There is little merit for a country or a region in having isolated brilliant schools, for example, when many or most of the rest struggle to achieve for the children or young people who have only those schools available to them for their education. Even 'pockets' of collaboration between a few good schools will not be sufficient for larger-scale improvement. Change is imperative!

Successful change of this kind also does not occur when it is planned either through large-scale and top-down mandates or through individual or mini-scale initiative. The first is described by Hargreaves and Ainscow (2015, p. 44) as 'counter-productive' and the second as 'inadequate'. The focus for successful change does not lie at the macro level of national government or international agencies; it is much more likely to occur at the level of 'family and community (the latter including schools)' (Brock 2011, p. 35). In developed countries, where a market-led school choice model operates, schools have inevitably become dislocated from their own communities and in many less-developed countries, issues of lack of resources, vast distances and historical divisions hinder opportunities for much national cohesion. Effective change, we suggest, is most likely to happen when a number of schools work or operate within networks or partnerships of various kinds, where they can together devise their own system(s) for innovation and development in learning and teaching. As noted previously, many different kinds of such networks exist. Hatcher (2008, p. 26) described the situation in England and Wales as:

> a multiplicity of networks of different types and scales, geographical and issue-based, ranging in scale from the local area to authority-wide and national, with formally structured partnerships, some involving new forms

of governance and less formal collaborations, and connecting the school to other public services and to the private sector.

Which kind of link or partnership between schools and their leaders is suitable for the particular region to develop as suiting and meeting their needs?

This chapter describes research carried out into various 'school to school' models in three different areas: a large urban conurbation in England with several areas of considerable social and economic deprivation; a region of Tanzania with a higher-than-average level of disadvantage and a province of South Africa with levels of deprivation higher than other provinces of the country. The research investigated various examples of cross-school collaboration, some of which were well established, some just beginning, others at the earliest stage of planning. A special emphasis in the research was on the role of school leaders in developing such collaborative models and/or participating in them. From the research, it was possible to consider models which offer the leaders and their schools opportunities to learn from each other, to share and spread effective practice, whilst recognising the uniqueness of each individual school and community, leading, perhaps, to an overall educational system improvement.

SCHOOLING IN THE COUNTRIES CONCERNED

England

School education in England has been the subject of almost constant review and reform for almost 30 years. There have been significant changes to all aspects of the system, including curriculum, assessment, inspection, increasing the period of compulsory education and reforming school organisation and funding (Abbott et al. 2013). A National Curriculum, introduced in 1988, has undergone significant reform alongside a national system of testing, which has been changed on numerous occasions. Performance in national tests is made public and school league tables have become a permanent feature. The Office for Standards in Education (Ofsted) was established in 1992 and all schools are subject to regular inspections with publication of the final outcome. All young people now have to remain in education or training until aged 18. Schools have been given greater financial autonomy, encouraged to compete for students and are now expected to manage their own resources. School leaders are expected to run their school as a business, alongside having expertise in pedagogy, assessment and curriculum development.

These changes have been driven by a desire to raise educational standards, in response to perceived underperformance set against widely reported improvements in schools systems in other parts of the world, such as Singapore, China and Scandinavia. In addition, education reform has been directed at improving social mobility and raising the aspirations of students from more deprived backgrounds with the aim of closing the gap between the most and least successful students. Underpinning this process has been continued reform of teacher training and professional development for head teachers and teachers (Middlewood and Abbott 2015).

Political interference in the system has increased as central government has taken greater control over what should be taught in schools and how it should be assessed. Education has become a significant political issue and it has increasingly been placed at the forefront of the political agenda although there has been broad political consensus between the two main political parties (Abbott 2015).

Local control of the system has diminished (Bell and Stevenson 2006) and at the same time schools have been given greater autonomy through increased local management of schools. In addition, successive governments have encouraged the establishment of a variety of schools. These include academy schools, which enjoy even greater autonomy, and free schools, which can be set up by groups and individuals including parents and teachers (Gorard 2009; Smith and Abbott 2014; Higham 2014).

The result of these reforms has been a move towards a free-market approach in education with students and parents being viewed as consumers of education and schools operating more like autonomous organisations rather than as part of a local network. At the same time, the central government has retained control of the key aspects of education including curriculum, assessment, school inspection and funding (Whitty 2008). The pace of change in the English education system has been rapid and schools have had to deal with wide-ranging reforms. This is against a background of a relentless drive to raise school standards and recently, since 2010, diminishing resources devoted to education. These changes have led to the development of a number of different models of collaboration and cooperation that we will return to later in the chapter. Our research took place in one of the largest cities in England.

South Africa

Despite progress since 1994, South Africa remains a 'two nation or two economies state' (Fleisch 2008) with the former white and Indian schools still relatively well resourced and achieving success in national exams and whose students are providing the majority of people who go on to universities and professional careers (Maringe and Moletsane 2015). They are joined by an increasing number of black children from the emerging middle classes (Maringe and Moletsane 2015). The remainder of schools cater for the poor working classes in rural areas, townships, mining and farming areas. These are often poorly resourced, with poor infrastructures, fewer trained staff and often principals who have had no training in such environments. Such schools are in the majority in the education system and very few students from them go on to higher education; in fact the drop-out rate from such schools is a huge issue. Much has been done to assist such schools (some 'no-fee' policies, help with transport, some free meals) but a discrepancy remains and this is reflected in the achievement gap between the advantaged and disadvantaged schools (Spaull and Taylor 2012).

All state schools are taught the same curriculum and enter the same examinations at senior levels.

Other issues adversely affecting the poorer schools include low expectations for pupils, especially girls, where the drop-out rate through pregnancy is still high, and the tendency of teachers to opt to work in better resourced schools. Such schools are nearly all found in urban areas, thus accentuating the urban/rural divide. Teacher training itself is very urban centred (Masinire et al. 2014) since virtually all universities are urban based and do not tend to provide much teaching experience in rural settings. Children from the poorer schools become doubly disadvantaged as they acquire a limited set of skills to apply to situations, leading to lower-level jobs in adult life, thus perpetuating the cycle (Fleisch 2008).

Our research was carried out in Limpopo, the northernmost province and the poorest in South Africa, with most schools lacking adequate facilities and services, according to its own government (Statistics, South Africa 2015).

Tanzania

Since independence was gained in 1961, Tanzania has been committed to improving access to and participation in education, and it adopted the Millennium Goals of 2000. Despite this, many challenges currently confront policymakers, administrators and school staff. The completion rates in education are low, with even at primary-level high truancy rates, and early marriage and pregnancy affecting girls at secondary level. By the age of 14, about half of the school population have left the system (UNESCO report 42). The actual quality of primary education is seen as poor, with many children leaving as illiterate. Secondary education also has low completion and high drop-out rates. A majority of girls do not complete secondary education and are outperformed by boys in achievement.

As elsewhere in Africa, a rural/urban divide exacerbates the problems and some rural areas have no schools at all or are very hard to reach for children. Children with special needs have extremely limited access to schools or services.

Tanzania has significant problems regarding the teaching force, with UNESCO arguing that the country has the lowest qualified force in sub-Saharan Africa (Hardman et al. 2012). Although the number of children in schools has increased, the teaching force has not expanded to meet the demand. There are serious shortages in science, maths and English teachers particularly—especially in rural schools. In addition, teacher absenteeism and attrition are high and staff are demotivated by poor facilities, overcrowded classes, heavy workloads and very limited opportunities for professional development—again, especially in rural areas (UNESCO 2014, p. 54). Our research took place in Mtwara, one of the poorest of the country's provinces.

LITERATURE REVIEW

Globally, schools are operating in a rapidly changing environment with significant changes taking place in the relationships between individual schools, local districts and national governments, all with the aim to bring about rising standards and school improvement. In many developed countries, a major part of this process is the promotion of school-to-school collaboration. A significant feature of this has been the development of system leadership which can be broadly defined as school leaders acting as 'practitioner champions' (Hargreaves 2010) or system leaders (Fullan 2005). Under this type of model head teachers aim to build and improve capacity in the broader school system by working with other head teachers to improve leadership knowledge, understanding and practice. Individual school leaders are seen as central to the process of school improvement.

Collaboration can take a number of forms including individual school to school, the organisation of chains of schools working together under loose terms of engagement, to more formalised federations of schools operating with common procedures and approaches (Robinson 2011, 2012). Townsend (2015; p. 735) has suggested that there 'is the need for leaders to share what they know and what they can do, not only with teachers within their own schools, but also outside of their schools with other leaders from different schools'.

The outcome of this process of collaboration has been identified as the emergence of a self-improving school system (Hargreaves 2010). Under this system, schools can provide mutual support to facilitate improvement and cooperate on a range of initiatives, working together to identify and respond to local needs. Particularly in developing countries, when local or district support is limited, due to resource issues or changing policy, and there is a lack of leadership development, collaboration with other schools and their leaders may be the only resource available. In many parts of Africa preparation for headship is certainly limited; see, for example, Bush and Oduro (2006); Bush and Glover (2013). There are some emerging signs of schools' awareness of the benefits of working with other schools. For example, in a study of township schools in South Africa, Prew (2009, p. 843) notes that improvement comes with 'partnerships built on trust and shared interest,' and suggests the benefits of schools looking outwards 'can be huge' (2009, p. 843). In an assessment of the impact of unequal resource allocation in South Africa, Mestry's (2014) analysis points to schools' working together as a possible way forward for greater equity and raising achievement for poorer schools.

The evidence for the impact of this type of development is limited and is not always necessarily positive. Chapman (2015, p. 47) argues that 'it is unsurprising the knowledge base pertaining to "what works" and "why" lags behind policy and emerging practice. Furthermore, the diverse and at times bizarre interpretation of policy mandates by educational leaders can lead to unintended and perverse outcomes and structural variations and diverse practices on the ground can present a complex and often confusing portrait.'

Limited data is starting to emerge that collaboration between schools of the type we have described can contribute to 'partnerships beyond the school, where partners multiply the impacts of each other's efforts' Ainscow et al. (2012b, p. 209). Abbott et al. (2014, p. 451) have reported on the support given by head teachers from highly effective schools to fellow head teachers in schools requiring improvement as 'being enthusiastically welcomed by head teachers of the supported schools'.

Whilst a useful tool, and one that is being encouraged by many policy makers, it is worth noting that school-to-school collaboration can only go so far in supporting educational improvement in any country and 'that without attending to the deeper structural issues rooted in society the quest for educational improvement, whether in isolation or collaboration remains limited' (Chapman 2015, p. 58). There is also a danger in taking a model developed in one context and dropping it into another; (see, for example, Eacott and Asunga 2014).

Methodology

The research methods used in all three places were primarily of two kinds: documentary analysis and semi-structured interviews. We needed access to the context, both in terms of resources and policy, and studied a selection of relevant documents for analysis, namely:

- Education Policy Statements, both regional and national
- School Improvement Plans, both at school and regional level

We chose to analyse these using the SWOT (strengths, weaknesses, opportunities, threats) method because it was hoped it would offer a picture of possibilities for the future as well as the current situation, and in a context of striving for educational improvement and the potential role of the university in this, this seemed essential. In analysing the documents, we were conscious that such documents are part of the culture which produced them (Cortazzi 2002) and were therefore careful to take account of the documents' sources and authorship, paying particular attention to distinguishing between evidence-based ideas and aspirational ones.

The second method was the use of interviews with various personnel who were closely involved with school improvement. We chose semi-structured interviews because these give scope for clarification and emphasis and 'can adapt to the personality of the interviewee and perhaps any circumstance relating to him/her' (Middlewood and Abbott 2012, p. 53). Given the wide range of contexts involved, this seemed essential. The main sample of interviewees consisted of school principals or head teachers. Not only were these people at the forefront of future developments, they were in the best position to comment on the reality of the impact of policy and use of resources, as well as potential in leadership collaboration.

In Birmingham, 10 head teachers of schools seen as requiring improvement or who had failed recent external inspections were chosen from a list supplied by the local authority (LA). Each of these 10 had been paired with the head teacher of a school deemed 'outstanding'. It did not prove possible in the research project to interview these. In the Mtwara region of Tanzania, eight principals were interviewed and in the Limpopo province of South Africa, there were nine. In both these cases, the schools and principals were chosen by the relevant educational body and were said to represent a reasonable range in terms of achievement. Of course, consideration necessarily had to be given to geography since travel to the schools had to be feasible, given the period of the research visit and the potentially long distances involved.

The other interviewees included: In Birmingham, two LA officers and two local government representatives; in Mtwara, academic officers, and in Limpopo, circuit managers, education board members and local university representative.

The purpose of the interviews was to ascertain the effectiveness, potential impact, positive and negative factors of collaboration between school leaders.

FINDINGS AND DISCUSSION

The SWOT analysis of the documents showed the following which had relevance to school leadership collaboration:

STRENGTHS

- A commitment by the overseeing authorities to proposals that would lead to school improvement.
- Willingness and commitment of school principals to working with other schools and their leaders.
- High level of professional capability of a number of school principals.
- Availability of facilitation facilities through a local university or LA.

WEAKNESSES

- Potential lack of financial resources to support the mechanics of collaboration.
- No significant history of structured collaboration between schools.

Threats

- Lack of time, both in time actually available for collaboration and in the sense of the urgency of something needing to happen fairly urgently. For example, external agencies such as inspection agencies could be seen as 'taking over' if improvement not forthcoming.
- Some cultural factors suggesting reluctance on the part of some community stakeholders to 'share' their practice with other communities.

Opportunities

- Investment in education likely to increase.
- The university involved has excellent records in educational leadership and management training.
- Basically, the findings showed evidence of a strong foundation for developing school leadership collaboration for school improvement and evidence of potential. If findings from the interviews about existing and possible future collaboration could support these, the proposal of an effective model was possible.

The Findings from the Interviews

England

- There was no one 'fixed' model of collaboration between school leaders; in fact a variety of different models offered both schools and their leaders more flexibility to develop a collaborative model which was customised to suit their particular context and circumstances. Most interviewees were strongly opposed to the idea that there was or could be one specific way of working with another. As head teacher C said, 'each school is unique and so are we as individual people and leaders. Whilst I am very ready to accept guidance from outside, only I and my team know this area and this school so well.' Other interviewees referred to the fact that individual human beings, whilst they worked in similar contexts, had different characters and personalities and forcing them into a single model of what an effective partnership should be just could not work for everyone.

- All interviewees felt that each particular collaborative partnership had to be negotiated so that the terms of the partnership were mutually agreed at the beginning. It was no good terms being imposed by an outsider or indeed by one of the two parties. This negotiation could be very hard-headed at times but was essential.

- The best way to view any such collaboration, all agreed, was as a professional working relationship, with the words 'professional' and 'working' being important. Although friendships might develop through any collaboration—and several did! It was agreed that those who were already friends were not the most suitable partners. A certain distance and objectivity was essential. Head teacher B said of her partner head teacher, 'I had met her at meetings and been impressed but did not know her otherwise. I could have had (A. N. Other) as my partner but I felt we knew each other too well and she might have been a little soft on me when I made mistakes!'

  Honesty and professional integrity were seen as at the heart of any successful partnership. 'In the end, we have to remember that it is all for the benefit of the children in our schools and any improvement in me as the leader is for that purpose' (Head teacher E).

- The recognition of the uniqueness of each school was central, according to a majority of head teachers interviewed. Although lessons could be learned from the school that was outstanding, it was not possible to simply try to replicate that school in the other one; they were different. There were a few instances where indications of this approach had been hinted at early on in the collaboration, but eventually *all* leaders came to recognise the other school's needs were specific to itself and its context. Even where the contexts of the two schools were similar, for example both in disadvantaged areas, it became clear in the effective collaborations that there were individual 'peculiarities' in the other school which meant that a particular 'solution' which had worked in one would not necessarily do so in the other.

- Whilst the partnership was essentially between the two individual school leaders, as the collaboration developed, considerable sharing of practices and ideas developed at various levels. Professional development was high on this list and several interviewees reported successful joint enterprises involving staff from both schools. The powerful thing here was that, whilst inevitably the outstanding school had most to offer and began by offering training in various areas for the other school's staff, eventually the 'weaker' school had something to offer the other one. We were reminded that no one has a monopoly of good ideas and practice and also that not every teacher working in an underachieving school is necessarily underachieving. Other examples of collaborating at different levels included a deputy head teacher working in the other school for a period and even office administrators visiting each other's schools. As interviewee A noted, 'Although we had been seen as a failing school, we were very good in our work with special needs children, and the other school's staff with those responsibilities came several times to pick our brains!'

- Inevitably, resources were discussed. The LA invested some resources in the scheme and there were bargains struck between the two schools in most cases. In only one case did an attitude of 'trying to sell me something' threaten to spoil the partnership and here a change of partner was negotiated! The LA here did have an important role in its monitoring of how the collaboration was or was not working and did intervene in this single case. Again, this underlined the need for a mutually agreed set of terms for a collaborative relationship.
- Finally, every interviewee indicated their own significant learning that had occurred through his collaboration. Head teacher F was typical, 'I learned more through working with X than I could from any number of courses and my staff tell me how much I have developed! My partner head teacher also told me how much SHE had learned, which was great.' Although the research project did not enable us to interview the partner head teachers, it is interesting to note that nearly all the interviewee head teachers reported this point; that is, their partners had learned as much as they had. 'Mutual learning' was how head teacher D described the whole process.

SOUTH AFRICA: LIMPOPO PROVINCE

A visit to the University of Warwick in England by a group of Limpopo school principals, with Education Officials and University of Venda staff, for a week's programme of leadership and management development occurred in Autumn 2014. During this time, the idea of structured collaboration between the principals began to take shape, with the recognition that it would need the support of local officers and university. Action learning sets were introduced during the visit and were enthusiastically taken up by the principals. After their return to Limpopo, six principals remained in regular communication using the action learning sets. Although these sets focused on helping each individual principal develop an action plan for their particular school, the crucial step forward was the sharing between the principals in the devising of these. Identified issues, introduced in the visit to England, such as strategy and vision, school culture, teacher development and team-building, were discussed and developed within a learning framework. Each principal learned to put their practice and projects in front of the others for ideas and comment and, where appropriate, criticism.

Communications were crucial to the success of this venture (Coleman 2011), as was the capacity to listen to others (Connolly and James 2006). Undoubtedly, the week together 'off-site' in England had laid the foundations for the most important element in effective collaborative models, that of developing trust (Gillinson et al. 2007). One of the interviewed principals said in January 2015 of the collaborative sessions that 'We don't have to feel we are in competition now, anything like as much as we did. Even if we did not say it, we felt it inside-watching how another school was doing. Now we trust each other, and when we contribute a good idea to another colleague principal, it's great when they like it—and I get as much pleasure from that as when I get something right in my own school.'

Principal L described the new collaboration as 'mutual learning' and hoped that the learning from others would lead to improvement at the most crucial level, that is, in the classroom. 'It is vital that we don't just focus on leadership and management but get to learning from each other about how things can be better in teaching and pupil learning.'

Principal F felt that the success was due to the fact that they are all equal in status. 'It is really peer-to-peer learning, isn't it? Although some schools are better off in resources and parental and community support than others, we are all principals doing the same job, so we understand each other's problems and can give and receive advice. AND, we do not have to take all the advice!'

This group of six principals included both secondary and primary school leaders and for Principal C, a primary school leader, this was important because 'We seem to want to play a blaming game between primary and secondary schools sometimes, when we should be working together to share good practice. It is easy in your own secondary school to sit and blame a primary school for not preparing children properly, or for a primary to say it is the secondary's fault for not building on good work. They ARE all the same children!' This aspect was one welcomed by the supporting administrator interviewees as it addressed the whole system issues rather than one specific part of it.

At the time of writing, models are still being investigated, including the possibility of principals of highly effective schools supporting principals of struggling schools. Collaborative working at leadership levels across schools has inherent tensions and a 'plethora of potential problems' (Coleman 2011, p. 310) and in Limpopo, as elsewhere in Africa, a major one is the urban/rural divide with its geographical and logistical issues to be tackled. Although there is some way to go before this is at all resolved, the early indications of collaboration between school principals being a route to school improvement are encouraging. One education board interviewee speculated that 'Soon perhaps, even a small meeting of school principals who are collaborating on ideas about improvement; if they managed to gather in a rural secondary, for example, a lot of eyes would be opened and everyone might gain!'

TANZANIA: MTWARA PROVINCE

The interviews with school principals made it very clear how isolated many of them felt. This was in some cases true geographically when a school was a long way from its nearest neighbour, but it was also true in the psychological sense for virtually all the principals. Headship or principalship has been shown through research to be a lonely job (Barrett-Baxendale and Burton 2009). There is after all only one of you in that role! When factors such as lack of resources, teacher absenteeism and low pupil achievement are added in to the situation, matters can be greatly exacerbated. One interviewee stressed that, whilst she was 'not blaming anyone—I know I have to do the job for these children—but I sometimes feel as if no one else cares about me.' For these school leaders, even a very occasional meeting with a regional officer was welcome. The relief that some expressed that could come from a simple meeting with one other leader was considerable. 'Then, you can just exchange news, hear about someone else's problems and so on' (Interviewee A).

When the possibilities of some kind of structured collaborative arrangement was mooted at interview, all the principals embraced the concept eagerly, and emotions of 'relief', 'eager anticipation' and 'enjoyment of peer-company' were expressed. However, beyond, the purely personal and human emotional side of any such collaborative venture, the professional benefits and also consequences were clearly expressed.

All interviewees were clear that collaboration between principals would 'make things better' (Principal C). Ideas about possible forms of collaboration were plentiful. Two specific ideas involved:

- New principals being linked with experienced ones in a form of mentoring arrangement. Bush (2008) shows that such mentoring schemes for school leaders are amongst the most common form of support given for school leaders, and can be especially helpful in countries where preparation for headship is minimal.
- Close collaboration between primary and secondary school leaders at the stage of transition was strongly advocated, particularly over a longer period than just the short time prior to pupil transfer. 'Leaders and other staff meeting and working together would make a big difference to how the children from primary felt about the new secondary school' (Principal B). At present, that period of transition in Tanzania is one where a number of children disappear from the system altogether.

Other arguments involved the sharing of skills, including leadership skills. As Principal E noted, 'We are all individuals with our different strengths and weaknesses. I am good—I think—with staff, but I seem to have no success with getting parents to feel supportive. I would like to link with a school leader who is good at that and get ideas from them.' Other skills mentioned in this context of sharing included:

- Staff and pupil motivational ideas
- Classroom support for weaker teachers
- Delegation
- Technical skills in assessment
- Professional development in for example English language teaching

An aspect of prospective collaboration that was both interesting and important was the wider view taken by several of the principals. They saw collaborative arrangements between school leaders as being significant in making a contribution to the development of the whole education system. Principal D said, 'We face problems and we need to work in partnership. We have to encourage people to work together in areas such as professional development. We have to develop links that will improve the system.'

Principal F endorsed this: 'There has to be support for head teachers from other heads across the local area. Greater team work across the system will lead to a more effective education system.'

And Principal C said, 'We need to have co-operation and commitment from everyone to improve the system. There has to be regional planning and setting of priorities with schools working together. Increased co-operation WILL make things better!'

Such comments point to an understanding that leadership collaboration can not only increase individual school leader effectiveness but can play a part in helping stakeholders to see that only by working together and ending or minimising school isolation can an education system eventually operate for the benefit of ALL those involved, despite disparity in individual circumstances.

CONCLUSION

Our research has identified three basic stages of leadership collaboration which exhibit differing levels of development. We do recognise the difficulties in attempting to transfer a Western-type model to other systems. At the same time, we advocate that collaborative models do need to be constantly aware of the variations which might occur in terms of specific regional and local needs and experience tells us that collaboration is not always the most effective strategy to adopt. Notwithstanding these caveats, the three basic stages of leadership collaboration are:

1. A recognition by head teachers of the benefits of leader-to-leader collaboration and a willingness to develop and introduce a limited model of cooperation. There is agreement about the benefits of the approach and a belief that collaboration can lead to improvements in schools on a micro and macro level. Pressure is starting to build from head teachers to move away from a top-down bureaucratic approach to school improvement to a system that enables school leaders to work together.

2. Building on the aforementioned, an informal network is established which is supported and facilitated by the Local Authority or District. Head teachers begin to talk together and to learn from each other, either on an individual basis or as part of an informal network. This is a loose arrangement without any formalised structure, but the benefits of increased collaboration are seen as important in bringing about school improvement.

3. A formalised and structured system established by a central body, the Local Authority or District, which facilitates one-to-one colla-boration between senior school leaders. This is designed to offer tailored support and aims to provide specific help and advice for particular issues relevant to the local situation. This more sophisti-cated model allows long-term relationships to develop in a secure and trusting environment which recognises the importance of a formalised system of collaboration.

As these different types of collaboration develop, there will be a need to understand the 'fluidity and flexibility of leadership relationships which spread both through and beyond schools, and which does not simplistically attribute concepts of success or failure to the actions of particular appointed leaders' (Townsend 2015, p. 734). The drive for school improvement will continue, but the models that we have described will continue to evolve as policy initiatives continue, circumstances change and head teachers become more accustomed to working in a collaborative manner.

REFERENCES

Abbott, I. (2015). Politics and education policy into practice: conversations with former secretaries of state. *Journal of Educational Administration and History*, *47*(4), 334–349.

Ainscow, M., Beresford, J., Harris, A., & Hopkins, D. (2012a). *Creating the conditions for school improvement*. London: David Fulton.

Ainscow, M., Dyson, A., Goldrick, S., & West, M. (2012b). Making schools effective for all: rethinking the task. *School Leadership and Management, 32* (3), 197–213.

Barrett-Baxendale, D., & Burton, D. (2009). Twenty first century headteacher: pedagogue or visionary leader or both? *Journal of School Leadership and Management, 29*(2), 91–106.

Bell, L., & Stevenson, H. (2006). *Education policy: process, themes and impact.* Abingdon: Routledge.

Brock, C. (2011). *Education as a global concern*. London: Continuum.

Bush, T. (2008). *Leadership and management development in education*. London: Sage.

Bush, T., & Glover, D. (2013). *School leadership in West Africa*. Paris: UNESCO.

Bush, T., & Oduro, G. (2006). New principals in Africa: preparation, induction and practice. *Journal of Educational Administration*, *44*(4), 359–375.

Chapman, C. (2015). From one school to many: reflections on the impact and nature of school federations and chains in England. *Educational Management Administration and Leadership*, *43*(1), 46–60.

Coleman, A. (2011). Towards a blended model for school-based collaborations. *Educational Management Administration and Leadership*, *39*(3), 296–316.

Connolly, M., & James, C. (2006). Collaboration for school improvement. *Educational Management Administration and Leadership*, *34*(1), 69–87.

Cortazzi, M. (2002). Analysing narratives and documents. In M. Coleman & A. Briggs (Eds.), *Research methods in educational leadership and management*. London: Sage.

Eacott, S., & Asuga, G. (2014). School leadership preparation and development in Africa: a critical insight. *Educational Management Administration and Leadership*, *42*(6), 852–868.

Fleisch, B. (2008). Primary education in crisis: Why South African schoolchildren underachieve. *Reading and Maths*. Cape Town: RSA, Juta and Company Ltd.

Fullan, M. (2005). *Leadership and sustainability: system leaders in action*. London: Sage.

Gillinson, S., Hannnon, C., & Gallagher, N. (2007). Learning together. In S. Parker and N. Gallagher (Eds.), *The collaborative state*. London: Demos.

Gorard, S. (2009). What are academies the answer to? *Journal of Education Policy*, *24*(1), 101–113.

Hardman, F., Abd-Kadiri, I., & Tibuhinda, T. (2012). Reforming teacher education in Tanzania. *International Journal of Educational Development*, *32*(6), 826–834.

Hargreaves, A. (2010). *Creating a self-improving school system*. Nottingham: National College.

Hargreaves, A., & Ainscow, M. (2015). The top and bottom of leadership and change. *Phi Delta Kappa*, *97*(3), 42–48.

Hatcher, R. (2008). System leadership, networks and the quest for power. *Management in Education*, *22*(2), 24–30.

Higham, R. (2014). 'Who owns our schools?' An analysis of the governance of free schools in England. *Educational Management Administration and Leadership*, *42*(3), 404–423.

Maringe, F., & Moletsane, R. (2015). Leading schools in circumstances of multiple deprivation in South Africa. *Educational Management Administration and Leadership*, *43*(3), 347–385.

Masinire, A., Maringe, F., & Nkambule, T. (2014). Rural education, education in rural schools of education for rural development: embodying rural dimensions in initial teacher education. *Perspectives in Education, 32*(3), 146–158.

Middlewood, D., & Abbott, I. (2012). *Achieving success with your leadership project.* London: Sage.

Middlewood, D., & Abbott, I. (2015). *Improving professional learning through in-house inquiry.* London: Bloomsbury.

Middlewood, D, A. I., & Robinson, S. (2014). Prospecting for support in a wild environment: investigating a school-to-school support system for primary school leaders. *School Leadership and Management, 34*(5), 439–453.

Mestry, R. (2014). A critical analysis of the national norms and standards of school funding policy in South Africa. *Educational Management Administration and Leadership, 42*(6), 851–867.

Prew, M. (2009). Modifying school improvement concepts to the needs of South African township schools. *Education Management Administration and Leadership, 37*(6), 824–846.

Rathbone, M, A. I., & Whitehead, P. (2013). *Education policy.* London: Sage.

Robinson, S. (2011). Primary headteachers: new leadership roles inside and outside the school. *Education Management Administration and Leadership, 39*(3), 63–83.

Robinson, S. (2012). *School and system leadership: changing roles for primary headteachers.* London: Continuum.

Smith, P., & Abbott, I. (2014). Local responses to national policy: the contrasting experiences of two Midlands cities to the Academies Act 2010. *Educational Management Administration and Leadership, 42*(3), 341–354.

Spaull, N., & Taylor, S. (2012, December 21). Effective enrolment-creating a composite measure of educational access and educational quality to accurately describe performance in sub-Saharan Africa. *Stellenbosch Economic Working Papers* (pp. 1–25). Matieland: Stellenbosch University.

Statistics, South Africa. (2015). Education Series 1. *Focus on Schooling in Limpopo,* Report 92-01-01, Pretoria, South Africa.

Stephens, D. (2012). The role of culture in interpreting and conducting research. In A. Briggs, M. Coleman, & M. Morrison (Eds.), *Research methods in educational leadership and management.* London: Sage.

Townsend, A. (2015). Leading school networks: hybrid leadership in action? *Educational Management Administration and Leadership, 43*(5), 719–737.

UNESCO-CFIT Project. (2014, June). Tanzania needs assessment report. http://unesdo.unesco.org/images/0023/002336/233665.pdf. Accessed 10 March 2014.

Whitty, G. (2008). Twenty years of progress: English education policy 1988 to the present. *Educational Management Administration and Leadership, 36*(2), 165–184.

David Middlewood, EdD, is a research fellow at the Centre for Educational Studies, University of Warwick, UK, having previously worked at two other UK universities. Prior to that, David worked in schools for many years, including 9 years as a secondary school principal. David has published nearly 20 books on a range of educational topics, including human resources, strategic leadership, practitioner research and professional learning. He has taught and researched in countries such as South Africa, Seychelles, New Zealand and Greece. His research interests include staff leadership, student voice, school collaboration and raising achievement for disadvantaged pupils.

Ian Abbott, EdD, is an associate professor and Director of the Centre for Educational Studies at Warwick University, UK, having previously worked in schools and colleges for several years. Ian has significant international experience, including working in countries such as Ethiopia, Tanzania, South Africa, Brazil and China. Ian's research interests include education policy and reform, school collaboration, initial teacher education and the use of Pupil Premium. He has published widely on all of these and other topics and has recently published, with David Middlewood, books on dissertation writing and improving professional learning.

Vhonani O. Netshandama, PhD, holds a Master's in Nursing Management from the University of South Africa and a doctorate in Nursing Education at University of Johannesburg, South Africa. She has taught in Higher Education for 17 years. Her research interests focus on nursing education, mental health and development and Indigenous Knowledge Systems (IKS). She is responsible at the University of Venda, Limpopo, for facilitating university programmes engaging with communities. She has published various journal articles and also works as a reviewer for a number of journals.

Phil Whitehead, MA, is Assistant Professor in Educational Leadership and Management at the Malaysian campus of the University of Nottingham, Selangor, Malaysia, following his work at the University of Warwick, UK. There, he was a course leader for two Master's programmes in education. He had previously worked in further education colleges in ITE and staff development. Phil has been involved in research in Tanzania and South Africa and taught at Master's level in Abu Dhabi. He has co-authored a book on educational policy and recently completed research on principals in further education colleges. Phil is on the international board for a journal on research in the post-compulsory sector.

CHAPTER 8

Leadership for the Attainment of Improved School Outcomes: A Brazilian, Australian and Maltese Study

Lindy-Anne Abawi, Ana Maria de Albuquerque Moreira, and Christopher Bezzina

INTRODUCTION

The quest for methods to ensure improved educational outcomes for young people is a worldwide 'holy grail'. Unfortunately what appears to be happening is the adoption of educational fashions that fade and re-emerge, often rebadged, as the great 'new' initiative. Today many leaders are sceptical of the latest trends when in many countries there is a flatlining of results or a decline (OECD 2013). Instead they seek real evidence of

L.-A. Abawi (✉)
University of Southern Queensland, Toowoomba, Australia
e-mail: Lindy-Anne.Abawi@usq.edu.au

A.M. de Albuquerque Moreira
University of Brasilia, Brasília, Brazil
e-mail: anaalbuquerque@unb.br

C. Bezzina
University of Malta, Msida, Malta
e-mail: christopher.bezzina@um.edu.mt

© The Author(s) 2017
P. Miller (ed.), *Cultures of Educational Leadership*, Intercultural Studies in Education, DOI 10.1057/978-1-137-58567-7_8

sustained achievement and how they can influence the work of teachers by providing direction, building capacities and creating a work environment that maximises opportunities for individual success (Gurr et al. 2006).

All three countries within this study have nationally established goals aimed at lifting the quality of secondary education outcomes which reflect a need to focus on more than just academic success. The Australian 'Melbourne Declaration on Educational Goals for Young Australians' (Ministerial Council on Education, Employment, Training and Youth Affairs 2008) outlined two overarching goals: to promote equity and excellence, and for all to become successful learners, confident and creative individuals, and active and informed citizens. In Brazil, the National Plan of Education (2014–2024) outlined the goals for secondary education: to universalise access for young people aged 15–17 years, and ensure quality and equity in secondary education (Ministry of Education 2014). In Malta the National Curriculum Framework (NCF) speaks of holistic education that 'supports all learners to achieve and succeed, whatever their background, needs and aptitudes; learning which is active, personalised, relevant and purposeful' (Ministry of Education, Employment and the Ministry of Education Employment and the Family 2011, p. 8).

Through our analysis we explore a sample of high achieving secondary schools in Australia, Malta and Brazil to determine overall factors contributing to student achievement. The Research Based Framework for School Alignment (RBF) (Crowther & Associates 2011) assisted researchers to focus on specific success indicators related to leadership and the alignment of diverse schoolwide practices.

Research Based Framework

School improvement literature focuses attention on a variety of quality practices: the creation of professional learning communities (Hord and Sommers 2008), justifications of practice according to measurable data (Hattie and Yates 2013), authentic learning and assessment (Burke 2009) and the benefits of distributed leadership (Harris 2004; Spillane 2012). What remains problematic is how the various elements of successful school practice work together to produce quality student outcomes. From a leadership perspective it is necessary to understand internal interactions for 'the distinctive characteristic of schools with superior evaluation systems is that their leaders can identify practices that they have stopped doing as a result of insufficient evidence of effectiveness' (Reeves 2009, p. 82).

The RBF allows understanding of internal interactions to be gained. It is grounded in authoritative theory relating to management and organisational alignment (Drucker 1946; Schneider et al. 2003) and complemented by research from the University of Wisconsin–Madison (King and Newman 2001). Alignment in educational organisations occurs when five fundamental variables (see Fig. 8.1) are mutually reinforcing,

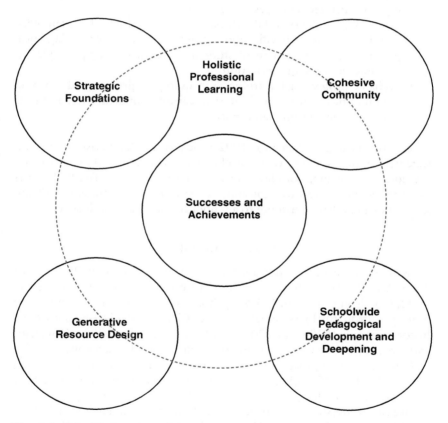

Fig. 8.1 Modified version of the Research Based Framework for Organisational Alignment (Crowther and Associates 2011, p. 175)

thereby enhancing the opportunities for heightened school outcomes (Crowther & Associates 2011, p. 175):

- Strategic foundations, for example, leadership roles and structures; vision and values; recognition of teacher professionalism; and decision making processes
- Cohesive community, for example, stakeholder support; community engagement processes; clear communication channels; and celebrations
- Generative resource design, for example, collective prioritising regarding curricula, technologies and environments
- Schoolwide pedagogical development and deepening, for example, a blend of context-specific and authoritative effective pedagogical practices; encouragement of student voice; linking of principles to systemic policy; and innovation
- Holistic professional learning, for example, professional learning communities; external and internal learning opportunities; and provision of learning time and space.

RBF elements align to Schein's (1992): the artefacts level (visions, mission statements); the espoused values level (values, structures and practice); and the norms and assumptions level (unwritten expectations). The RBF assists in bringing these levels to light and, in the case of this study, identifying strong practices that contribute to a school culture that breeds success.

Utilising 'Snapshots'

Loosely based on a case-study approach (Denzin and Lincoln 2005; Noor 2008; Yin 1993), we took 'snapshots' of each context (Crowther et al. 2002; Goodson et al. 2002). A 'snapshots' approach relates to naturalistic inquiry (Patton 2001), personal narrative (Clandinin and Connelly 1995), historical inquiry (Wineburg 2001) and case study (Yin 1993). Our snapshot approach portrays a cross section of time-specific materials.

Our snapshots approach adheres to a number of Yin's Case Study design criteria (2014, p. 45): using multiple sources of evidence; pattern matching and explanation building; theory based; and the development of a database. Unlike case study, snapshots are not collated over an extended time period but within a window of time framed by a specific preconceived investigation intent which in this study is the investigation of school leadership within secondary schools displaying high achievement data.

Data Collection and Analysis

Schools were randomly chosen from government web site data collations indicating high achieving schools—socio-economic status was not a consideration. Selection was refined according to geographical availability and the willingness of the principal and teachers to be involved.

Digitally recorded semi-structured interviews (Noor 2008) based on questions related to school practices and procedures were transcribed and combined with related data sources (e.g., web sites), then analysed for indicators suggesting why each school had achieved high levels of academic success to determine (1) similar elements, or (2) context-specific elements. Findings are summarised under each of the RBF domains and illustrated with one or two brief data extracts indented and placed in italics following the summary.

Each school has a fictitious name identified by italicised initials with participant contributions identified by abbreviations: principal (P); teacher (T1, T2, T3 and T4).

Australian Snapshot

Australian education systems vary from state to state, and from government-funded schools to Catholic and independent schools with 65 % of students attending government schools (Australian Bureau of Statistics 2014). Education is compulsory between the ages of 6 and 16 with 90 % of students attending pre-schooling options. In 2012 the Australian Curriculum was launched. Core curriculum subjects such as English, mathematics and science were the first to be implemented Australia-wide within both primary and secondary school settings. Additional discipline areas have now been added.

The Australian Qualifications Framework, established in 1995, is a national policy governing higher education pathways and secondary schools must meet government standards. Post-school higher education options for students include vocational education and training providers and varied university pathways. According to the 2012 PISA (Program for International Student Assessment) data, although mathematics and reading results are slipping, Australian schools consistently perform better than the OECD average. The biggest issue for Australian educators is the gap between the lowest and highest achievers (Thomson et al. 2014).

AUSTRALIAN CASE STUDIES

According to the Australian national database (MySchool) student achievement results for the case-study schools have been consistently above, or well above, those of schools similar in size, socio-economic background and demographics.

Westlake College (WC) is a non-denominational, co-educational, metropolitan private school in Victoria. It caters for over 1,300 students up to Year 12 with 30 % of enrolments being from an 'English as another language' family background. No students identify as being of Aboriginal or Torres Strait Islander descent. The leadership structure consists of a principal, a deputy principal and two heads of school (junior and senior) assisted by heads of departments. Students come from families of high-economic status (MySchool).

Fairmont State High (FSH) is a regional government secondary school in Queensland. The student population comprises of approximately 1,400 students in years 7–12. The leadership structure consists of one principal, three deputy principals and heads of departments. Demographically the school sits within an average to slightly lower than average socio-economic index range with 13 % of students coming from diverse cultural backgrounds and an additional 5 % identifying as Indigenous. Emphasis is placed on community partnerships and catering for individual student needs. There is a large special education programme in place.

In each school **strategic foundations** were characterised by a strong school culture reinforced by verbal, visual, relational and aural expectations based on a shared vision and consciously developed shared understandings of processes and practices.

Both schools articulated beliefs and values systems placing student welfare at the centre of decision-making. The principal of Fairmont demonstrated a strong moral commitment to social justice. In both schools education of the 'whole child' was a priority. Social and emotional well-being were fore-fronted and students were explicitly taught to demonstrate respect for others. Distributed leadership practices were evident with professional learning communities and networks for actioning in place consisting of teacher leaders, student leaders and community leaders.

> [The Principal] has her little catchphrase . . . If you come to school you are going to be safe, you are going to be respected and you are going to learn. (FSH T1)

> We are each expected to be leaders in our own right—if we take her a problem we...even students...have to....suggest a solution. (FSH T3)
>
> The Principal's catch cry of 'Every child—Every moment' can be seen and heard. (WSC T1)
>
> School values—community, scholarship, courage and creativity—help to create a sense of purpose. (WSC P)

Both schools show evidence of a **cohesive community** characterised by diverse learning experiences built on positive relationships based on trust and reinforced by the explicit teaching of school values and expectations.

Parents are acknowledged and welcomed as integral to student learning success. FSH has a visible parent presence in the first 2 years but this diminishes over time. WSC has less of a visible parent presence. Both schools have parent information blogs on school web sites and WSC has a parent portal where student progress and achievement is continually mapped. Text messages and phone calls keep parents informed. Wider community connections, including with the local university, offer ongoing partnerships for providing extended learning opportunities. At FSH medical practitioners are a part of the partnership because many students have varied physical, emotional and cognitive needs. Generally students and staff feel safe and respected. At FSH safe spaces and places are readily accessible to students in need. Celebrations of achievement are targeted, varied, visible and regular. WSC has removed punishment and reward scenarios and replaced these with celebrations and goal-setting activities aligned to a restorative justice approach, whilst FSH developed support strategies to 'head problems off at the pass'.

> We're a team and we won't accept anything else. So when you come into this room you are going to be safe and you are going to be respected. (FSH T5)
>
> We believe in developing growth mindsets—within staff and students. (WSC P)

Generative resource design was characterised by resourcing to meet individual student needs and interests according to collectively established priorities informed by data and schoolwide pedagogical approaches.

Principals spoke of resourcing according to need as aligned to vision. At FSH strong relationships developed with feeder primary schools means information is at hand prior to a new school year commencing and additional resources, whether they be physical or human, can be accessed and put in place where required. Both principals talked about funding priority-driven targeted professional development opportunities for staff—both teachers and teacher aides. Digital technologies that support curriculum delivery and learning were a high priority. WSC is well resourced in this area whilst FSH talked about the need to cleverly stretch budgets in order to purchase iPads and other learning manipulatives to assist particular students with learning. Learning spaces are also consciously adjusted to meet the needs of specific individual learners.

> When we knew Student x would be joining us...we had to start getting supports in place. Aides did additional training and we approached district office to cover the financial cost of air-conditioning, a specially tailored desk and support chair. (FSH T4)
> At times student interests take us in different directions and we have prioritised purchase of new desks, chairs, computers and learning hub hotpoints to provide options. (WSC T1)

Both schools illustrated forms of **schoolwide pedagogical development and deepening** characterised by data-driven focused discussion developing pedagogical understandings about contextualised ways of working across the school.

Pedagogical conversations take the form of team meetings, data analysis sessions, professional learning communities and in the case of WSC shared action research projects. At WSC they use the SOLO taxonomy (Biggs and Collis 1989) and four pillars for learning as a schoolwide pedagogical framework. Differentiation and inclusion are the major focuses for FSH staff. In both contexts new staff are oriented into the school's ways of working. Effective communication strategies ensure messages are consistent across both schools. There is a sense that staff, students, parents and any of those closely involved in each school are 'on the same page'.

> We have the same expectations—the same language. (FSH T1)
> Students also relate to the various stages of the SOLO taxonomy—from pre-structural thinking into extended abstract thinking. (WSC T1)

Holistic professional learning was a strong focus with principals indicating the ongoing desire to support professional knowledge acquisition, and the sharing and building of leadership capacity.

Principals praised their staff's willingness to be involved in additional professional development and conversations about improving practice regardless of whether after-school time commitment was required or not. Teachers spoke about '*doing what it takes*' to ensure positive outcomes for students. School cultures embraced open-collaboration and discussion. Teachers received assistance and shared their expertise. Many of the responses to interview questions indicated a lack of acceptance with the status quo and a continual striving for new ideas and ways of working. Change overload appeared in conversations but was related to external impositions rather than the internal goal-driven changes to which the majority of staff were committed.

> A lot of our PD ... has been about differentiation ... we've got kids coming in and although we've got a SOSE class, you've still got to teach reading because some kids can't read. (FSH T2)
>
> The Principal and Curriculum Leader really want us to develop an ongoing research culture and for many of us this will lead into doing our Masters. (WSC T3)

BRAZILIAN SNAPSHOT

Brazilian education is structured at two main levels: basic and higher education. The basic level comprises of three stages: early childhood education (from 0 to 5 years old), primary education (from 6 to 9 years old) and secondary education (from 15 to 17 years old). Higher education options for students include university bachelor's degree, the licentiate, technologic graduate and postgraduate studies. Education is compulsory between the ages of 4–17.

Brazil has a federative regime consisting of public and private schools which vary significantly across three management levels: Federal Union, State and Municipality. Secondary education is currently a great challenge. According to the System of Social Information (2014), in the population of 15–17 year olds, 15.2 % did not study and did not commence secondary school and only 54.3 % of young people aged 19 completed the final years of education. According to the 2012 PISA data, although Brazil performs below the OECD average, its performance in mathematics has improved between 2003 and 2012. Current issues relate to access to education and reducing dropout rates thus raising retention rates and ensuring quality and equity.

Brazilian Case Studies

The two schools were selected as 'snapshots' because they presented results above the average in the public system of the Federal District at the National Secondary Education Examination (ENEM). The information comes from ENEM's 2014 database, published by the National Institute of Educational Studies and Research of the Ministry of Education.

Anisio Teixeira Secondary School (ATSS) is located at north quarter, in the town centre of Brasilia, District Federal. ATSS's mission is that all students should attain 3 years of secondary education. According to ENEM's database, students are mostly of high socio-economic status. The staff consists of one principal, one deputy principal, one supervisor, three coordinators and two pedagogic advisors. Results show high grade point averages in all evaluated fields: language, mathematics, human sciences, natural sciences and writing. More than 50% of the students who conclude their education at ATSS enter university. However, first-year dropout rates are a concern.

Juscelino Kubitschek College (JKC) is located at south quarter in the town centre of Brasilia, District Federal. Four hundred and fifty students attend JKC for their 3 years of secondary education. JKC is an inclusive school catering also for visually impaired students. According to ENEM, students are mostly of high socio-economic strata living in Brasilia and its suburbs. Results show grade point averages are higher than the norm in all evaluated fields. Students who concluded their secondary education at JKC enter university. The staff consists of one principal, one deputy principal, two supervisors, four coordinators and three pedagogic advisors. Dropout rates and outcomes in maths, physics and chemistry are a concern.

In each school the **strategic foundations** are characterised by an administrative focus on a strong adherence to school values, shared mission and a culture of all-round education.

The two schools present clear guidelines regarding school objectives and learning outcomes to be achieved. These determine decision-making processes but are limited by funding constraints. Differences are observed regarding the focus on student achievement. The principal of ATSS declared that the school's objective is the all-round education of the students; nevertheless, there is a large panel at the entrance with a list of successful students and the universities they have entered. Meanwhile, the principal of JKC clearly states a focus on preparing students for admission into higher education courses which is more difficult for students from basic public schools. Both demonstrate commitment to student welfare and secondary school completion.

Mission statements, beliefs and values guide planning and day-to-day activities. Both schools identify student profiles and develop strategies to increase engagement with ongoing learning.

> Our focus is the welfare and educational background given to the student. (ATSS P)
>
> (Our focus) is to include students and prepare them to the university entrance exams. (ATSS T2)
>
> Almost 98 % of students aspire for higher education. So we concentrate a lot in obtaining results for ENEM and PAS exams, but do not leave aside values and discipline in the day-to-day school routine. (JKC P)
>
> The School aims to educate citizens ... Teachers are always concerned in directing students to the universities. (JKC T2)

Cohesive community is characterised by the engagement of teachers and students with the pedagogical and cultural activities of the school and a positive relationship between the different segments of the school.

In both schools the principals spoke about the cultural diversity and the importance in promoting activities with the objective of enhancing student well-being. A positive relationship with the teachers is considered very important. This is based on trust and dialogue.

> Relationship between teachers and direction must be built. Today we live a good relationship of trust with the teachers ... You must listen to the teachers and convince them of the importance of building a vision of school. (ATSS P)

The two schools are considered by the community as above average in the public system of the town and attract students from various locations. This choice shows the acknowledgement and confidence of families in how the schools are run. Nevertheless both principals pointed out the lack of participation by parents in meetings and school activities. Mostly, parents only come to school after receiving a communication to do so. The principal of ATSS stresses that parents are present to receive students' scores and grades at the beginning of the school year as well as in the first year but afterwards the frequency of their involvement declines. The low involvement of families in secondary public schools has been observed in other studies (Moreira and Aires 2015).

JKC is located in the town centre and student families do not live in the neighbourhood. As a consequence parent participation is low ... parents respond when called individually. (JKC P)

Parents are present at meetings during the 1st year, then their frequency declines ... the school calls the parents as any problem comes up, this is important to them and increases confidence in our work. (ATSS P)

Generative resource design is characterised by the emphasis on pedagogic objectives and the participation of representatives of different sectors of the school in the decision making process.

As established by Brazilian legislation, both schools are maintained by public funds administrated by the Secretary of Education of the Federal District. In both cases, school leaders manage the school space, the material, technological and financial resources according to school characteristics and the need to raise quality according to the school's pedagogical plan.

Management of resources is done in partnership with school community representatives in adherence to specific criteria. The School Council—constituted by the principal, teachers, students, parents and school personnel—contribute to decisions about allocating funds. However, problems persist in areas where resources are not sufficient and school autonomy is limited.

Financial and administrative resources are intended exclusively for the pedagogical area and development of extra-curricular projects. ... (JKC P)

We're missing some resources such as the update of the library. (JKC T1)

We concentrate our available resources for the development of the pedagogical activities and we receive financial resources from the national program for innovative secondary education to apply in extra-curricular projects ... but last year we did not received these resources. (ATSS P)

In general resources are scarce due to low public investment in schools. (ATSS T1)

In both schools **schoolwide pedagogical development and deepening** is characterised by innovative projects aimed at developing creativity and improved schools outcomes.

The curriculum developed by both schools follows National Curricular Directives for Secondary Education (DCNEM). Core subjects are languages, maths, human and natural sciences. Schools also follow guidelines from the 'Curriculum in Motion' materials set by the Secretary of Education of the Federal District, but they have autonomy to develop their own projects regarding the contents of the disciplines. Therein lies the key to pedagogic innovation in the school. Pedagogic activities are systematically planned for and evaluated during professional conversations by teachers working in discipline areas or areas of concern.

Broader involvement with community and partnerships with universities and other institutions are aimed at developing projects that enhance student success. Beyond those projects both schools promote a series of thematic workshops aimed at improving specific student abilities. These initiatives stimulate pedagogical innovation in an attempt to reduce drop-out rates and raise the quality of learning.

> The development of projects contributes to the exchange of information and experience and shows students that knowledge should be learned in an interdisciplinary way. (JKC T1)
>
> Workshops are carried out ... and have an impact on performance and to make the student like school. (ATSS P)
>
> Improvements have occurred in the performance of students with the methodology of the curriculum in motion. (ATSS T1)

Holistic professional learning is characterised by democratic management, the sharing of knowledge and experiences, and the constitution of shared leadership in the school context.

Both schools are going through a process of democratic management that includes a wide range of members developing the capacity for 'attentive listening', participation and responsibility contributing to the establishment of shared leadership. Both schools systematically organise meetings to discuss pedagogic planning. Shared understandings are developed showing that an important part of a teacher's knowledge is relational and tacit, whilst another is acquired and developed during professional activity and the sharing of experiences. Learning and sharing processes tend to consolidate into a 'shared know how' that enhances the distributed leadership culture across each school.

> During the gatherings to discuss school planning, all personnel participate, including cleaning and surveillance people, so that they all feel responsible for the student's formation. (JKC P)

We joined forces, experiences and knowledge to improve the process of teaching and learning. (JKC T2)

Teachers are encouraged to use external coordination in order to do further training courses or other educational entities. (ATSS P)

The projects focused in interdisciplinarity and transdisciplinarity learning and assist teachers professionally. (ATSS T1)

MALTESE SNAPSHOT

The Maltese education system has three main sectors—a State-run system catering for around 60 % of the student population, a Roman Catholic Church school sector catering for just over 30 % and an independent fee-paying sector catering for around 6 % of the student population. Recently co-educational schools have started to be established but the majority remain as single sex schools. Current reforms are seeing the Catholic school sector increasing its population as a number of schools have started catering for both primary and secondary students. Education is compulsory for children aged 5–16 but with the majority of children in the 3–5 bracket attending kindergartens across the three sectors. All secondary schools follow programmes leading to national and international examinations leading to higher education.

Maltese schools must follow a National Curriculum prescribed by the education authorities. The country is bilingual with most schools teaching subject areas in Maltese and English. Malta took part in the 2009+ PISA and achieved mean scores in reading, mathematics and science results are lower than both the EU and OECD averages. Of major concern is the gap that exists between the lowest and highest achievers. Given a drive to devolve greater responsibilities to school sites, schools have been encouraged to develop School Development Plans which bring staff and community members together to identify and address school needs. Each plan highlights the vision, aims and targets that schools are addressing at a given period of time. It is meant to be a living document—'celebrating what we stand for'—as one principal put it.

MALTESE CASE STUDIES

Malta is a small island state and yet social and economic differences exist in particular regions and the social fabric influences student achievement. This is further exacerbated by increasing levels of diversity as the migrant population increases. Regardless of context-specific differences the two case-study schools have similar characteristics. One school caters for girls in the northern region of the island and the other for boys in central Malta.

Westbrown Secondary School (WSS) is a single-sex girls' school. The leadership structure consists of one principal, two deputy principals and three heads of department. This is officially recognised as the School Management Team (SMT). The college attracts students from towns and villages in the northern part of the island. The student cohort comes from families of average to above average economic status. It caters for 520 students aged between 13 and 15 years. The majority of children hail from Maltese-speaking parents, although there is a growing population of foreign students, currently making up 16 % of the school population and coming from 20 different nationalities. There is an emphasis on creating and maintaining a safe and welcoming environment for all, supporting children whatever their needs and celebrating and rewarding all forms of achievement.

St Clementine (SC) is a secondary school for boys in the central part of the island. The student population comprises approximately 1,200 students between the ages of 11 and 16. The SMT consists of one principal, five deputy principals and four heads of department. Demographically, the school population sits within the average to slightly above average socio-economic index range. There are strong links between the primary and secondary schools within the network and teachers speak highly of their students. Structures are in place to make students feel safe and proud to belong to this school. Similar to WSS, the priority is to celebrate and reward students who make that extra effort to obtain better results. They also support students whose social and economic milieu may preclude them from having a pleasant and profitable school experience.

In both schools **strategic foundations** are characterised by a strong emphasis on a shared set of values that underlie a shared vision, one directed towards providing a holistic education to all children. Both schools share a drive to provide 'educational experiences' that help develop the skills and values needed to live an engaging life in local communities that are becoming progressively more multi-faith and multi-ethnic.

Social developments, together with a drive to engage a more participative approach to decision making, show a commitment to greater involvement by teachers through various forms of collaboration.

> The school management team makes it a point to meet and engage with teachers on a regular basis encouraging them to take on responsibilities. (WSS P)
>
> We have introduced a system where more experienced teachers help out newly-qualified teachers through a mentoring scheme. (SC T1)

One principal noted that 'we need to work more to adequately reach out to the community' (SC P) emphasising that whilst the principle of networking and community outreach are within the school policy this is still deemed as a challenge.

Each school shows evidence of a **cohesive community**, one characterised by a positive relationship between the different school members and the development of external partnerships.

Lines of communication between teachers include email contact and weekly staff meetings. The members of the SMT are involved in departmental meetings. Student voice is evident through the active role that the student council plays and they also contribute towards the type of extracurricular activities offered.

Both schools do their utmost to support diverse student needs. The SMT celebrate good practices through personal conversation and notes of thanks. Some respondents noted that whilst a number of teachers state that they assume responsibility for individual students by providing them with time to address their needs, whether academic or personal, others were less explicit but still did so in practice, emphasising the altruistic nature of educators.

> As time goes by I am realising that students need to see the person in us rather than the teacher only interested in teaching his or her subject. I make it a point to show and give them time to come to me and talk about their needs...This does not come easy and at times is quite draining. (WSS T2)

Both schools recently established a partnership with the Faculty of Education within the University of Malta to support a mentoring scheme for teachers in the Initial Teacher Education stage. This is a new initiative and the intent is to see a strong relationship established between school members and faculty staff as they explore and engage in different initiatives.

In a context that is based on a college network system **generative resource design** sees a collective effort by the two principals who work within a system that sees needs identified, discussed and decisions taken collectively.

Information is shared, disseminated and discussed with central authorities who then provide the human and physical resources needed. These requests are linked to national priorities, college and school development plans.

As established by Maltese legislation both schools are maintained through public funds. All structural costs are covered by central authorities with schools being provided with maintenance funds to address running costs. Both central authorities and the school authorities through different bodies can generate funds or allocate funds to address particular needs as stipulated by the SDPs.

Even in a context inundated with reform and with teachers experiencing reform fatigue, both principals noted that teachers do their utmost to reflect and improve their practice.

> Through our SMT meetings we are always asking questions such as 'how are we doing?', 'how can we improve our practices?'. We are also engaging other educators to help us reflect on the way we do things around here. (SC P)

Both schools illustrate some form of **schoolwide pedagogical development and deepening** with documents expressing this as a priority area to enhance student achievement.

St Clementine staff spoke of the need to address issues of inclusion as more and more students were identified as facing learning difficulties leading to teachers facing doubts about their ability to support all students.

> The number of students identified as facing learning difficulties is on the increase. I often feel so helpless not knowing what to do next, how to go about addressing particular needs. (SC T3)

Both principals noted that reflection sessions take the form of departmental meetings headed by heads of department. Specific discourse also focuses on national data provided by the assessment unit where student achievement is measured against national benchmarks.

Holistic professional learning is recognised by both schools as a pivotal component to enhance teacher knowledge and skills and improve student learning.

Both principals spoke of the collegial learning processes that are in place to ensure that 'teachers share and discuss their practice'. This takes place with strong adherence to the schools' vision and as agreed upon by staff. Both mentioned mentoring schemes that support newly qualified teachers (NQTs), and the seeking of help or assistance from both internal and external educators.

One principal noted a mentoring process that created a possibility for educators to enter into a dialogic communication with a more experienced mentor. In fact one of the teachers noted that:

> I have learnt to share things that have worked for me with my colleagues . . . when we find something that works we share it together . . . (WSS T2)

Another spoke of the sense of empowerment felt as the school principal allowed them to share their initiatives.

Spotlights

It is important to acknowledge the differences of policies, practices, school management, funding regimes and stages of secondary education in the three countries. Further investigations also need to be carried out, especially in schools that fall below the mean socio-economic index (as by chance only one school fell into this category). Nonetheless, these Australian, Brazilian and Maltese snapshots reveal significant themes related to leadership in high-achieving contexts (see Table 8.1). The intent is not to generalise but to highlight key observations, views and opinions shared by staff from six schools in three different countries.

In each of the schools within this study, focus was placed upon meeting diverse student needs through extra-curricular activities, establishing quality relationships between teachers and students, and seeking partnerships beyond school boundaries. Parental engagement was generally difficult to obtain. Partnerships with universities were either developed or being developed in all contexts. All examples reveal the importance of the school leader not working alone but being open to exchange and dialogue with diverse 'others'.

Defining students' needs and interests was a priority and achieved through collaborative processes involving data collection and collegial discussions between principals, teachers and coordinators. Leaders created clear connections to shared understandings and shared vision. They articulated the

Table 8.1 Prominent themes within the domains of the RBF

Strategic foundations	Cohesive community	SWP development and deepening	Generative resource design	Holistic professional learning
Leaders connect vision to practice	Parental engagement difficult	Shared sense of direction	Overall funding is governed by the government body	Professional conversations
Clear direction distributed leadership structure	University partnerships	Shared understandings and expectations	Australian schools have a little more autonomy in the prioritising of funding—particularly in the independent system	Teachers are constantly seeking new ways to improve student engagement and outcomes
Student-centred decision making	Celebrating and catering for diversity	Collaborative data collection and interpretation	Resourcing according to student need	Regular discussions between leaders and teachers
Leaders make clear efforts to have open communication channels	Broader community relationships	Identifying students interests—extra-curricular options		Opportunities to learn from colleagues were valued

importance of ongoing professional conversations and commitment to distributed leadership. Although actioned a little differently according to context, mechanisms were in place to promote leadership with distributed leadership concepts embedded horizontally and vertically (Torrance and Humes 2015).

From this study implications arise regarding the concept of alignment according to the five dimensions of the RBF. We believe that the data situated within the 'holistic professional learning' domain is a key indicator of how alignment might be attained and maintained in schools. Brazilian and Maltese school leaders appeared to have less financial autonomy in this area than Australian school leaders, but regardless of differences or limitations all school leaders used what was available to mobilise pedagogical improvement.

Regardless of the challenges, leaders consciously built distributed leadership capacity and created an environment that enabled the sharing and building of pedagogical knowledge at all levels of the school community, thus establishing a culture that enhances student achievement.

CONCLUSIONS AND RECOMMENDATIONS

When looking across the 'snapshot' cases presented it should be immediately apparent that all the principals are highly capable leaders, having common ideals that embrace the needs of students. They have set and maintained a sense of common purpose which sees them working with and through people to accomplish goals that help to improve the life chances of students. Each principal, in her/his own way within their respective community, strives to establish strong networks which allow people to come together. The networks are not only vertical and horizontal within each respective school but extend to other stakeholders, such as universities.

We particularly like the phrase used of developing 'safe spaces and places' for people to grow and develop. We see a leadership style directed at the creation of engaging learning experiences for students and teachers alike. A lot of energy went into applying systems thinking to the task of developing distinctive, enabling structures that would promote personal, interpersonal and organisational learning throughout the schools. Principals encouraged personal and collective learning through the sharing of information, valuing differences, raising awareness of the school's big picture and enabling all to see and take responsibility for the consequences of professional actions and preferences.

Another interesting point that emerged is that principals placed a lot of effort in creating enabling management structures. Decision making and planning occurred across levels and teachers were brought together to address issues that they themselves identified and wanted to be directly involved in tackling. The opportunities for reflection promoted dialogue and encouraged critical conversations. Such discourse meant that teachers gained a sense of what Holden describes as 'a personal sense of personal agency, empowerment from this conscious and deliberate interaction with the culture of the school' (2002, p. 12).

These snapshots confirm previous findings that successful improvement depends on transformational leadership, one based on a clear and unifying vision, an emphasis on learning, a commitment to teamwork and time for reflection. To some extent they also show that whether working in decentralised systems (Australia and Brazil) or centralised ones (Malta), in contexts that are data-driven and focused on academic results/achievement, the schools that make a difference are those that utilise distributed leadership practices focused not only on academic issues but which also address the affective domain. Rather than merely following prescription or the dictates of central authorities, quality change and quality improvement depends on the inner potential of school staff—on the 'heads, hands and hearts' of educators who work in schools (Sirotnik and Clark 1988, p. 660). The responses from principals and teachers show that relationships are the key to improvement. Hard work, sacrifice and commitment lead to enhanced student engagement in learning and their potential for growth and development.

From these findings a number of recommendations can be articulated that could help in the way we look at the impact of leaders and leadership on school improvement, and the way that leaders and aspiring leaders can look at the way they relate with their roles and responsibilities.

Creating a safe and inviting environment requires that principals model good practices – that they are seen to be focusing their energies for staff and students alike. All principals, in whichever context they may be in, can reflect on their own beliefs and practices. We are not presented with rhetorical flourishes aimed merely at acknowledging policies; instead there is evidence of commitment to deeply held beliefs leading to the creation of safe, welcoming environments.

Recommendation 1 is for principals and aspiring principals to look into the way they articulate beliefs in everyday practice – to see what they do to engage staff and nurture collective responsibility. The Research Based Framework helps us to appreciate that the principals made strong strides to establish the appropriate strategic foundations that nurture communities of good practice through the focus on a holistic professional learning. These in turn are central to the way staff engage with curriculum and pedagogical matters.

Another point that leads to the next recommendation can be articulated through a series of questions. What skills are needed by school principals to take our schools forward? What is expected of school leaders today? Such questions can easily be answered through existing policy documents – through an analysis of what is being presented in each respective country. The challenge is to know how principals use these skills in practice – what is behind the principles and beliefs they uphold.

Recommendation 2 is that aspiring principals be provided with opportunities to observe and be mentored into the leadership role. Whilst there is a lot of understanding of the core skills school leaders need to contribute to the improvement of student learning we know less about how such individuals acquire the practical application of these skills. District/state or national authorities need to develop school leader preparation programmes which include the possibility of mentoring partnerships or, even better, internship placements in different types of schools and settings. Ideally, such placements should be in schools with leaders who have a proven record of success in improving student learning. Mentoring could also take the shape of giving recently retired successful school leaders the opportunity to visit and consult with schools.

Another issue worth pursuing is to explore the concept of altruism. In a context often determined by central authorities with schools having to follow the dictum of the state, it is extremely comforting and encouraging to see how teachers and school leaders are willing to go that extra mile, to give of themselves so that goals are reached, that collaborative practices are introduced.

The study shows the need for further research in this area. How far are schools conditioned by the roles and responsibilities assigned to them? Of what benefit are external partnerships? How willing are we to challenge the status quo, the prescription of the authorities? Answers to these questions are essential if we are to fully understand what teachers and leaders do to achieve student-centred goals which brings us to our final recommendation—Recommendation 3. Readers should engage with the responses within each of the framework domains. How do the varied responses impinge on your own beliefs and how do these translate into practice in your context?

This study has merely scratched the surface of the complex and demanding world that educators inhabit. However, the framework does allow us to reflect on how different elements come together therefore allowing us to better understand what school leaders do, and can do, to make a difference.

REFERENCES

Australian Bureau of Statistics. (2014). *Commentary on student numbers.* http://www.abs.gov.au/ausstats/abs@.nsf/mf/4221.0. Accessed 11 December 2015.
Biggs, J., & Collis, K. (1989). Towards a model of school-based curriculum development and assessment using the SOLO taxonomy. *Australian Journal of Education, 33*(2), 151–163.

Burke, K. (2009). *How to assess authentic learning*. Thousand Oaks, CA: Corwin.

Clandinin, D. J., & Connelly, M. (1995). *Teachers' professional landscapes*. New York, NY: Teachers College Press.

Crowther, F., & Associates. (2011). *From school improvement to sustained capacity: the parallel leadership pathway*. Thousand Oaks, CA: Corwin (Sage).

Crowther, F., Kaagan, S., Ferguson, M., & Hann, L. (2002). *Developing teacher leaders: how teacher leadership enhances school success*. Thousand Oaks, CA: Corwin Press.

Denzin, N. K., & Lincoln, Y. S. (Eds.) (2005). *The SAGE handbook of qualitative research* (3rd edn). Thousand Oaks, CA: Sage.

Drucker, P. F. (1946). *Concept of the organization* (revised edn). New York, NY: John Day.

Goodson, I., Knobel, M., Lankshear, C., & Marshall Mangan, J. (2002). *Spaces/social spaces*. New York, NY: Palgrave Macmillan.

Gurr, D., Drysdale, L., & Mulford, B. (2006). Models of successful principal leadership. *School Leadership and Management*, 26(4), 371–395.

Harris, A. (2004). Teacher leadership and distributed leadership. *Leading & Managing*, 10(2), 1–9.

Hattie, J., & Yates, G. (2013). *Visible learning and the science of how we learn*. New York, NY: Routledge.

Holden, G. (2002). Towards a learning community. *Professional Development Today*, Spring: 7–16.

Hord, S., & Sommers, W. (2008). *Leading professional learning communities: voices from research and practice*. Thousand Oaks, CA: Corwin Press.

King, M. B., & Newman, F. M. (2001). Building school capacity through professional development: conceptual and empirical considerations. *The International Journal of Educational Management*, 15(2), 86–94.

Ministerial Council on Education, Employment, Training and Youth Affairs. (2008). *Melbourne declaration on educational goals for young Australians*. http://www.curriculum.edu.au/verve/_resources/National_Declaration_on_the_Educational_Goals_for_Young_Australians.pdf. Accessed 11 January 2016.

Ministry of Education Employment and the Family. (2011). *Towards a quality education for all: the national curriculum framework 2011*. Floriana: Ministry of Education, Employment and the Family.

Ministry of Education. (2014). *Planejando a Próxima Década: Conhecendo as 20 metas do Plano Nacional de Educação*. http://pne.mec.gov.br/images/pdf/pne_conhecendo_20_metas.pdf. Accessed 19 November 2015.

Moreira, A. M. A., & Aires, C. J. (2015). *A avaliação do Pacto Nacional pelo Fortalecimento do Ensino Médio na percepção de gestores escolares do Distrito Federal*. Lisboa, Brasil: EDUCA/Secção Portuguesa da AFIRSE.

Noor, K. B. (2008). Case study: a strategic research methodology. *American Journal of Applied Sciences*, 5(11), 1602–1604.

OECD. (2013). *PISA 2012 results: excellence through equity.* http://www.oecd.org/pisa/keyfindings/pisa-2012-results-volume-II.pdf. Accessed 9 November 2015.

Patton, M. Q. (2001). *Qualitative evaluation and research methods* (2nd edn). Thousand Oaks, CA: Sage.

Reeves, D. (2009). *Leading change in your school.* Alexandria, Virginia: ASCD.

Schein, E. H. (1992). *Organizational culture and leadership* (2nd edn). San Francisco, CA: Jossey-Bass.

Schneider, B., Godfrey, E., Hayes, S., Huang, M., Lim, B., Nishii, L., et al. (2003). The human side of strategy: employee experiences of strategic alignment in a service organization. *Organizational Dynamics*, 32(2), 122–141.

Sirotnik, K. A., & Clark, R. W. (1988). School-centred decision making and renewal. *Phi Delta Kappan*, 69(9), 660–664.

Spillane, J. (2012). *Distributed leadership.* San Francisco, CA: Josey-Bass.

Torrance, D., & Humes, W. (2015). The shifting discourses of educational leadership: international trends and Scotland's response. *Educational Management Administration & Leadership*, 43(5), 792–810.

Thomson, S., De Bortoli, L., & Buckley, S. (2014). *The PISA 2012 assessment of students' mathematical, scientific and reading literacy.* Victoria, Australia: Australian Council for Educational Research.

Volpi, M., Silva, M. S., & Ribeiro, J. (Eds.) (2014). *10 desafios do ensino médio no Brasil: Para garantir o direito de aprender de adolescents de 15 a 17 anos.* Brasília, DF: UNICEF.

Wineburg, S. (2001). *Historical thinking and other unnatural acts.* Philadelphia: Temple University.

Yin, R. (1993). *Application of case study research.* Thousand Oaks, CA: Sage.

Yin, R. (2014). *Case study research: Design and methods* (5th edn). Los Angeles, CA: Sage.

Lindy-Anne Abawi, PhD, is Associate Dean for Learning and Teaching in the Faculty of Business, Education, Arts and Law at the University of Southern Queensland, Australia. She has worked across multiple educational sectors and is a member of the Leadership Research International group based at the University of Southern Queensland. Her research interest is driven by the desire to build the capacity of educators in order for them to reach their full potential, thus ensuring positive outcomes for all learners. She researches in the fields of school improvement, institution-wide alignment and the development of inclusive educational institutions and class contexts.

Ana Maria de Albuquerque Moreira, PhD, is a professor at the Department of Planning and Educational Management, Faculty of Education, University of Brasilia, Brazil. She holds a doctorate in Public Policies and Management of Education, and her thesis was about the influence of institutional factors regarding the student's performance on science graduates. Her more recent research interest areas are related to management practices and theories at both the tertiary and secondary school levels, and she continues to research in the fields of policies, planning, funding and management of basic and higher education.

Christopher Bezzina, PhD, FCCEAM, is Professor of Educational Leadership at Faculty of Education, University of Malta, Malta. He is currently Deputy Dean and Head of the Department of Leadership for Learning and Innovation at the University of Malta. He has taught and done consultancy work in various countries. Research interests include the professional development of school leaders and teachers, as well as nurturing professional learning communities, governance, the self-evaluation of schools and policy-making. Also serves on a number of editorial advisory boards. Christopher is President of the Malta Society for Educational Administration and Management and Vice President of the Commonwealth Council for Educational Administration and Management (CCEAM).

CHAPTER 9

Sustaining Growth of Novice Teachers to Leadership Through Mentorship Process: A Study of Praxis in Brazil, Canada, Pakistan, and South Africa

Elizabeth F. Majocha, Marco Antonio Margarido Costa, Mamotena Mpeta, Nargis Ara, Catherine A. Whalen, and Terezinha Alves Fernandes

E.F. Majocha (✉)
Gabriel Dumont Institute, Saskatoon, Canada
e-mail: jp.majocha@shaw.ca

M.A.M. Costa
Universidade Federal de Campina Grande, Campina Grande, Brazil
e-mail: marcanco@terra.com.br

M. Mpeta
University of Venda, Thohoyandou, South Africa
e-mail: mamotena.mpeta@univen.ac.za

N. Ara
Government Girls Post Graduate College, Chishtian, Pakistan
e-mail: natriumn1@hotmail.com

C.A. Whalen
University of Northern British Columbia, Prince George, Canada
e-mail: Catherine.Whalen@unbc.ca

T.A. Fernandes
Universidade Federal da Paraíba, João Pessoa, Brazil
e-mail: terezinhaafernandes@hotmail.com

© The Author(s) 2017
P. Miller (ed.), *Cultures of Educational Leadership*, Intercultural Studies in Education, DOI 10.1057/978-1-137-58567-7_9

INTRODUCTION

Encouraging promising novice teachers in the public school system to become leaders is an issue of international interest, because statistics have revealed that the highest rate of teacher attrition occurs within the first 5 years of professional service (Alliance for Excellent Education 2005; Cooper and Alvarado 2006; Harfitt 2015; Ingersoll 2001). Awareness and understanding of novice teachers' needs is essential to understand their high rate of early attrition. Harfitt argued that the problem of retaining beginning teachers, particularly in the first 2–5 years following graduation, is a worldwide phenomenon.

Recent educational literature has stated that it is a challenging time to be a teacher in the public school system (Stone 2015). Western countries, in particular, reveal an international trend of frustration in the education system in that sufficient numbers of teachers are trained to teach, but many novice teachers leave the field within the first few years (Cooper and Alvarado 2006; Harfitt 2015). Research evidence has shown that teacher effectiveness spikes sharply after the first 3–5 years in the profession, but teachers commonly exit the profession prior to attaining this level of expertise (Kain and Singleton 1996; Worthy 2005). The Organization for Economic Co-Operation and Development ([OECD] 2009) emphasized the global importance of novice-teacher attrition rates and the reasons for these high rates: 29 % of teachers work in schools without a formal induction process for novice teachers, and 25 % work in schools without a mentoring programme for novice teachers.

The main challenges that novice teachers face are increasing with the complexity of teachers' work environment (Alberta Teachers' Association (n.d.); LeMaistre and Pare 2010). The OECD (2005) described this challenging situation as remarkably similar across countries. Encouraging promising novice teachers to become leaders is an issue of international interest because many leave the profession within their first 3 years of teaching (Lovett 2011). They need to feel prepared, empowered, supported and committed to building a professional learning environment for their students and their school. Bureaucracies and centralized educational systems that fail to support effective performance and career progression in spite of the increasing demands for teachers to teach and lead in their classrooms can hinder teaching careers (Zembylas and Papanastasiou 2006) despite very different social, economic and educational structures and traditions (OECD 2005). For example, the shift in societal expectations for teachers and schools to meet the needs of more racially, culturally and linguistically diverse students places demands and stresses on teachers and prevents them from doing their jobs effectively (Gernin-Lajoie 2008).

Novice teachers are often frustrated when they enter their classrooms because of their lack of comprehensive preparedness for the complex issues in classrooms (Stone 2015). The work of Darling-Hammond and Bransford (2005) and Hargreaves (2003) also pointed to the lack of understanding of teachers' specific roles and responsibilities in preparing and educating students for equitable participation in a democratic society. Contrary to the information in the literature, Wagner (2008) contended that highly skilled teachers who are prepared and whom the system supports influence educational outcomes. Novice teachers consistently face praxis shock, which is the trial-and-error mode of coping with the realities of the classroom for which their university training and internship have not sufficiently prepared them (Goddard and Foster 2001; Whalen 2010). Teachers experience stress because they feel undersupported in their efforts to adjust their practice to meet the demands of rigorous standards and new assessments, in addition to having to incorporate technology to meet individual student needs (Stone 2015). When novice teachers feel vexed and pressured because they have inadequate time or support, they begin to doubt themselves and lack confidence, which can lead to teacher burnout over time (Stone 2015). It is imperative that novice teachers have the time and opportunity to network with colleagues, reflect on the difficulties that they face in leading students and develop strategies to strengthen their classroom management skills (Jones 2012). The evidence in the literature strongly supports novice-teacher mentorship as a nurturing and caring practice in which mentor and mentee form a professional and personal relationship whilst adhering to the professional code of ethics to foster understanding, self-confidence and trust, which are foundational to successful leadership development (Alberta Teacher's Association (n.d.); Ralph and Walker 2011; Robertson 2008; Robertson and Timperly 2013). Even when situations and circumstances present opportunities for novice teachers to lead, they are hesitant to see themselves as leaders in their school environment and district (Pucella 2014).

The purpose of this phenomenological study was to investigate and uncover the needs of novice teachers that their colleagues must meet to enable them to sustain their leadership in their classrooms and schools. Through the lens of constructivism, the focus of the study was on the experiences and perspectives of novice teachers within the first 3 years of their professional practice. The focal point of their lived experiences was the needs that they require their teacher colleagues to meet. Before delving into the study, we believed that it was essential to become familiar with the education system and teacher education programming in each of the four countries (Brazil, Canada, Pakistan and South Africa) included in this research. We hoped that, by providing informed research data and articulating and amplifying novice teachers' needs through their stories, the differing global perspectives would illuminate the perception of the silence surrounding novice teachers.

EDUCATION IN BRAZIL, CANADA, PAKISTAN AND SOUTH AFRICA

For the most part, the four countries' respective local/county, state/ provincial, or federal governments oversee education. Even though none of the participating countries have a central federal education office, the foundation of learning stems from a specific constitution. This body of fundamental principles in each country's constitution guarantees the right of education to the general population. We categorized the education system in the four countries in general terms such as primary education, secondary education and vocational/postsecondary.

National-government education policies in Brazil, Canada, Pakistan and South Africa are concerned with preparing citizens who can engage with their respective communities to improve the local economy and participate in a global market. Economic and social transformations help teachers and students to acquire extensive knowledge of their own culture, along with the necessary skills and dispositions to engage with citizens within their own communities and globally, in many different cultures and countries. We reviewed teacher training programmes from a global perspective and came to the consensus that the common theme is the amalgamation of rapid social changes with the heightened expectations of teachers to be prepared for the diverse challenges of teaching. It is evident that all four countries strive to ensure quality education for all students regardless of economic background and that each nation has its own unique practices. The stages of the education systems and country modules differ in Brazil, Canada, Pakistan and South Africa, along with their learning policies, which can vary within the same jurisdiction.

Brazil

The general student population must progress through two tiers to be prepared to take their places within a business-oriented society. The first tier, basic education, is comprised of early childhood, which lasts 5 years; elementary and lower secondary education, which lasts 9 years; and upper secondary education (high school), which lasts 3 more years and prepares students for entrance exams for private or public universities. Students then advance to higher education, which is the second tier. During these two levels of Brazilian education, a series of additional options are blended with students' learning activities: (1) education of young people and adults, (2) special education, (3) technical-vocational education and (4) Indigenous education.

The government financially supports public universities. Specifically, teacher education policies are the responsibility of all levels of government. Because programmes are frequently offered to teachers to allow them to update their skills, the National Council of Education is responsible for the elaboration of the national curriculum at all levels and for all modalities of courses offered in Brazil. Many students and teachers live a great distance from major universities, so the government established a distance-education programme at the Open University of Brazil. It focuses on distance learning as the best means of providing opportunities to those who would not otherwise have access to education in their own communities.

Canada

In Canada, students progress through two levels of education: public elementary (6–8 years) and secondary public (4–6 years). Upon successfully completing their secondary education, students can choose to enrol in postsecondary education. Canadian students are obliged to attend both primary and secondary schooling. Legally, Canadian students cannot drop out of school until Grade 10. Learners in primary education take generalized courses that are mandatory for all students. In the secondary-school education system students choose electives in addition to the compulsory or core courses such as English, mathematics, science and social studies. Canadian students begin to specialize or stream according to interest to pursue further study or training in the trades in postsecondary institutions that prepare them for the job market.

Education is a constitutional responsibility of the individual provinces. All major Canadian universities are now publicly funded but maintain institutional autonomy and the ability to make decisions on admission, tuition and governance. Specifically, in Canada the 4-year bachelor of education degree has two main routes, the elementary and the secondary stream, but within each are specific speciality levels. Elementary school is comprised of primary, junior and intermediate grade levels, whilst secondary school is comprised of junior and senior grade levels. Many higher education institutions specifically offer Aboriginal/First Nations teacher training, Aboriginal education assistant and Aboriginal special-needs educator preparation/certification programmes. In addition, the jurisdictions have different models of teacher education programmes that 'are affected by curricula and pedagogies, recruitment and support programs for teacher contenders along with areas of expertise of university professors' (Van Nuland 2011, p. 410).

Pakistan

Even though Pakistan's education system focuses strongly on primary education, it is compulsory for students to attend both primary and middle education. In Pakistan's two-tier education system, learners must progress through layers that consist of preprimary; primary, which is 5 years in duration; middle elementary, which takes 3 years; secondary/trade vocational, which takes 2 years; and higher secondary, which is 2 years in duration. This multiple education system consists of multiple languages of instruction, multiple curricula, multiple examination systems, multiple scoring systems and multiple admission systems.

Pakistan reviewed its National Education Policy with regard to the development of teacher education to create an effective mechanism to accredit teacher education institutions and programmes. At the elementary level of education, teachers require a bachelor of education; whereas at the secondary and higher secondary levels, by 2018 teachers will require a master's degree as well as a bachelor of education degree. The National Professional Standards for Teachers in Pakistan, with the assistance of the United States of America for International Development, initiated the Strengthening Teachers Education in Pakistan project to ensure high-quality trained teachers.

South Africa

All South Africans have the right to a basic education. Even though this country has traditional primary (Grades 1–7) and secondary (Grades 8–12) education, the system consists of two broad bands of education: General Education and Training (GET) and Further Education and Training (FET). GET, or basic education, is further divided into three phases of schooling and takes approximately 10 years of training. FET, from Grades 10 to 12, includes career-oriented education and training that other FET institutions such as technical, community and private colleges offer.

The National Policy Framework for Teacher Education and Development was designed to develop a teaching profession that would meet the needs of the people of South Africa. This country has a 4-year bachelor of education programme in which graduate teachers will be qualified to teach in either primary or secondary schools. To qualify as teachers, graduates who hold a 3-year non-education bachelor's degree must work towards a 1-year initial teacher qualification postgraduate certificate in education (PGCE). In addition, programmes are offered to upgrade unqualified teachers and reskill those who want to assume special roles such as leadership. Special government funding allows access to teacher education, particularly for students from disadvantaged backgrounds. The beneficiaries of such grants are placed in schools with positions for which they qualify. Because of the challenge of retaining graduate teachers within the teaching profession, a programme of induction for beginning teachers is offered to motivate newly graduated teachers to stay in their chosen profession.

The information that we gained in this research study clearly indicates that the novice teacher participants lacked formal induction or mentorship programming, which leads us to believe that transferring theory to practice is not reducing the new-teacher attrition rate globally. If the intent of school systems is to facilitate the transition from preservice programming to in-service professionalism and leadership capacity building, mentorship is not evident in the individual countries, let alone globally.

NOVICE TEACHERS' PROGRESS TOWARDS TEACHER LEADERSHIP

The literature emphasized the need to cultivate teacher leadership early in a teacher's career (Barth 2001; Darling-Hammond and Bransford 2005; Katzenmeyer and Moller 2009). According to Katzenmeyer and Moller, teacher leaders can provide leadership support in three ways: leadership of students or other teachers as facilitators, coaches, mentors, trainers, or curriculum specialists; leadership in school study groups; and leadership of operative tasks by serving on goal- and service-oriented committees or in decision-making processes as members of school improvement teams. In short, novice teachers gain leadership expertise by observing and learning from their colleagues. Furthermore, classroom teachers are taking on more leadership roles and activities within their institutes, school districts and communities (Kutz 2009). However, the perspective that despite the increasing opportunities for novice teachers to lead, they are hesitant to see themselves as leaders (Pucella 2014) challenges the previous statement that novice teachers are becoming more involved in leadership positions in their school communities.

Pedagogy, Content and Knowledge

As graduates of colleges of education, novice teachers bring with them new ideas to improve student learning. During their first 3 years, novice teachers struggle with knowing what to teach, determining the resources that they must use to teach, finishing certain materials quickly, engaging different types of learners and preparing students for high-stake tests (Jones 2012). At the same time, novice teachers must build relationships with colleagues, learn the administrative task of grading and learn how to purchase resources through the school, all with the knowledge that their teaching evaluations are fast approaching (Alberta Teachers' Association n.d.; Jones 2012). Novice teachers also face the task of integrating content, pedagogy and knowledge into the contextual arena of their instructional material according to the Alberta Teachers' Association's (n.d.) *Mentoring Beginning Teachers: Program Handbook.* Pedagogical content knowledge (PCK) is a form of knowledge that contributes to teachers' success in supporting student learning, based on the work of Shulman (1986), who explained that PCK involves both 'the ways of representing and formulating the subject that make it comprehensible to others' in addition to 'an understanding of what makes the learning of specific topics easy or difficult' (p. 9). This concept is best interpreted in a Venn diagram (Fig. 9.1).

The first circle of the Venn diagram in Fig. 9.1, labelled *content*, refers to the subject material that is being taught (Koehler and Mishra 2008). The second circle, *pedagogy*, refers to the methods or techniques that the teacher uses in the classroom, along with the strategies to assess students' understanding. The third circle, *knowledge*, is the ability of an individual to accomplish a variety of tasks and develop different ways to accomplish a given task. At the point at which all three circles intersect emerges the concept of PCK, which is the interaction of content, pedagogy and knowledge in the framework with relevant classroom ideas and strategies. Each component—content, pedagogy and knowledge—must be included in a given contextual framework to integrate new data in the classroom.

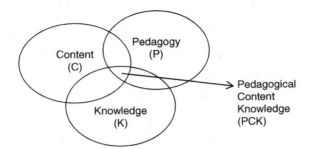

Fig. 9.1 Shulman's (1986) PCK framework and its knowledge components

PCK prompts a novice teacher to ask, 'How can I combine content, knowledge and pedagogy to become an effective teacher?' This framework of learning, knowledge and pedagogy characterizes the knowledge upon which novice teachers draw (Darling-Hammond and Bransford 2005). Furthermore, novice teachers who become teacher leaders demonstrate the interdependence of knowledge, pedagogy and content, which results in transferrable knowledge that will fit any teaching environment, to make learning relevant to their students.

Teacher Leadership: The REACH Model

Merideth (2007) identified five characteristics that exemplify teacher leadership: risk taking, effectiveness, autonomy, collegiality and honour. Teachers who wish to lead thrive on challenges and pursue professional growth to increase student achievement (Merideth 2007). This concept is related to personal efficacy, which is teachers' evaluation of their teaching capabilities. To be effective, they need to grow intellectually with the assistance of relevant professional workshops to acquire content and sustain the professional expertise that will help them to lead their students and colleagues in the school. However, teachers must work not only with the mind, but also with the heart, which is the passion that defines their reality (Merideth 2007).

Teachers who are autonomous will display initiative, independent thought and responsibility when they acquire knowledge to improve the learning experience of their students. In turn, they must have a community that respects them as contributing professionals (Alberta Teachers' Association n.d.; Merideth 2007).

Merideth (2007) also advocated the notion that teachers must seek and maintain collegial relationships, which require trust for professional suste-nance, as many researchers have shown (Ralph and Walker 2011; Robertson 2008; Robertson and Timperly 2013). Collegiality involves 'both support and cooperation—give and take between professionals' (p. 9), which requires that teachers work together to meet the common goal and support the vision of student learning.

Last, teachers must convey trust and honour to their colleagues whilst they learn to integrate content, knowledge and pedagogy. Novice teachers need to demonstrate their willingness to attain a common vision to ensure that their colleagues will support their goals for student learning.

METHODOLOGY

The use of phenomenology to explore the lived or existential experiences of novice teachers gave us a better understanding of and brought perso-nal meaning to the novice teachers' stories about their experiences dur-ing their first 3 years of teaching (Van Manen 1990). Because of the complexity of novice teachers' role, they turn to colleagues to help them to become successful and effective leaders of student learning in their classrooms (Pucella 2014). The literature prompted the first research question:

1. How do novice teachers maintain their leadership role within the classroom?

During the first year of teaching, novice teachers must build teamwork and collaborate with their peers and students (Caspersen and Raaen 2014). This particular fact led to the development of the second research question:

2. How do novice teachers earn respect from their colleagues and students?

The third research question stemmed from the evidence-based fact that novice teachers face an adjustment period within the first 3 years of professional practice and search for professional development workshops and opportunities to learn to deliver their content more effectively and develop other classroom strategies (Fantilli and McDougall 2009).

3. How do novice teachers benefit from professional development workshops?

The qualitative nature of the study ensured its reliability and external validity through the triangulation of the data that we collected and synthesized from the novice teacher participants' reflections, semi-structured interviews with eight different participants and a survey that school administrators oversaw. For the purpose of this study, we defined novice teachers as teachers who were working within the first 3 years of their professional practice after having received a bachelor of education degree.

The questions that we used to guide the participants' reflections fit an interpretative paradigm (Patton 2002) that included their descriptions, interpretations and explanations in their attempt to make sense of situations and experiences.

1. In what ways do novice teachers need to be supported?
   1.1 In what areas of their work would novice teachers need support?
   1.2 What support would novice teachers need to become effective teachers?
2. How do novice teachers build and maintain their leadership roles in their schools?
   2.1 What activities could help novice teachers to establish their leadership roles?
   2.2 How can novice teachers maintain their developed leadership abilities?
3. Based on your experiences during your first year of teaching, what theme (or topic) would you suggest as mandatory for preservice teachers?
   3.1 Can you pinpoint a moment or situation when you were teaching when a class (or a lecture/seminar) that you attended (or heard) at the university made sense to you (the moment when you can say, 'Only now I understand what my teacher said')?
   3.2 In lesson planning and classroom management, what have you learned from your colleagues? Give examples.

We recorded all of the participants' reflections on the guiding questions for a period of one month as the primary source of data. We then conducted audiotaped semi-structured interviews after the reflective practice as a means of corroborating the participants' reflections (Gordon 1975). The transcripts of the recordings became the secondary data source. The interview questions were as follows:

1. In what ways did your colleagues support you in the teaching profession?
2. How did the support you received from your colleagues assist you in the teaching profession?
3. What leadership abilities did you develop as a result of the support you received from your colleagues?
4. Explain how your preservice classes either effectively or ineffectively assisted you now that you have begun to teach?
5. What would you like school administrators and policy advisers to know about your experience during your first year of teaching?

Last, we emailed a Likert-scale survey to school administrators for distribution to the participating teachers to correlate the views of the participants with those of their colleagues. The sample survey (Table 9.1) consisted of 50 statements that we derived from the participants' reflections and the interview data. The intent of the survey was to give their colleagues a way to express their perceptions to enable us to correlate the data (Bourque and Fielder 2003).

Research Ethics

The novice teacher participants were required to sign the study information sheet and consent form. We used pseudonyms to protect the privacy and ensure the anonymity of the participants, as well as the school leaders and schools affiliated with the research study.

Data Analysis

Because the research was exploratory in nature, after multiple readings of the collected data, which included reflective entries, transcripts of the semi-structured interviews and the survey, we used content analysis to scrutinize the data. We also developed codes as patterns emerged from the

Table 9.1 Novice teachers' leadership

Colleagues' support to assist novice teachers	Definitely agree	Agree	Definitely disagree	Not sure
12. Novice teachers acquire confidence through colleagues' support.	☐	☐	☐	☐
13. Colleagues' support create positive work relationship.	☐	☐	☐	☐
14. Colleagues' support create positive working environment.	☐	☐	☐	☐
15. Novice teachers take the time to know teachers.	☐	☐	☐	☐
16. Novice teachers take the time to know educational assistants.	☐	☐	☐	☐
17. Novice teachers listen to their colleagues.	☐	☐	☐	☐
18. Novice teachers focus on curriculum.	☐	☐	☐	☐
19. Novice teachers are to be aware of testing expectations.	☐	☐	☐	☐
20. Novice teachers are to be aware of importance of deadlines.	☐	☐	☐	☐

data and later grouped and organized them according to the novice teachers' needs to maintain their leadership in their classroom and institutes. This resulted in four categories that we then organized into levels of the novice teachers' teacher–leader developmental skills.

Methodological Challenges

The major limitation of this study was the authenticity of the data sources. Were the novice teachers' reflections their own views, or did they reiterate the perspectives that they acquired in their teacher training? The participants' insights into and perspectives on the needs of novice teachers reflected their own country's context. However, the novice teachers supported their reflections with explanations and contextualized them within their particular school experience by using local anecdotes and stories. With regard to the authenticity of the data, to prevent the novice teachers from writing what they thought the researchers wanted them to write, we clearly asked them to write their own views and express their own thoughts in the reflective entries and responses to the interview questions.

Descriptions of Participants

The research study involved eight full-time novice teachers who represented four different countries (Brazil, Canada, Pakistan and South Africa) and had 3 years or less of teaching experience. As we stated previously, to protect the participants' privacy and ensure their anonymity, we used pseudonyms.

One participant from Brazil, Fátima, had been a secondary public school English-language teacher for 3 years and was currently working at both the state and municipal levels. Fátima also tutored students who were enrolled in distance education programming. At the time of this study, she was not involved in any school or personal projects or research because of her commitment to 17 groups of approximately 20 students each in a face-to-face mode of course delivery. The second Brazilian participant, Maria, had also been an English language teacher for the past 3 years. Maria was currently working with 10 groups of students, with an average of 30 per group. Apart from her regular groups, she taught a modality entitled 'Education of Young People and Adults' to students who could not access or continue their studies at the appropriate age. Over the last 3 years she had carried out projects with her students on the use of cellphones as a pedagogical resource; they received state government awards for their achievement.

The two Canadian participants, Anna and Zylen, had graduated from a college of education in their own locale and were currently working in the public school system. Anna had had 3 years of teaching experience and was consciously integrating different hands-on approaches into student learning. She eagerly shared her teaching successes and perspective that overall improvements in classroom teaching are urgently required. Prior to working in her current school, Anna had taught overseas, where she had quickly learned to appreciate her students' cultural values. This overseas experience made Anna aware that she needed to share her passion to improve student learning through a more hands-on approach to teaching. Anna was an advocate of learning programmes for her students in her current role.

The second Canadian participant, Zylen, was a first-year teacher who was actively implementing and promoting Aboriginal language studies in his school. His school administrator as well as school administrators from another school who are interested in his work supported his work to promote the beauty of Aboriginal culture and language. Like Anna, Zylen was passionate about improving student learning by becoming involved in the school community. At the time of the interview, Zylen had set up a Language Warrior programme to revitalize students' learning and improve their oral, written and reading ability in their Aboriginal language.

In Pakistan, the two female participants, Alina and Saba, each had 3 years of teaching experience, and were currently teaching in the public school system. Both had acquired a master of science and a bachelor of education degree and had passed the National Testing Services test to become certified as primary school teachers. They have gone through one-teacher school experiences and faced many challenges with regard to their conveyance allowance. Both participants felt confident about their teaching-learning process and had set their sights on higher positions as teachers, for example, at the secondary or college level.

The participants from South Africa, Tumi and Papi, had PGCEs from a 1-year training programme. Tumi was currently in her third year of teaching and had the stability of having taught at her current school for 2 years. She believed that learners need to be supported in their school work as well as in extramural activities, which had kept her engaged in community work that involved learners from her school. This, according to Tumi, demonstrated leadership. She collaborated with colleagues on different ways of doing things and had gained the trust of those with whom she worked. She was currently enrolled in a bachelor of education (honours) degree programme to improve her teacher qualifications.

Papi was in his second year of teaching and was leading school processes at an early stage of his career. He ascribed this to his computer skills and acknowledged that he had learned a great deal in the meetings that he attended in his leadership role in his school. The process further enhanced his knowledge and computer skills.

Findings

The following section includes quotations that illustrate the participants' views and capture the richness and complexity of their experiences as novice teachers in becoming leaders in the classroom and school. Wherever appropriate, we have interwoven direct participant quotations and reflective thoughts to augment and solidify the context of the data in which these teachers described their lived experiences and their needs.

Encouragement from Colleagues

The interview responses revealed that all of the participants felt confident because of their colleagues' support in their classroom teachings, strategies and content delivery. When the novice teachers struggled, they wanted their colleagues to listen and help them to analyse their classroom trials and tribulations to enable them to develop strategies to overcome the problems. Fátima explained that 'communicating and sharing what I am struggling with helps me analyze the problems I am facing and develop different methods to deal with old problems we have in the public teaching context.'

The novice teachers acknowledged that they needed to listen attentively to their colleagues when they proposed alternative teaching and classroom management strategies to help them to resolve the challenging issues. Saba's colleagues had offered her assistance to effectively deal with student and classroom management. Tumi's colleagues encouraged her to persist in her teaching activities, and one colleague offered this advice: 'Do not get discouraged but persevere even when it is difficult.' However, Zylen emphasized that novice teachers 'need to take the time to know staff— teachers and educational assistant—for they already have great rapport with students.'

Building Leadership Skills

All of the novice teacher participants appreciated the encouragement of their colleagues to become part of a team. For example, Fátima specifically stated, 'I noticed [that I had acquired] some abilities [that] I thought I wouldn't be capable of, such as coordinating events and activities, solv[ing] problems, and guid[ing] meetings, and becom[ing] more tolerant of different opinions.' Papi had been asked to lead the schoolwide integrated quality management system process and wrote a report that was approved. Tumi's colleagues had supported her involvement in community activities in which she led learners in sports; these activities extended to surrounding areas. Zylen implemented a new Michif language (a combination of French and Cree languages) in the school and had initiated the Language Warrior programme as part of the school curriculum with the support of his administrators and other school-district administrators. Likewise, Alina had an opportunity to become involved in teamwork and collaboration in a division of six classes that focused on building and maintaining teacher leadership. Zylen contended that novice teachers must follow experienced teachers to decide which type of leadership roles they preferred: 'If you sign up with an experienced teacher, then you are able to experience how to be a leader in one area of the school.' Furthermore, he stated that 'creating a relationship with your colleagues will help novice teachers establish leadership roles by learning how to use your strengths and guide those around you.'

In Need of Mentors

The participants from Brazil, Canada, Pakistan and South Africa asserted their need to partner with mentors. Their message was that novice teachers in mathematics and English language arts classes in Canadian schools require mentors for assistance; the South African teachers added that they needed assistance with mathematics as well and that they had been assigned classes in the lower grades with reasonable workloads to allow them to gain confidence.

The evidence in the literature suggests that new teachers need to work with other teachers towards a common goal and a vision for student learning (Merideth 2007). However, the participants from South Africa and Pakistan believed that novice teachers need to receive regular workshop training based on practical performance to learn new theories and technologies. Similarly, Fátima reflected, 'I cannot be in this career without studying and seeking higher qualifications, so I think novice teachers should be in training courses constantly.' Alternatively, Saba pointed out that the head of the school and the teachers should be involved in lesson planning and class management in a positive manner. Novice teachers who lack mentorship opportunities become frustrated during their first year of teaching. Fátima clearly expressed her vexation:

> The first time in a real class can be really difficult and frustrating if you cannot achieve what you have planned. So being honest with the people you work with can make all the difference to get help and guidance when needed.

Similarly for Saba and Alina, the experience of isolation in a one-teacher school was a serious factor in their frustration and has the potential for early attrition rates.

Contemplation on Preservice Classes

All of the novice teachers considered some of their university classes helpful in transferring their knowledge from their training to the school classroom. The participants from Pakistan and Canada lamented the massive amount of reading on effective classroom management throughout their teacher training programmes; yet, when they were confronted with the situation in real life, they found the expectations in the classroom overwhelming. The participants described real-life classroom management as a 'real learning experience' for novice teachers. In addition to classroom-management challenges, new teachers face resources issues dealing with teaching developing resources and teaching strategies. Fátima reported her experience:

> I did not have enough time to understand how the planning and the teaching processes work; there was not enough time to practice all the theory I had studied. The most clear, positive aspect of those classes was developing real, consistent teaching material by myself.

Papi also reflected on the matter: 'From my own experience, I am able to understand that if learners do not answer correctly, that does not mean they will fail, so I am able to assist learners to improve.'

DISCUSSION

The commonality amongst all of the novice teacher participants from Brazil, Canada, Pakistan and South Africa is that their more experienced colleagues were supportive and encouraging during their first years of teaching. This concept supports Meredith's (2007) REACH model of collegiality, which explains that novice teachers need professional communities that respect them as contributing professionals. The Alberta Teachers' Association (n.d.) also stated this principle in its *Alberta Novice Teacher Induction Handbook*. When novice teachers struggle, they seek support from their colleagues for teaching strategies to overcome issues that impede student learning. Therefore, collaborative dialogue between novice and experienced teachers results in mutually respectful learning opportunities through personal and professional support (Mitchell and Sackney 2005). Conversely, novice teachers must listen to their colleagues attentively when they offer alternatives and solutions to improve student learning. Novice teachers must also take the time to get to know their colleagues as experienced members who already have a strong rapport with each other and their students.

Colleagues' support and encouragement for novice teachers is necessary in teaching teams. Katzenmeyer and Moller (2009) and Merideth (2007) emphasized that novice teachers must work with others in the best interests of all students rather than only 'my students'. This form of teamwork helps novice teachers to become leaders when they learn that leadership is not an isolated function; rather, they lead all students and staff within the school environment, as the participants from Brazil, Canada, South Africa and Pakistan noted. Fátima clearly expressed the value of teamwork:

> Working with people who care about you helps us get our work well done. So the main way my colleagues support me is being able to work together. One great example of that in working together is developing projects. In addition, we talk about our students, pointing out their characteristics, behavior, strengths, and weaknesses; developing strategies to help them improve their learning process.

The participants reflected on the notion that experienced teachers consider their leadership role in supporting them as distributed leadership (Grant and Singh 2009). Furthermore, new as they are in a school, the administrators have already in some cases assigned novice teachers leadership tasks in recognition of certain abilities. They gain confidence, and their desire to enhance their skills further in the teaching profession demonstrates this.

The participants from Brazil, Canada, South Africa and Pakistan stressed that, to understand the protocol of their respective schools, they needed to work with mentors. Even though their colleagues played a critical role in making sense of the teaching expectations (Jones 2012), the novice teachers from these countries wanted to become engaged in more active forms of learning, such as lesson planning and the analysis of student work with their mentors, rather than just sharing materials with colleagues. The Alberta Teachers' Association (n.d.) fully supported the need for formal mentorship programmes rather than informal mentoring relationships in that mentees' growth and development is significantly greater when they have formal mentorship. All of the novice teachers expressed a desire to observe the lessons of experienced teachers in their subject field or at their grade level. In addition, all of the participants stressed that professional development on a regular basis has strengthened their practical teaching performance in their respective classrooms.

Even though the novice teachers expressed the need for regular teaching workshops, they reported that their university training had prepared them for their current classroom teaching. Unfortunately, Zylen, Anna, Fátima and Saba were concerned about their lack of preparation in their university preservice programming, specifically in the area of classroom management, which made the reality of their experience upon entering the classroom as professional teachers overwhelming. For example, Fátima explicitly noted that she did not have enough time to apply all of the theories that her professors had taught her to her teaching. Overall, we determined that education systems involve various levels of mentorship, as the participants, who represented the global perspective, revealed. Most important, we discovered that few formal mentoring and induction programmes are available to novice teachers to enhance their professional and personal growth and development into future school leaders.

CONCLUSION

The findings of this study reveal the views of the eight participants as a global perspective on the need for collaboration, support and mentorship for novice teachers within the first 3 years of professional service. This global perspective in this particular research study is limited to the growth and professional development of two participants from each of the following countries: Brazil, Canada, South Africa and Pakistan. Therefore, the ability to generalize to other contexts might be limited.

Although this study had obvious limitations, teachers, educational administrators, policy advisers and researchers might consider these findings useful as a point of reference to improve teaching policies for novice teachers. Thus, the topic of the needs of novice teachers requires a case-study approach to further research. The findings of this study have the following implications.

1. Novice teachers need support from colleagues. Although some teachers assume that they are prepared to teach after they have completed a teacher training programme, many do not immediately feel that they are teachers. The normal experience appears to be trial

and error, and eventually novice teachers will realize that they need to turn to colleagues for assistance and support.

2. Novice teachers need mentors to help with lesson planning and familiarize them with necessary administrative practices such as testing and student-file management. In addition, they need mentors who will encourage them to consider leadership roles in their school communities.

3. Novice teachers need to work collaboratively as a team in their subject areas and/or at their grade levels. Staff and school-community engagement will also help them to gain experience in leading others within their schools.

The key implication of this research study is the importance of novice teacher support in professional learning communities that offer opportunities for dialogue with colleagues as well as reflective practice. The result of collaborative work with colleagues is quality educational services for students, who ultimately benefit with achievement and success when their teachers gain confidence and efficacy.

REFERENCES

Alberta Teachers' Association (n.d.) *Mentoring beginning teachers: program handbook* (1st edn). Edmonton, AB: Alberta Teachers' Association.

Alliance for Excellent Education (2005, August). *Teacher attrition: a costly loss to the nation and to the states.* Washington, DC: Alliance for Excellent Education.

Barth, R. (2001). *Learning by heart.* San Francisco: Jossey-Bass.

Bourque, L. B., & Fielder, E. P. (2003). *How to conduct self-administered and mail surveys.* Thousand Oaks, CA: National Academy Press.

Caspersen, J., & Raaen, F. D. (2014). Novice teachers and how they cope. *Teachers and Teaching: Theory and Practice, 20*(2), 189–211.

Cooper, J., & Alvarado, A. (2006). *Preparation, recruitment, and retention of teachers* (1st edn). Brussels: The International Academy of Education.

Darling-Hammond, L., & Bransford, J. (2005). *Preparing teachers for a changing world: what teachers should learn and be able to do.* San Francisco, CA: Jossey-Bass.

Department of Education, R. o. S. A. (2006). *The national framework for teacher education and development in South Africa.* Pretoria: Department of Education, Republic of South Africa.

Fantilli, R. D., & McDougall, D. E. (2009). A study of novice teachers: challenges and supports in the first years. *Teaching and Teacher Education, 25*(6), 814–825.

Gernin-Lajoie, D. (2008). *Educators' discourses on student diversity in Canada: context, policy, and practice* (1st edn). Toronto, ON: Canadian Scholar's Press.

Goddard, J. T., & Foster, R. Y. (2001). The experiences of neophyte teachers: a critical constructivist assessment. *Teaching and Teacher Education, 17*(3), 349–365.

Gordon, R. L. (1975). *Interviewing: strategy, techniques, and tactics* (1st edn). Chicago: Dorsey Press.

Grant, C., & Singh, H. (2009). Passing the buck: this is not teacher leadership! *Perspectives in Education, 27*(3), 289–301.

Harfitt, G. J. (2015). From attrition to retention: a narrative inquiry of why beginning teaches leave and then rejoin the profession. *Asia-Pacific Journal of Teacher, 43*(1), 22–35.

Hargreaves, A. (2003). *Teaching in a knowledge society: education in the age of insecurity.* London: Open University Press.

Ingersoll, R. (2001). Turnover and teacher shortages: an organizational analysis. *American Educational Research, 38*(3), 499–534.

Jones, B. K. (2012). A new teacher's plea. *Educational Leadership, 69*(8), 74–77.

Kain, J. F., & Singleton, K. (1996, May/June). Equality of educational opportunity revisited. *New England Economic Review*, 87–111.

Katzenmeyer, M., & Moller, G. (2009). *Awakening the sleeping giant: helping teachers develop as leaders* (3rd edn). Thousand Oaks, CA: Corwin Press.

Koehler, M. J., & Mishra, P. (2008). Introducing TPCK. In J. Colbert, et al. (eds.), *Handbook of technological pedagogical content knowledge (TPCK) for educators* (pp. 3–29). New York: Routledge.

Kutz, S. (2009). Teacher leadership. *Leadership, 39*(1), 12–14.

LeMaistre, C., & Pare, A. (2010). Whatever it takes: how beginning teachers learn to survive. *Teaching and Teacher Education, 26*(2010), 559–564.

Lovett, S. (2011). Career pathways: does remaining close to the classroom matter for early career teachers? A study of practice in New Zealand and the USA. *Professional Development in Education, 37*(2), 213–224.

Merideth, E. M. (2007). *Leadership strategies for teachers* (1st edn). Thousand Oaks, CA: Corwin Press.

Mitchell, C., & Sackney, L. (2005). *Sustainable improvement: building capacity for a learning communities that endure* (1st edn). Rotterdam: Sense Publisher.

Organization for Economic Co-operation and Development (2009). *OECD teaching and learning international survey.* Paris: OECD Publications.

Organization for Economic Co-operation and Development (2005). *Teachers matter: attracting, developing and retaining effective teachers.* Paris: OECD Publications.

Patton, M. (2002). *Qualitative research & evaluation methods* (3rd edn). Thousand Oaks, CA: Sage.

Pucella, T. J. (2014). Not too young to lead. *Clearing House, 87*(1), 15–20.

Ralph, E., & Walker, K. (2011). *Adapting mentorship across the professions* (1st edn). Calgary, AB: Detselig Enterprises Ltd.

Robertson, J., & Timperly, H. (Eds.) (2013). *Leadership and learning* (1st edn). Victoria: Hawker Brownlow Education.

Robertson, J. (2008). *Coaching educational leadership: building leadership capacity through partnership* (1st edn). Victoria: Hawker Brownlow Education.

Shulman, L. S. (1986). Those who understand: knowledge growth in teaching. *Educational Researcher*, 15, 4–14.

Stone, E. (2015). If not us, then who? *Kappa Delta Pi Record*, 51(3), 127–130.

UNESCO (2009). The National Professional Standards for Teachers in Pakistan. *Read Pakistan*, 29 March.

Van Nuland, S. (2011). Teacher education in Canada. *Journal of Education for Teaching*, 37(4), 409–421.

VanManen, M. (1990). *Researching lived experience: human science for an action sensitive pedagogy* (1st edn). New York, NY: State University of New York.

Wagner, T. (2008). Rigor redefined. *Educational Leadership*, 66(2), 20–25.

Whalen, C. (2010). *The phenomenon of novice teachers who teach students with diverse learning needs*. Doctoral dissertation. Calgary: University of Calgary.

Worthy, J. (2005). It didn't have to be so hard: the first years of teaching in an urban school. *International Journal of Qualitative Studies in Education*, 18(3), 379–398.

Zembylas, M., & Papanastasiou, E. (2006). Sources of teacher job satisfaction and dissatisfaction in Cyprus. *Compare*, 36(2), 229–247.

Elizabeth F. Majocha is an Office Administration instructor at Gabriel Dumont Institute as well as a facilitator for teacher leadership workshops. She holds an EdD in Educational Leadership from the University of Calgary, Canada, and has taught for 30 years where 3 years were in the public school system and the remaining years in the adult education sector. As a result of her research work towards her doctorate degree attained through University of Calgary in 2011, she published her work on teacher leadership, entitled "Passage Through the Threshold of Technological Change: Insights into Leading Qualities of a Teacher." Currently, she is pursuing research studies on teacher leadership and technology along with mentorship.

Marco Antonio Margarido Costa is a professor at Universidade Federal de Campina Grande, Brazil. He holds a PhD in English Language from Faculdade de Filosofia, Letras e Ciências Humanas da Universidade de São Paulo (FFLCH/USP), Brazil. While attending his doctoral programme, he was also a visiting scholar at the University of Wisconsin–Madison, USA. He conducted a postdoctoral research at FFLCH/USP and at the University of York, Toronto, Canada.

He is a member of a national Teacher Education Project called "Literacies: Language, Education, Culture and Technology," coordinated by professors from the USP. His recent research focuses on English language teaching/learning, applied linguistics, literacy studies and teacher education.

Mamotena Mpeta, PhD, is Senior Lecturer in Life Sciences (Biology) methodologies at the University of Venda, South Africa. Her research has included looking into how teachers' beliefs about the content they teach influence their teaching of that content. She is currently Head of the Department of Professional Studies and was coordinator of teaching practice until December 2015. She was once involved in research investigating the effectiveness of Induction Programme in Lesotho, the result of which saw an improved mentoring system in order to strengthen support of beginning teachers in schools. Her teacher education work includes training of mentors in schools where student teachers undergo teaching practice. She is currently investigating the experiences of student teachers in schools during teaching practice in relation to their practical knowledge and support they receive.

Nargis Ara, PhD, is Dean of the Faculty of Science, Head of the department and an associate professor at Government Girls Post Graduate College, Saidu Sharif, Pakistan. She holds double bachelor (BSc, BEd), double Master's (MSc, MEd), double MPhil (MS Chemistry, MS Education) and a PhD in Education. She has taught 2 years in K-10 class at a convent school and 27 years at postgraduate college level. She is a member of British Educational Leadership Management and Administration Society (BELMAS), UK; the Motherhood Initiative for Research and Community Involvement (MIRCI), Toronto, Canada; and a peer review group at Intellectbase International Consortium, USA. She has attended seven international conferences, two national conferences, and one international and four national workshops on teacher administration and leadership. Next papers for presentation have been accepted by BELMAS Conference in July 2016 and MIRCI Canada in October 2016. Nargis is currently working on a book on advanced research in ABC of Chemistry. She has published educated mother comparison by the *International Journal of Technology and Inclusive Education*; children performance by *Review of Higher Education and Self-Learning*; and "teachers training and technology" and gender discrimination by *Interdisciplinary Journal of Contemporary Research in Business.*

Catherine A. Whalen, EdD, teaches Bachelor of Education and the Master of Education programmes offered at the University of Northern British Columbia (UNBC), Canada, in the areas of Inclusive Education, Exceptionalities in K-12 Students, Policy and Politics in the Education System, Culturally Responsive Teaching, Instructional Leadership and Multidisciplinary Leadership. Her current research interests are focused on the K-12 education system in the areas of Novice

Teacher Mentorship, Student Well-being and Achievement, Inclusive Education and Diversity, Culturally Responsive Teaching, Education Policy and Politics and Multidisciplinary Leadership. In addition to these, she is involved with UNBC community service as a Senator and on the Senate Sub-Committee for Academic Affairs.

Terezinha Alves Fernandes is working at Universidade Federal da Paraíba (UFPB), Brazil, as a technician for educational affairs in the area of distance education and is conducting her Master's degree research at the Graduate Program in Linguistics and Teaching at the same university. She holds a degree in Languages and in Pedagogy from UFPB where she also attended a specialization course in Methodology and Social Science Research. The main focus of her recent research is to investigate the existing coherence between goals and procedures in teachers' reports about their pedagogical practices concerning the teaching of writing in a project called "The National Pact for Literacy at the correct age." She held various positions in the Secretary of Education of Paraíba and was a member of the State Education Council of Paraíba.

CHAPTER 10

Cross-Cultural Stories of Practice from School Leaders

Joan M. Conway, Dorothy Andrews, Leentjie van Jaarsveld, and Cheryl Bauman

INTRODUCTION

It could be assumed that research into school leadership might be exhausted and it is now only a matter of actually doing the job. Most educational systems are currently advocating for the evaluation of school leaders and their leadership against a set of adopted or developed principles: the Australian Institute for Teaching and School Leadership (AITSL) Professional Standards for Principals in Australia (AITSL 2014); the South African Standard for Principalship (DBE 2014); and the Ontario Leadership Framework (OLF) (Ontario Ministry of Education 2013). So the standards of expectation are set.

J.M. Conway (✉) · D. Andrews
University of Southern Queensland, Toowoomba, Australia
e-mail: joan.conway@usq.edu.au; Dorothy.Andrews@usq.edu.au

L. van Jaarsveld
North West University, Potchefstroom, South Africa
e-mail: Leentjie.VanJaarsveld@nwu.ac.za

C. Bauman
Independent educational consultant, Ottawa, Ontario, Canada
e-mail: cheryl.bauman.buffone@gmail.com

© The Author(s) 2017
P. Miller (ed.), *Cultures of Educational Leadership*, Intercultural Studies in Education, DOI 10.1057/978-1-137-58567-7_10

Linda Darling-Hammond and others debunked the myth that principals are just born, and presented the case that they can be made (Darling-Hammond et al. 2007). This might be a turning point for acknowledging that school leaders experience the highs and lows of professional learning on the job, and that a deeper awareness and understanding of their experiences might present richer appreciation for the complexities of school leadership across different cultures.

Of significant interest to this study is that the same research method has been used to expose the data of school leaders from Australia, South Africa and Canada. Albeit small samples from each of the countries, the quality of the data is in the richness of the personal stories that have been gained because of the generous and authentic sharing of each participant. The three sets of data have been analysed by country with an emphasis on exposing the emergent themes, and then brought together to bring the findings to a heightened level of understanding of, and empathy for, the differences and similarities of school leadership across three countries.

BACKGROUND TO SCHOOL SYSTEMS IN THREE DIFFERENT COUNTRIES

Australia

Australia is a federation of states and territories with funding for education coming from both the state/territory and federal governments. A joint Government body (Council of Australian Governments—COAG) provides a forum where State and Federal Ministers agree on areas of cooperation (https://www.coag.gov.au/schools_and_education). They have established an independent statutory authority, The Australian Curriculum, Assessment and Reporting Authority (ACARA), to develop and coordinate but not implement structure and policy in these areas (http://www.acara.edu.au/). Also established is AITSL (http://www.aitsl.edu.au/), which is governed by an independent board of directors appointed by the Federal Minister for Education and Training. This institute has established a Professional Standards for Principals framework (AITSL 2014), which sets out what principals are expected to know, understand and do, and provides guidance for state and territory governments in relation to principal accountability.

Australian schooling is offered through public and private operations. The public systems are controlled by each state and territory government and determine all matters of education, developing their own implementation strategy for national curriculum, system organisation and professional development. The private system consists of religious education systems and other individual authorities with each school registered to offer education relevant to the state in which they reside and directly funded by the federal government, with some states providing additional funding.

Both the public and private systems have developed their own policies related to principal selection, professional development and appraisal processes. Across Australia there is no common preparation requirements for principalship; however, aspiring and established principals are encouraged to upgrade formal education and participate in professional learning opportunities offered by public and private education systems, AITSL and/or professional associations. In a recent OECD report (TALIS 2014) only 27 % of Australian principals reported receiving weak leadership training in their formal education. Most principals rise from the classroom and are promoted into leadership positions, essentially learning on the job.

The Australian schools explored in this chapter are located in the Catholic Education system of South Australia (CESA). A typical role description for employment would include leadership in faith and religious education; a community leader; the one responsible for the smooth operation of the school's resources; and ensuring excellent teaching and learning. Selection criteria would not include the requirement of formal education and training (see cesa.catholic.edu.au/working-with-us/).

South Africa

The education system of South Africa consists of two national departments, namely the Department of Basic Education (DBE) (primary and secondary schools) and the Department of Higher Education and Training (tertiary education and vocational training). There are nine provinces in South Africa with their own education departments that are responsible for implementing the policies of the national department. Provincial officials and circuit managers act on behalf of the department (DBE 2014).

The South African education system might be described as a mixture of First and Third World institutions consisting of a few top functioning schools but many dysfunctioning schools with poor teaching and learning cultures. The education system deals with many difficulties such as violence in schools, long distances travelled by learners, learner dropout, learner–teacher ratio, language of instruction, socioeconomic status and poverty (Chikoko et al. 2015). Furthermore, teachers in South Africa find it difficult to cover the curriculum due to absenteeism, unforeseen in-service training, union and departmental meetings during school hours and poor teacher content knowledge of subjects (Carnoy et al. 2015).

South Africa does not require compulsory training and specific qualification for school principals. The only requirement for school principals is a teaching qualification and teaching experience: the way to become a principal is to 'go through the ranks' (teachers, head of department, deputy principal, principal). Formal preparation is not mandatory, but the Department of Education has established the South African National Professional Qualification for Principals focusing on 'providing a practical, professional, certificated program for aspirant principals' (DBE 2014); and the Standard Generating Body registered the Advanced Certificate in Education (School Management and Leadership) (ACE) for the professionalisation of school principalship with the South African Qualification Authority. The ACE was recognised as a first step towards serving principals aspiring to become principals (Bush et al. 2011).

Canada

Education in Canada for the most part is publicly funded and is overseen by the federal, provincial and municipal governments. In Canada, education is under provincial jurisdiction, and all three schools in this study are within the Province of Ontario. It is the Ministry of Education of the Ontario Government (http://www.edu.gov.on.ca/eng/) that governs policy, funding, curriculum planning and direction in all levels of public education. This ministry is responsible for curriculum guidelines for all elementary and secondary schools in the province. The ministry is also responsible for all 72 publicly funded school boards across Ontario, but it is not involved in the day-to-day operations.

All principals/vice-principals require special qualifications to become recognised by the Ontario College of Teachers (http://www.oct.ca/) and to work within the province of Ontario in publicly funded schools.

To become a principal/vice-principal, a person needs an undergraduate degree in education, 5 years of teaching experience, certification in three divisions, two specialist or honour specialist additional qualifications or a master's degree, and they are required to complete the Principal's Qualification Program (http://www.oct.ca/members/additional-qualifi cations/schedules-and-guidelines/principals-development?sc_lang=en).

In line with a growing body of knowledge, research and literature highlighting a direct connection between effective leadership and improved student achievement and well-being, principals and vice-principals are viewed and expected to play a prominent role as instructional leaders in Ontario's schools. The OLF provides guidelines that direct leaders and organisations by outlining traits of effective leaders; the characteristics of effective organisations; and common leadership language. This framework is in place to help facilitate effective dialogue, professional learning and collaboration (Ontario Ministry of Education 2013).

THE GLOBAL VIEW OF SCHOOL LEADERSHIP

Definitions of leadership are many, often incomplete and as Dimmock (2012, p. 6) argues, the 'concept itself is complex, multi-dimensional and inseparable from the social and organisational context and conditions in which it operates' [and defines leadership as] 'a social influence process guided by a moral purpose with the aim of building capacity by optimizing available resources towards the achievement of shared goals' (p. 7). Drawing on the research of others he establishes five conditions for leadership, that is, it exists within social relationships and serves social ends; involves purpose and direction; is an influence process; is a function and may not be confined to formal positions; and is contextual and contingent.

When the purpose of leadership is for successful school improvement it should be viewed as a 'highly responsive and contextualised relational process' (Hallinger and Heck 2010, p. 106) and, many argue, should be broader than the principal. Authors, for example, Harris (2013), Hopkins (2013) and Spillane (2006), indicate that extending (distributing) leadership is a way of increasing and extending a school's capacity for better use of its 'intellectual and social capital, with improved leverage strategies for teaching and learning' (Dimmock 2012, p. 113). Furthermore, Harris (2013), Hopkins (2013) and Lambert (2007) argue that it is the way people think about leadership that determines the leader's practice, and research evidence indicates that without the full support of the principal establishing structural and cultural condition, a broader view of leadership will not be a reality (Day et al. 2009). Hallinger and Heck (2010) have captured the essence of the current debate when they conclude that no single approach will work to improve all schools; leadership in itself is insufficient to bring about improvement; there is need to focus on culture and capacity for improvement; and there is need for inclusion of a broader range of leaders in school improvement capacity building processes.

What then is the role of the principal in school improvement? Ultimately, given the current established role positions, the principal is responsible and accountable for the effective operation of the school. Established in the research is the notion that principal leadership is the second most influential factor that accounts for variation across schools (Leithwood et al. 2008) and that principals may influence learning by shaping teachers' working conditions and motivation (Louis 2007; Louis et al. 2010; Walker et al. 2014). Other research has explored the contribution of principal leadership to improving school outcomes (Crowther & Associates 2011; Hopkins 2013; Robinson 2007; Walker et al. 2014). Functions such as goal setting, resource mobilisation, enabling and engaging with other leaders within the school, effective communication, engaging with staff in professional development and culture building have been included in the list. Such a list provides a starting point for the research in this chapter as we explore from a cross-cultural perspective, the role of the principal in school improvement.

THE SHARED DATA COLLECTION APPROACH

The methodology for this qualitative study used the interpretive perspective to collect and analyse data from school leaders in three different countries. The overall purpose was to explore the role of the school leader in leading school improvement with a focus on the following questions:

What did the school leader do to lead school improvement?
What impact did this have on how they viewed their role?
How has this experience enabled ongoing leadership?

The participants were nine school leaders, three from each of Australia, Canada and South Africa, who had been in their current schools for three years or more, and had been appointed to the position based on prior leadership experience. This study has focused on school leaders in their leadership of school improvement.

Each school leader was interviewed one-on-one by the researcher of each country for approximately one hour. The interviews were semi-structured and school leaders were provided the questions prior to the interviews. The research questions included the following exploration:

a. *What did the school leader do to lead school improvement?* [Structural processes/procedures/strategies—implementation and the relationality of how this was done.]
b. *What impact did this have on how they viewed their role?* [The school leader's personal reflections in relation to personal and professional growth.]
c. *How has this experience enabled ongoing principal leadership?* [The school leader's reflection on themselves in terms of current leadership practice.]

The analysis was completed in two phases. First, the researcher from each country interrogated their interview data set to expose themes and independently presented the findings. The second phase involved a collaborative comparative analysis of the themes to determine what similarities and differences in school leaders' roles could be identified and thus enabled discussion in response to the overarching question: *what emerges as the role of the school leader in leading school improvement across three countries?*

The Stories from the Principals (The Nominated Nomenclature for 'School Leader' from Each Data Set of This Study)

From Australia

Each of the principals selected for the Australian contribution adopted a systemically supported school improvement project, IDEAS (Innovative Designs for Enhancing Achievements in Schools) (Crowther et al. 2001), which provided a processual way of meeting the mandatory CESA school improvement framework. Whilst none of the schools were compelled to adopt a school improvement process, each of the principals independently had determined there was room for improvement. Each of the schools is located in the capital city of South Australia but differs in their socio-economic position, total enrolment and reason for embarking on the school improvement project.

The principals' individual responses have revealed a number of themes which, although quoted in different ways, have resounding affirmation in all three schools.

Commitment to Context, Cultural History and Sustainability

Having examined the results of the diagnostic survey built into IDEAS, each principal was able to clearly articulate why he/she had committed to it. As illustrated in the quotes following, their reasons were different. Interestingly, all connected under the themes of context, recognition of a specific cultural history and a need to build capacity for sustainability.

Principal AU1 said 'It was a bit of a traditional school. Not a lot of working together... more working as individuals. So here, they've got a principal who wants to actually come in and see what they're doing and chat' which he believed needed to change in this already successful school if there was to be sustainable school outcomes and student achievement into the future.

Principal AU2 wondered, 'How can we reenergise what's actually happening across the community; more importantly, how do we move forward in a way that's going to strengthen and improve teaching and learning?' This was also recognition of what was already in place and how it was to be sustained.

Principal AU3 reflected on his position in relation to the staff: 'I had a review... and the staff indicated that they were feeling a little bit out of the loop in terms of some of the things that were happening in the school. It was fairly clear to me that I needed to change my style... in terms of how I brought the school along. So when the opportunity to be involved in a project which opened leadership up to be a more sustainable way that more people's opinions and ideas could be part of it, I was very keen'.

Ownership and Trust

Each principal readily stressed the importance of ensuring that whatever was to be successful would have to involve whole community—staff, students and parents.

For me sometimes I just have to make sure I'm not in the way, that I don't get in the way of things happening ... when the people feel empowered I think the trust builds up and builds up and people come in and have quite a vigorous discussion ... it's the trust and valuing of people. (Principal AU3)

I trust their knowledge and I trust their experience, and I trust they know their students really well. Much more than I would know because I'm not in the classroom often. And I trust their professionalism. I probably trust their, how can I put it, their desire to improve learning here. It is about that deep respect isn't it, for each other. (Principal AU1)

During the interviews the principals spoke in varying ways about the importance of building trust, developing a trusting community through collaboration, taking risks and 'letting go'.

Educative

For each principal in their own way and in response to their contextual needs, there was an appreciation for their role as the lead educator of this whole school improvement process. Although not boastfully expressed, each one of them demonstrated this role:

Principal AU1 ensured that staff developed their professional knowledge aligned to their classroom practice: 'Methodology has changed enormously. We work on things that are well researched. Now we've aligned literacy right across the whole school ... and there's guaranteed things happening in every room of our school.'

Principal AU2 drew staff into the conversation about the moral purpose of education: 'This is what we're working on, it's what we believe is really important for our children and their learning, and how they can improve.'

Principal AU3 demonstrated a strategic approach to ensuring that the staff could see the purpose of their involvement: 'I was fairly enthusiastic about the project and I tried to let people know that it would include a fair bit of work but a lot of good times too ... that we would do things together. I thought that the power of the people that were picked [as teacher leaders] took a lot of people with them.'

Personal Leadership Learning

Of significance during these interviews was the readiness of each principal to share what it was that they believed they had learned about themselves, and particularly themselves as leaders.

Principal AU1 unreservedly admitted to the difficulties throughout the process but reflected on the necessary pathway that had to be forged: 'So the frustrations that I was feeling as the principal in this school forced me I think to reflect a lot more on my work as a principal in this school. Looking back, it's far easier than when you are in the moment.'

Principal AU2 reflected on the importance of collaboration and the capacity building of teachers taking leadership: 'I think the biggest learning for me in that process was around the importance of teachers being leaders, and I don't think we would have made so much ground without that committee, or that team, being involved.'

Principal AU3 admitted to having changed his perspective when he finally realised he had to trust the leadership of those with whom he had chosen to share the journey:

> Probably the biggest point I had was when we were discussing—about our vision … and I was thinking we should be going down a particular line. It wasn't until I let that go and let other ideas come in that everyone just sort of started to think this is great and I had to take a big step back. But that took a bit of soul searching I suppose to actually think that through.

Common to all three principals was the respect and trust for the moral integrity of each person involved and the power of effective communication to ensure that all were engaged. This motive was eloquently summed up by Principal AU3:

> Always thinking about where people are at, what's their depth of understanding, what's their depth of knowledge, and then what do we need to either refine, recap, refine, build on, so people can see the development? So planning, communicating, just filtering I think, all the things, the demands that come in around what teachers have to deal with. Communicating in different formats.

From South Africa

The principals interviewed in the South African context were selected from two provinces and were representative of a primary and two secondary schools. The socio-economic status of the schools as well as the learner–teacher ratio are similar. Each year the schools must adhere to the compulsory school improvement plan (SIP), being completed and sent back to the department. The SIP, provided by the department, is an instrument for measuring the progress in specific areas in the school in order to develop a culture of teaching and learning. Although the three schools share similarities, one of the schools has experienced many challenges and therefore does not perform as well as the other two schools. However, an initial analysis of the three principal interviews has revealed several common themes of interest to this study.

Appreciation of Teamwork
Each of the principals indicated the importance of appreciation. Teachers want to feel that they are appreciated for the work they have done, whether it is teaching, extra mural activities or duties assigned to them, especially the evaluation of the school which is part of the SIP. During the evaluation of the SIP, all nine areas are evaluated. The nine areas include basic functionality; leadership, management and communication; governance and relationships; quality of teaching and learning, and educator development; curriculum provision and resources; learner achievement; school safety, security and discipline; school infrastructure; and parents and the community. Without the necessary appreciation from their side as principals, the evaluation of the school becomes a one-sided process and the basic purpose of the evaluation fails. This was clearly articulated by each of the principals of this study.

> I think we've got very hardworking educators who are doing extra miles for these learners in terms of what they are ordered to do. So, I think you must appreciate the fact that educators at this school are working as a team and they're going all out despite all challenges that we must face to provide to this community. (Principal SA1)
>
> Our vision is basically bringing about excellence in learners, to bring about improvement in learners, improvement of the teachers that will lead to improvement in the school as a whole. We have a good set of teachers. The teachers are particularly hard workers. (Principal SA2)
>
> I think it's a way of varying the contribution of every member who is part of the staff and then recognising the fact that you cannot know all. You allow them to come up with their views and they must see you showing appreciation of their views so that they would also at least be able to also feel their confidence and they should realise that what we are doing is appreciated. (Principal SA3)

Without the efforts of the teachers the principals would not be able to evaluate the SIP on their own. The principals are aware of this and therefore appreciate the contributions of the teachers.

Challenges

All three principals agreed unanimously that it is a difficult task to bring about school improvement when there are various challenges that place pressure on them as principals.

> Our challenges become greater, they [the learners] are coming from socially disadvantaged homes and they don't have the facilities that are necessary for them to develop properly, they lack all the basic facilities. The parents are not equipped to help their children and then it comes back to us. The Department forces us to pass learners that are not equipped for the next academic year. It has a very negative effect on us. (Principal SA1)
>
> The parents are not involved in the education of their children. The children are exposed to drugs, violence and crime. Poverty plays a vital role in our education system. (Principal SA2)
>
> The main concern is finances. We are not receiving enough money from the Department. Therefore there is a lack of facilities, resources and staff members. (Principal SA3)

The socio-economic situation in the quintile 1, 2 and 3 schools results in a lack of finances, proper resources and a lack of parental involvement. These are the challenges the principals have to face on a daily basis.

Awareness of Self and Others

One of the aspects that came to the fore during the interviews was the concept of awareness. Although the SIP is compulsory and could be seen as 'something that must be done', the principal became aware of a number of important issues.

> Principal SA1 acknowledged: The SIP makes me very much aware of the greater needs of the teachers and then I can determine the weaknesses of the teachers and probably use their strengths to put it in other areas where it is needed.
>
> Principal SA2 viewed opportunities for himself and his teachers: I think I am this person who's very open to different proposals. In fact, when people question me I regard that as an opportunity for me to provide answers. I always think that with everything you do you can always better your performance, but

whilst it's working we should check on better things so that we don't think that we've arrived in this way that we're arriving or that we arrive again. I don't think that I have arrived yet. So, every time I feel we must keep on with innovations in terms of how we implement things and check whether we improved the value.

Principal SA3 used the requirement as a checkpoint for his leadership: The SIP is like a 'wake-up call'. You think that everything is running smoothly in your school and you as a principal is well in control of everything. But during the evaluation process your staff identify needs and then you realise that you need them.

Furthermore, Principal SA3 also acknowledged the need for personal development and learning by explaining that 'The thing that I've realised about myself is that you need to have skills, skills to manage, plan, delegate, to serve the school to the best'.

The SIP changes one to become aware of the needs of others and to look out for the needs of all the stakeholders involved in the school.

Continuity

The principals agreed that continuity is of importance for improvement. Not only continuous assessment regarding the evaluation of the school but also assessment and development of oneself, the teachers and the learners.

Every day you learn how to deal with different things in different ways on different levels. It is important to look for different solutions on a day to day basis. You cannot leave the SIP till the end of the year, once a month it is necessary to have a meeting regarding the Plan. You must continuously identify the needs of the school, the needs of staff development, your own [sic] personal growth. Often we neglect ourselves by giving the opportunity to teachers to develop and not ourselves. (Principal SA3)

The SIP is continuous. It's from the beginning and it is continuous and every year we leave a new necessity in the Plan. If an issue arises, if it's a serious issue that looms immediately, you know when we find what the issue is an issue will determine what strategies you would put together. (Principal SA1)

Needs must be addressed in the SIP so that when you check your progress column to indicate whether we are doing each of that, because the progress column will then be able to give the evidence. People come and check whether we are moving towards the right direction or not. (Principal SA2)

All three principals appeared to agree that to ensure improvement, the SIP must be first priority to ensure continuous updating and development in the interest of the staff members as well as the whole school.

From Canada

All three schools in this study are under the direction of their District Board of Education and the Ontario Ministry of Education. All 72 publicly funded school boards in the province of Ontario must submit a yearly board improvement plan (BIP) to the Ministry of Education. The SIP processes expected of each school must involve all school partners to ensure success.

The principal, responsible for administering the school and for providing instructional leadership, is ultimately responsible for improvement planning. However, the entire school community is expected to be involved in all stages of the process: planning, implementing, monitoring and evaluating progress. The SIP process is focused on three areas of priority: curriculum delivery, school environment and parental involvement.

As the interviews took place and the data were analysed, themes emerged and are discussed later in the chapter.

Developing and Maintaining a Positive Attitude

All three principals discussed having a positive attitude towards their work–life responsibilities and their interactions with others. This attitude provides hope during the SIP process.

> Principal CA1 confidently admitted that 'By looking at the positive I am able to magnify my strengths and the strengths of my staff and students.'
>
> Principal CA2 posed that 'If we remain positive we have a much better chance to work together on the school improvement planning and focus on what is important.'
>
> Principal CA3 affirmed that 'We all believe in students, and this belief helps to provide a positive atmosphere in the school at all times.'

Positive Relationships

All three principals discussed in great detail the importance of positive relationship building and maintaining of these relationships in terms of the school improvement process. They all saw their role as being instrumental in creating and maintaining positive relationships built on trust.

I believe that when the students see staff getting along that this tells them how to act. The students look to us as adults as to how to form relationships and what is expected here. (Principal CA2)

When I first arrived at this school, the behaviour was so out of control. The police were here all the time. Slowly through setting expectations for behaviour and learning with both staff and students and building relationships, the behaviour problems are almost non-existent. Three years ago when I arrived I would not have been able to sit here for this long without being interrupted many times. (Principal CA3)

Part of building trust was also being open, honest and authentic. 'When I mess up, I admit it,' stated Principal CA1, and went on to say, 'I always apologise if I know I have done something wrong. It shows trust and respect.'

Decision Making

All three of the principals discussed the importance of the decision-making process when it came to school improvement as a collaborative process. The principals actively shared the decision-making process with the teachers, parents and students.

Not one single person has all of the necessary skills and knowledge to lead this school. (Principal CA2)

Staff volunteer to take on roles and to lead initiatives at the school. (Principal CA1)

Principal CA3 explained a process where the entire school community was mobilised to support the emotional, social, physical and academic needs of the students. This principal believed in the philosophy that 'it takes a village to raise a child'. The other two principals also provided instances of whole school engagement in decision making relative to their contexts:

I give my staff freedom to make decisions. (Principal CA1)

The staff and students make decisions as to how to allocate resources, what programs should stay and what programs should go, based on our needs. It was tough to make some of these decisions, as some of the after school programs and sports teams were cut due to resource allocation and staff being stretched too thin. (Principal CA2)

As Principal CA3 stated, 'sharing decision making is critical to moving the school in a forward direction, believing that all students can succeed'.

Allowing the Reflections and Voices of Staff to Influence Their Decisions
Principal CA3 stated that when he first arrived at the school there were many changes to be made from student achievement to student behaviour. This principal explained:

> By the end of my first year student discipline issues had declined and we were seeing more sustainable improvements in student attendance. A few staff members approached me and said, 'we really like the changes you are making, but can you slow down a bit, we can't keep up'. I considered this a courageous conversation and was forced to take a look at the fast pace of these changes.
>
> Although all the changes were great the staff were telling me that they could not continue at this very fast pace. I did not realise the impact this was having on the staff. I am glad that they approached me, as I started to involve them more in the decision making at a pace that we all agreed upon.

This is a powerful acknowledgement by a school leader willing to work reflexively with the staff in order to enhance personal leadership style.

Providing a Voice through Conversations
Two out of the three principals talked about the importance of having conversations with all key stakeholders surrounding what leadership is in the school.

> I want leadership to go on well past when I am not here any longer. It needs to. I hold one-on-one conversations with staff as well as conversations in group settings. Through these conversations I give the staff and school community members a voice on how they define leadership...what is their participation in the leadership process...this helps to work on developing a vision for future sustainability of leadership after I have left. (Principal CA3)
>
> I like it when my staff come to talk with me about decisions or issues. My door is always open. The parents know this too. Students come to talk with me. All voices must be heard...it helps me to decide what is important and what isn't. (Principal CA1)

Formalised Measures for Capacity Building and Sustainability
All three principals spoke of their leadership practices being grounded in theory and informed by the educational leadership philosophy of the OLF

(Ontario Ministry of Education 2013). However, despite formalised measures in place for sustainability in terms of SIP in the districts and the province of Ontario, the three principals lamented assurance of leadership sustainability:

> I cannot guarantee that the school improvement planning process as it is now will continue when I leave. (Principal CA1)
>
> There are no measures to ensure that what we have done here at this school will last or even be continued on with the next principal. (Principal CA2)
>
> Ummmmm … no (shaking their head and frowning) all of the hard work may or may not continue when I leave, it all depends on who is placed here … I don't know … I can't say. (Principal CA3)

DISCUSSION

The emergent themes from each data set viewed together reveal six roles of similar and different value as to how principals work with the task of developing a plan for school improvement. These roles have been named and categorised in Table 10.1. Further interpretation of each role is explained following Table 10.1.

Producing the Plan for School Improvement

Each of the educational systems had requirements for each school to have a plan for school improvement. Despite the overall similarity linked to the tenet of improving school outcomes, the structure, the development and the expectations differ across all three selected systems. Australian schools

Table 10.1 Principals' roles in leading school improvement

Role	*Contextual category*
1. Producing the plan for school improvement	Structural
2. Diagnosis	Structural/cultural
3. Relationship building	Relational
4. Educative	Relational/cultural
5. Developing a personal leadership style	Cultural
6. Addressing the context	Cultural/structural

individually develop their relevant plan framed by the systemic school improvement framework. The South African Education Department produces a mandatory systemic SIP and all principals explained how they must adhere to it and report in order to meet the requirements. Canadian schools work within the parameters of the BIP and each of the principals spoke of their responsibility to ensure the development of an SIP which must engage all stakeholders in the particular context.

Diagnosis

Each of the principals spoke of some way of diagnosing how they responded to the task of school improvement, however, how it was done, and for what purpose differed in each context. The Australian principals responded to a diagnostic survey that had engaged staff, students and parents, which provided a basis for engaging staff in conversations that responded to specific needs of their contexts. The South African principals spoke of having to tick off each item of the SIP as 'something that must be done'. The Canadian principals explained that they responded to the annual mandate of the board by prioritising the focus of their school.

Relationship Building

Overwhelmingly, all principals of this study were concerned about the importance of building and maintaining relationships between themselves and the teachers. However, the way in which that was expressed differed in each data set. The Australian principals appeared to be genuinely concerned about a sense of ownership and trust developed amongst the staff. The South African principals focused on teamwork and appreciation for the teachers' contributions. The Canadian principals focused on relationship building as a key focus for working towards attaining positive relationships built upon trust and respect.

Educative

This role appears to be an extension of the previous focus on building relationships. It is termed the educative role of the principal in relation to the organisational culture whereby there is an intention to move the culture of leadership beyond the sole responsibility of the principal. In the Australian schools there was repeated evidence of the principals working towards fostering the leadership of teachers in the school improvement process. The principals of the South African schools tended to go beyond their role as school leaders by encouraging other stakeholders to complete the SIP with a teamwork approach. The Canadian principals had a commitment to lead that carried with it an ownership for the collective as well as for themselves.

Developing a Personal Leadership Style

The relationship of the personal leadership style to the culture of the system within which the principal operated emerged as a factor in determining how the educative role of the principal influenced the development of a personal leadership style. Whilst this study is in no way intended to draw generalised conclusions, analysis has drawn attention to the complexity of context and culture whereby what appears to be valued in the relationship between systems and schools, principals and teachers have bearing on the resulting styles of leadership. The Australian principals appeared to operate liberally and open-mindedly as learners of leadership, encouraging and letting others take a lead, make decisions and demonstrate leadership. The South African principals appeared to feel somewhat curtailed by the prescription of the mandated SIP with little scope for the principals to show initiative in recognising growth in their personal leadership styles. The Canadian principals spoke of continually discussing their learning with regard to their leadership style as they listened to voices from all stakeholders, reflected upon their practices and used data to inform their decisions.

Addressing the Context

This final role presents a more startling revelation that could be studied in greater depth to reveal how the principal has responded to perceived challenges in their specific contexts. For the Australian principals the important challenge was how to engage and motivate the staff to be involved in school improvement processes, and then to know how to sustain that engagement. For the South African principals the challenge was far more confronting as they faced many issues, such as poverty, illiteracy and lack of resources (Van Wyk and Van Der Westhuizen 2015, p. 172). Evidence suggests that they applied themselves with diligence to the task of completing the SIP, but found difficulty in taking ownership of it in their context or seeing the value of the exercise as an opportunity to develop themselves. In Canada, the educational system has put in place mechanisms to try to ensure sustainability, but there is no framework in place to support the building and maintaining of a culture of sustainability, and the principals expressed concern for what they have in place might not necessarily be continued after they left.

CONCLUSION

The greatest value in this relatively small study has been the richness of the principals' voices. Each principal generously shared their perspectives and provided opportunity for valuable conclusions within the parameters of this chapter. Of significance is the interpretation of the principals' roles in relation to the context categorised as structural, relational and cultural. The authors propose that this categorisation provides a sound basis for a larger research study. Such a study would extend the interpretation reached in this chapter, to enable a deeper understanding of the challenges faced by principals in leading school improvement in different cultural contexts structurally, relationally and culturally.

Overall, there is evidence to suggest that two specific factors contribute to the way in which the individual principal perceives the role of school leadership—the nature of the context, and the relationship between the system and the school.

REFERENCES

AITSL (Australian Institute for Teaching and School Leadership). (2014). *Australian professional standard for principals.* Victoria, Australia: Education Services Australia, Carlton South.

Bush, T., Kiggundu, E., & Moorosi, P. (2011). Preparing new principals in South Africa: the ACE school leadership programme. *South African Journal of Education, 31*(1), 31–43.

Carnoy, M., Ngware, M., & Oketch, M. (2015). The role of classroom resources and national educational context in student learning gains: comparing Botswana, Kenya, and South Africa. *Comparative Education Review, 59*(2), 199–233.

Chikoko, V., Naicker, I., & Mthiyane, S. (2015). School leadership practices that work in areas of multiple deprivation in South Africa. *Educational Management Administration & Leadership*, *43*(3), 452–467.

Crowther, F., & Associates. (2011). *From school improvement to sustained capacity: the parallel leadership pathway*. Thousand Oaks, CA: Corwin.

Crowther, F., Andrews, D., Dawson, M., & Lewis, M. (2001). *IDEAS facilitation folder*. Toowoomba, Australia: Leadership Research Institute, University of Southern Queensland.

Darling-Hammond, L., LaPointe, M., Meyerson, D., Orr, M. T., & Cohen, C. (2007). *Preparing school leaders for a changing world: Lessons from exemplary leadership development programs*. Stanford, CA: Stanford University, Stanford Educational Leadership Institute.

Day, C., Sammons, P., Leithwood, K., Harris, A., & Hopkins, D. (2009). *The impact of leadership on pupil outcomes. Final report*. London, UK: DCSF.

DBE (Department of Basic Education). 2014. *The South African standard for principalship, enhancing the image of and competency school principals*. Pretoria: DBE. http://www.saou.co.za/images/stories/library/Nuus_van_Nas_kan toor_2014/standards%20for%20principalship%20gazette%207august2014. pdf. Accessed 12 January 2016.

Dimmock, C. (2012). *Leadership, capacity building and school improvement: concepts, themes and impact*. Ambingdon, OX: Routledge.

Hallinger, P., & Heck, R. (2010). Collaborative leadership and school improvement: understanding the impact on school capacity and student learning. *School Leadership & Management*, *30*(2), 95–110.

Harris, A. (2013). Distributed leadership: friend or foe? *Educational Management Administration & Leadership*, *41*(5), 545–554.

Hopkins, D. (2013). Exploding the myths of school reform. *School Leadership & Management*, *33*(4), 304–321.

Lambert, L. (2007). Lasting leadership: toward sustainable school improvement. *Journal of Educational Change*, *8*(4), 311–323.

Leithwood, K., Harris, A., & Hopkins, D. (2008). Seven strong claims about successful school leadership. *School Leadership & Management*, *28*(1), 27–42.

Louis, K. S., (2007). Trust and improvement in schools. *Journal of Educational Change*, *8*, 1–24.

Louis, K. S., Dretzke, B., & Wahlstrom, K. (2010). How does leadership affect student achievement? Results from a national U.S. Survey. *School Effectiveness and School Improvement*, *21*(3), 315–336.

Ontario Ministry of Education. (2013). *Ontario leadership framework*. http://www.edu.gov.on.ca/eng/policyfunding/leadership/framework. html. Accessed 25 January 2016.

Robinson, V. (2007). *School leadership and student outcomes: identifying what works and why.* ACEL Monograph no 41. Winmalee, NSW: Australian Council for Educational Leaders.

Spillane, J. (2006). *Distributed leadership.* Jossey-Bass, CA: San Francisco.

TALIS (Teaching and Learning International Survey). (2014). *Education at a Glance 2014: OECD Indicators.* www.oecd.org/edu/Education-at-a-Glance-2014.pdf. Accessed 15 January 2016.

Van Wyk, A., & Van Der Westhuizen, P. C. (2015). Resistance to change in impoverished schools of a South African province. *Problems and Perspectives in Management, 13*(4), 172–180.

Walker, A. D., Lee, M., & Bryant, D. A. (2014). How much of a difference do principals make? An analysis of between-schools variation in academic achievement in Hong Kong public secondary schools. *School Effectiveness and School Improvement, 25*(4), 602–628.

Joan M. Conway, PhD, FACEL, FACE, is a senior lecturer in the Faculty of Business, Education, Law and Arts at the University of Southern Queensland, Australia. She is a member of the Leadership Research International (LRI) team and is a consultant researcher of the Innovative Designs for Enhancing Achievements in Schools (IDEAS) Project. Joan teaches, supervises and publishes in the area of educational leadership with a strong focus on the benefits of collaboration and collective intelligence for sustainable school improvement. She continues to engage in research projects investigating the relationship between teacher leadership, sustainable school improvement and professional learning.

Dorothy Andrews, PhD, FACEL, FACE, is an associate professor in the Faculty of Business, Education, Law and Arts at the University of Southern Queensland, Australia. She is Director of the Leadership Research International (LRI) and National Director of the Innovative Designs for Enhancing Achievements in Schools (IDEAS) project. IDEAS is a whole school revitalization project established in 1998. Its current form represents years of research and development by the research of the LRI-USQ. Dorothy teaches, supervises and publishes in the areas of educational leadership and school improvement, and her research interests are in the areas of leadership, pedagogy and sustainable school Improvement.

Leentjie van Jaarsveld, PhD, is Lecturer in Education Management Leadership in the Faculty of Education Sciences at North-West University (NWU), Potchefstroom Campus, South Africa. Since November 2013 she has been a full-time lecturer at the NWU and was appointed as the BEd Honours programme leader during 2014. Her research focuses on school leadership approaches and has published two articles on this.

Cheryl Bauman, BA, Bed, Med, EdD, teaches at the faculty of education departments at several universities. She is a member of the Leadership Research International team and is President of JSI (John Snow, Inc.) consulting, an educational consulting firm. Cheryl teaches in the area of educational leadership with a strong focus on the motivational benefits of individuals working both autonomously and collaboratively for sustainable school improvement. She engages in research projects investigating the relationship between principal and teacher leadership, sustainable school improvement, and autonomy and collaboration in organizations. Cheryl has held a number of roles in the educational system including principal, vice-principal, learning support consultant and guidance counsellor.

CHAPTER 11

Whole School Development Across Borders: Leading Intercultural and Cross-Cultural Learning

Paul Miller and Ian Potter

INTRODUCTION

The current discourse on school improvement, particularly in England, tends to focus on interventions to improve academic outcomes and insufficiently takes a holistic view about the psyche of a school in how it builds capacity for sustained development. This chapter argues that notions of outreach and schools looking beyond their own boundaries, which have been espoused and there is some evidence to support its impact in practice, should extend to looking internationally. The rhetoric of system improvement often manifests itself in structures of schools working as part of collaborations, or in partnerships. The research presented in this chapter illuminates how institutions of learning can broaden their perspectives

P. Miller (✉)
School of Education & Professional Development, University of Huddersfield, Huddersfield, West Yorkshire, United Kingdom
e-mail: P.Miller@hud.ac.uk

I. Potter
Bay House School, Hampshire, United Kingdom
e-mail: ipotter@bayhouse.hants.sch.uk

© The Author(s) 2017
P. Miller (ed.), *Cultures of Educational Leadership*, Intercultural Studies in Education, DOI 10.1057/978-1-137-58567-7_11

about how it can build capital through engaging with other institutions and individuals beyond national borders. The evidence collected is from staff and students from England who participated in study tours to Jamaica, Malawi and Albania and a group of teachers from Jamaica who participated in a study tour to England. In all four countries where visits occurred, participants took part in a range of learning activities across several institutions and organisations. The aims of these visits were to encourage a 'study-like' paradigm by providing staff and students with (1) developing strong cross-cultural communication skills, and an ability to appreciate social and cultural differences leading to a higher level of self-confidence as potential global citizens; and (2) exposure to and opportunities for international partnership working and collaboration.

A case study narrative is presented that shows how students and teachers in different parts of the world engaging in links with schools in other countries lead to whole school development. The countries evidenced are from several continents and therefore enriches the data that informs the thinking. The school links are not with schools described as 'International Schools' but are with publicly funded primary and secondary schools and other educational establishments. This is ground-breaking research in that it captures capacity-building activities that are uncommon between schools across the globe and because it also includes the voices of both students and staff engaged in 'Study Tours'. The impact on participants' own school and how this supports school development is analysed and evaluated. The impact on the schools visited is also part of the evidence leading to the conclusion that there is sufficient finding in this type of activity that deserves serious consideration and widespread adoption.

There is also the evidence of the reflections of the 'adults' accompanying the students on these trips and their learning. Therefore, the research data informing the writing of this chapter leads us to explore how study tours can produce a type of learning that is 'qualitatively different from other types of learning experience' (Miller and Potter 2014, p. 21). The impact on both staff and students is examined and illuminates Miller's (2012a) proposal that global trends are driving policy makers and schools alike as they reconceptualise and 'do education differently' (p. 1). The principle of experiencing through doing draws on and underscores Mintzberg's (2004) notion that there is need to develop a 'worldly mindset' where one's own mindset gets enlarged through other people's worlds. In the words of Fullan (2004, p. 16), 'Nothing beats learning in context'. In other words, nothing beats experiencing through doing.

We argue in this chapter that through these study tours, participants were introduced to a qualitatively different form of capital, which we describe as 'contextualised capital', not obtainable from the textbook or in the everyday in-school learning experience.

The construct of 'capital' draws on the work of Hargreaves and Fullan (2012) where they build a concept of 'Professional Capital' that recognises various forms of capital that prevail within a school. It is the confluence of three kinds of capital: human, social and decisional capitals (p. 88). Together they engender a professional culture and community that build capacity. Implicit in the theory is professionals working collaboratively. It cannot be rushed and 'there are no easy short cuts' (p. 119). Hargreaves and Fullan state that: 'Building collaborative cultures is a patient developmental journey' (p. 119). Dimmock (2012) argues for 'A new conceptualisation of educational leadership for the twenty-first century' (p. 18), where leadership is 'aimed at marshalling resources in ways that maximise capacity' (p. 18). His model presents a construct of holistic organisational approaches where capacity and capital increase through a mindset that sees synergies in partnership. He argues that: 'one is able to arrive at a fuller and more holistic understanding of leadership and schooling by placing them in the larger social context of which they are a part' (p. 202).

Therefore, our construct of 'contextualised capital' draws from these perspectives, in addition to the notion of contextualised knowledge production (Gibbon et al. 1994; Nowotny et al. 2001), where knowledge mobilisation is enhanced through its production happening within context. Thus, our construct is a synthesis of the idea of building capital and capacity through an appreciation of context. Hence, a knowledge-generation method that makes sense of one's own context through appreciation of another's increases not only an understanding of the situation in which one resides but introduces one to new knowledge of another's situation. It is a process of constructing and deconstructing one's experience to build a better understanding.

The building of capital amongst participants and their schools was believed to be important for two main reasons. First, the staff and students who participated in the tours can be seen as 'ambassadors'. Second, effective and transformational leadership models recognise that capacity can be built from 'bottom up' and not only through 'top down' approaches. In other words, the participation of staff and students on tour was a form of capacity building not only for them but also for others in their school communities. That is, as institutional 'ambassadors', participants were simultaneously tasked with the responsibility of positively marketing their own institutions and country abroad; and to ensure the knowledge and understandings of another country, gleaned whilst on tour, were, on their return, sensitively and responsibly communicated to others both inside and outside school.

This nuanced approach to capacity building represents the importance of a simultaneously 'contextualised' and 'de-contextualised' educational experience for staff and students operating successfully and competently in an increasingly global environment. This is consistent with providing experiential learning activities that focus on both the group and the individual, and that enable participants to explore new territories and cultures.

CONCEPTUAL FRAMEWORK

Transformational leadership

Transformational leadership is an approach to leadership that causes change in individuals and social systems. It creates valuable and positive change in the followers with the end goal of capacity development amongst followers. According to Burns (1978), transformational leadership is a process in which leaders and followers help each other to advance to a higher level of morale and motivation. In its simplest form, transformational leadership is suggested to enhance the motivation, morale and performance of followers through different mechanisms.

Hallinger (2003) proposed that transformational leadership involves targeted capacity development. Enacted at the level of a school, the linking, modelling and challenging that the leader does is applied across all categories of members of a school community and not only staff or teachers. But for this to be successful, it must arise out of the leader's knowledge of his followers. When met with out-the-box thinking, transformational leadership can result in increased student achievement, motivation and confidence at school. Wilkins (2013, p. 3) argues that school leadership:

- Utilises its agency in space-making on three levels: (1) the leaders' own personal spaces; (2) the spaces within the institution the leader manages; and (3) the networks of places and organisations with which the leader and the school have links.
- Is cosmopolitan, promoting global citizenship, multi-layered affiliations and respect for and understanding of other spaces.

- Creates infrastructure for capacity building by connecting homes, workplaces and civic spaces through the school's networks.

In facilitating students' participation in the study tours, the organisers have shown a clear understanding of all three points in relation to the academic and personal development of the students. Furthermore, the student's participation in the study tours also signalled the importance of students developing cosmopolitan, global and multi-layered identities and understandings of the world, particularly in the context of 'shifting borderland narratives' (Miller 2012a, p. 5). Hallinger (2003) argued that 'transformational leaders increase the capacity of others in the school to produce first-order effects on learning...' (p. 338). The study tours created a forum for students to recalibrate their knowledge and understanding of cultural spaces and people. And in doing so, the organisers and co-ordinating institutions created opportunities and a climate in which 'multiple actors' could engage in learning of a 'different' kind; the result of which would be benefits to individual students and the school community.

LITERATURE REVIEW

Study Tours

A body of literature has steadily emerged over recent years, in the management and marketing literature describing and supporting international study tours as valuable educational experiences (Tucker and Weaver 2013). There is, however, a paucity of empirical research on study tours in education and/or schooling (Miller and Potter 2014). Nevertheless, much of the available literature have focused primarily on the design and implementation of study tours, with only limited attention impacts on participants. The limited empirical research on the impact of study tours is somewhat surprising given their increasing popularity, especially amongst business students especially ('Business Students Flock' 2002).

Aims and Benefits of Study Tours

Study Tours can have different aims. For example, they can be about exposing participants to a particular experience or culture. However, they can also be about raising the profile of a host institution, which can lead to a boost in recruitment due to 'hosting' visitors from overseas and also due to the practice that local students may themselves be engaged in some reciprocal arrangement.

Study tours are reputed to provide individuals and groups with both tangible and intangible benefits. For example, Commins et al. (2010) proposed such benefits as personal development, whereas Williams (2005) proposed such benefits as intercultural adaptability and inter-cultural sensitivity. Moreover, Woolf (2007) argued participants can become more appreciative of their own country and culture, as well as for others. Similarly, study tours are said to provide essential opportu-nities for stereotypes about peoples and the host country to be clarified (Pariola and Pariola 2006). In other words, a study tour offers parti-cipants a real opportunity to acquire a socio-cultural understanding of another place and space, not previously had (Sachau et al. 2010).

From the available literature, one might summarise the benefits of study tours as follows:

- Increased cultural sensitivity (Anderson et al. 2006)
- Improved student confidence (Tucker and Weaver 2013)
- Heightened appreciation for other cultures (Pence and Macgillivray 2008)
- Increased international functional knowledge (Chieffo and Griffiths 2004)
- Deeper understanding of global interdependence (Sutton and Rubin 2004)
- Increased interest in working or studying in a different country (Orahood et al. 2004)
- Interest in interdisciplinary studies (Lewis and Niesenbaum 2005)
- Enhance cultural connectivity and professional development (Harrison 2006)
- New professional perspectives (Miller et al. 2015).

Allen and Young (1997, p. 169) notes, '... learning occurs more readily when students are able to experience (i.e., see, smell, taste, hear, feel) stimuli and actively participate in the education process.' By experiencing a culture first-hand, study tour participants develop a much deeper under-standing of and appreciation for that culture than they would by simply reading about it (Brokaw 1996; Porth 1997). However, organising and delivering a successful study tour is dependent on a range of factors, including availability of staff, geography, language and cost involved (Commins et al. 2010).

International Dimension in Education

A number of education ministries and institutions worldwide have committed to an 'international dimension'. The United Kingdom's Department for Children Schools and Families (2009), for example, has an international dimension that seeks to:

- enable people to understand *the links* between their own lives and those of people throughout the world;
- increase understanding of the *economic, cultural, political and environmental influences* which shape our lives;
- develop the *skills, attitudes and values* which enable people to work together to bring about change and take control of their own lives; and
- work towards achieving *a more just and sustainable world* in which power and resources are more equitably shared.

Students today demand much more from their educational experience, often taking a more active role in their learning (Pariola and Pariola 2006). Study tours, through a series of well planned activities and programmes can provide students with opportunities to achieve skills, attitudes and experiences they need to successfully compete in a global marketplace. Indeed, as Woolf (2007) observes, globalisation is exploding classrooms, such that 'the foreign landscape itself becomes the classroom' (p. 1); and Taylor (1969) acknowledges that in order for teachers and students to function effectively they need a first-hand understanding the world. As noted in the RAND Report, the traditional ways that *learning institutions* conceive of internationalising their curricula—by developing academic area studies and language training—may no longer be suitable for the kinds of students and professionals required. Instead, institutions of learning need to devise ways to give students a grounding in thinking and acting across cultures . . . (Bikson et al. 2003).

METHODOLOGY

Our approach draws on a combined descriptive and auto-ethnographic research methodology. Descriptive research aims to provide a detailed and accurate picture of a particular situation; in this case, the attitude of students participating in a study tour (Nueman 2006). Auto-ethnographic research aims to provide accounts from participants' viewpoints. By combining these two approaches, it was felt the findings and accounts would be more authoritative (Etherington 2004; Sikes 2013). These approaches were used because of the relatively small sample size, the need to recall student experiences over a period of time and the expectation that the data collected would contribute to a more sophisticated study. It is important to note that this study did not attempt to measure actual learning outcomes; rather, it aimed to describe students' perceived learning outcomes and experiences (Chieffo and Griffiths 2004). Each participant maintained a diary whilst on tour and took part in, daily, individual and collective reflection activities. The data presented in the next section derives from those diary entries. Whereas diary entries were organised based on institutions visited, the data presented in this chapter is based on apparent themes.

Sample

The data is taken from accounts of four study tours from England to Jamaica, Malawi and Albania; and one study tour from Jamaica to England. Albania, Jamaica and Malawi are developing countries whereas England is a developed country. The four countries are located on three continents. The study tours were operationalised using a comprehensive inclusion model, in that participants were encouraged and allowed to participate in the planning and design of activities. For tour 1, eleven Jamaican teachers and principals (two males and nine females) travelled to England in July 2013. The study tour lasted 21 days and had specific outcomes linked to their practice and studies in educational leadership and management. There were two principals and nine classroom teachers. Six were primary school teachers and five work in secondary and the post-compulsory sectors. For tour 2, five students (three males and two females), aged between 12 and 13 years travelled to Jamaica in April 2014. The tour lasted for 10 days and students were accompanied by four adults, two males and two females. The group was also accompanied to Jamaica by a master's student in educational leadership from a London university. For tour 3, eight students (6 males/2 females), aged between 14 and 18 years travelled to Malawi in July 2015. The tour lasted for 10 days and students were accompanied by two adults, both females. For tour 4, six students (four females and two males) travelled to Albania in June

2015. The tour lasted for 7 days and students were accompanied by two adults, one male and one female teacher. Four additional adults from the local Rotary Club also accompanied the group to Albania because the Rotary Club was a main sponsor. Unlike the other tours which were based on a cultural orientation, Study tour 1 was based on both a cultural and professional/academic orientation linked to the participants' work. In addition to attending and participating in cultural extravaganzas in each host country, amongst participants there were visits to museums, distilleries, places of worship, schools, colleges and universities.

Analysis

The main question asked of staff was: 'What impact did participation in the study tour have on you personally, professionally and what are the implications for practice?' The main questions asked of students were: 'What are the main observations made on tour in relation to teaching, learning and the availability and use of resources?' And 'How has participation in the tour impacted your personal development?' Analysis is through the lens of organisational development, accounting for the possible impacts that engagement in such intercultural exchanges can have on the ways in which schools can develop meaningful learning through cross-cultural learning.

FINDINGS (REFLECTIONS)

The reflections presented in the following pages are organised into two parts: Staff and Students' reflections.

Staff reflections will include accounts from the Jamaican teachers/principals who visited the United Kingdom and the adults who accompanied students on tours to Jamaica, Malawi and Albania. Reflections are presented under three categories: personal learning, professional learning and practice implications.

Staff Reflections

Personal Learning

Empowerment, Personal Efficacy and Reflectivity

The trip to the United Kingdom has simply been another in the series of steps towards my personal and professional progress. Perhaps the most challenging thing for me is to encapsulate this experience in words. I have been forced to be extremely reflective of my practice as a teacher and faced with answering the harsh question of the degree to which I have been effective in the last fourteen years of my career. Each day brought new insight, challenged or rather demolished existing epistemologies concerning who I am, what I really have a passion for and in what direction I want my life to be headed. Confronting these issues has been tumultuous to say the least as once again I attempt to 'come to rhythm'. Certainly, I am deeply cognizant of the fact that the process is not a linear one and in the days subsequent to my return, there has been significant introspection with the resulting emotional ebbs and flows.

I realised how important the local community is and what a large part they play towards making schools a success.

Albania taught me many things: Most importantly, I learned about the culture and people of Albania. What overwhelmed me the most was the hospitality, the generosity and the humility of the Albanian people.

Professional Learning

Research, customer service, collaboration, capacity development and a new professionalism

[S]chools in England are run like businesses and teachers are like business managers fully in charge of their classes. As with any business, customers are the target persons and their satisfaction is the primary concern. In order for a business to be successful, it must cater to the needs of the customers and create a product or service that will suit their needs. In addition to this, business owners and managers must make themselves available to the customers for advice on how to use the product and/or for feedback on their services. Accountability and documentation are also parts of the business. Timing of delivery of products and/or services is also important. The schools in England had all the facets of businesses and much more. Timing was a key factor in the organization of the schools. Everything was done on time and on target to satisfy the customers, the students. This was evident in every activity, every day.

It is interesting to experience the formalities that individuals follow in Malawi compared to the UK. Teachers at both secondary schools school show such respect for their learners and value education, possibly more than is seen in the UK.

[I] have realised that as a leader the greatest success is when you can take a school that is deemed failing to be an outstanding school according to the inspection team. I have learnt some new strategies for curbing poor behaviour and I have also learnt that needs assessment should be congruent with learning in order to be effective. Assessment should help to advance learning as well as determine whether it has taken place. If we are going to include everyone in our teaching, we have to plan effectively. We have to be clear what we want the children to learn. I have also learnt the meaning of working collaboratively. Despite our beliefs and abilities, teachers and the school as a whole, can achieve great things if we work collaboratively.

I have become acutely aware of my professional inconsistencies. It is very easy to complain about the things that are inherently wrong in our education system and even within our own school environment. However, it is more difficult to turn the spotlight on oneself and ask the searching question of how well one measures up to what the highest standards of a teacher are and should be. I know that I am a good teacher and that I have sacrificed much for my students but having travelled to the UK I realize that I have settled into a mire of mediocrity and for me that was the most difficult revelation. I remember the overwhelming emotions experienced at that point of revelation when I realised that I was fast becoming what I had, on occasions, vehemently criticised. I am happy for the opportunity to have gained a fresh perspective and to become aware of the fact that I am the solution to the problems I encounter and even the problems I may have indirectly helped to create.

Albania is a truly beautiful country and not at all as I expected. I learnt a lot about another part of the world that I previously knew nothing about.

Practice Implications

Unlearning, Relearning and Doing Teaching and Leadership Differently

I have been inspired to change my approach to teaching and learning. I now realise that I must unlearn some of my preconceived notions about education and adjust my teaching style to cater to the needs of all my students. My teaching has to be relevant, practical and exciting for learners so they can maximise from the learning experience. I have purposed to utilise all that I have learnt on this study tour to spark creativity among my students and to revolutionise teaching in my school.

Perhaps the most fundamental implication for transforming my practice is the change in my attitude towards my practice. Very often I begin the school year with a myriad of ideas but somewhere during the process they become forgotten. I am going to find a way to engage the students in those ideas and have them assist in making them come to fruition. I will encourage my colleagues. Instead of being dragged into a cycle of bickering I will enact my leadership skills to help them to find ways to improve their own practice.

I will find opportunities to relay what I have learnt about Albania to pupils/students in the classroom. I am a keen advocate of world literature so any opportunity to discuss different cultures is something that I relish.

The importance of careful planning. Decision-making based on caution; communication and managing the host's expectations, never underestimate the importance of building relationships and maintaining partnerships.

Students' Reflections

Students' reflections will include accounts from the British students who visited Jamaica, Malawi and Albania. Reflections are presented under two categories: observations related to teaching, learning and schooling; and observations related to personal development and country. These are presented in turn next.

Teaching, Learning and Schooling

Teaching Strategy

Assemblies were not just about passing on information to students. Their assemblies have a message and a meaning. There was singing, painting, dancing and presentations, which allowed students to show off their talents and be more confident.

I find teaching approaches in Jamaica refreshing. Teachers find a way to bring the whole class together. I think this is how teaching should be. It is very different from what I am used to, which—for me, is amazing.

At every school we visited, I feel the kids have just been the best. They have been so welcoming. I have also seen a new teaching style which mixes fun with serious work. I think even without the resources we have in the UK they are still able to reach just as high standards as us which is amazing because they are shaping the Jamaica of tomorrow.

Subject Choices

I was able to sit in on a practical cosmetology lesson. Cosmetology is about hair styling and the detail behind it. I strongly believe we should create more lessons like this in England because it will open up so many career opportunities.

I found learning about agriculture amazing. I also find it fascinating how they use recycled objects to make useful things . . . .I have never experienced a college like this before so it was brilliant to see not just agriculture college but also to visit an actual farm. I learnt things today that every student need to know.

Community in School

When we went into a classroom the first thing I noticed was that the children could hug visitors, unlike in Britain.

They are all about embracing other people, cultures and religions as a way of learning and improving their education. I have never sensed such community inside a school.

Resources and Resilience

Shocking to see the little resources. Could not imagine ever learning in that environment, but amazing to see what they've achieved with what they've got. 40 people per tiny classroom. Chalk boards make you appreciate home.

There is not much similarity between my school and theirs. We have so much and they have so little. Our school is completely different to all the schools I've seen but it I saw students learning and having fun. . . .

I think teachers and students do a great job at teaching and learning. Lessons observed were of a high standard and classrooms learning was always very good, particularly with the lack of resource.

Two rural primary schools we visited are particularly under-resourced. I think their location makes things harder for them. However, students and teachers show a great attitude and determination. Learning was once again outstanding.

At first I felt nervous about adapting to the different culture. However, as time went on, I felt amazed. It was very overwhelming looking around the schools and I felt very excited to be meeting the students although I felt very emotional due to the lack of facilities. We all made a fantastic and strong connection and I believe it will carry on in our futures.

Personal Development and Country

Students reflect on the experiences of visiting Jamaica:

I learnt lots about interacting with different cultures. I now understand a lot more about Jamaicans and their culture, for example, knowing what to avoid, and about their food and music.

It impacted in a major way on my cultural sensitivity. I am now much aware of differences in values, beliefs and lifestyles when dealing with people internationally. As a result, I have become very conscious of the way I deal with people from other cultural backgrounds especially regarding an underlying stigma towards that particular groups.

I can definitely see the huge benefits of the tour: it highlights areas for future studies and possible employment.... you get to experience 'work and play' in countries foreign to you and you meet great people. I have met many persons whilst on tour and I am still in touch with many of them even now.

Jamaica is one of the most important and rewarding experiences of my life. I have enjoyed going around all the schools and absorbing the Jamaican culture so much that I feel like an honorary Jamaican. The children at the schools were some of the most welcoming and polite and friendly children that I have ever met. Plus, they were really enthusiastic about their learning and the way that they conducted themselves around the schools. I would love to go back in a few years and see how much has changed....

Others reflect on their experiences of visiting Albania:

While waiting at the airport, I found that I began to feel nervous about the trip and what it entailed. I felt at ease with the people I was with although I have never been to a country as deprived as Albania is, or should I say, as deprived as I have heard it is.... It reminded me that money does not buy happiness but it can help you lead to it.

It's interesting to see the difference between the wealthy and the poor in Albania, because although they are wealthy their wealth is not as great as the UK's when they all work just as hard, or harder. Unfair. All so welcoming.

Parts of the town were rundown and untidy but the further up the hill you get you get to homes like outs in interior. I felt very spoilt how I had everything but a welcome seeped out of every crack—the people were some of the nicest I have ever met and I felt that the people of Albania may not have a lot, but they live with what they have.

DISCUSSION

Three discrete, yet overlapping themes—Admiration and Community, Perplexity and Change, and Contextualising Capacity Building—have emerged from the reflective findings presented above. These are discussed in turn next.

Admiration and Community

Overall, staff and students were appreciative of their time in the tour country. They enjoyed meeting other staff and students, engaging with persons from different school communities and visiting different institutions. The 'openness' and 'warmth' experienced by staff and students was noticeable amongst participants in all countries. For UK students the physical display of affection and 'warmth' between staff and students in tour countries, for example through 'hugs' and 'high 5s' was different to what students were accustomed in England. Nevertheless, such observation simultaneously highlighted cultural differences and pointed to a need for increased cultural sensitivity (Anderson et al. 2006).

Similarly, both staff and students praised the teaching approaches used by teachers and the resilience of learners. They commented on the use and influence of music in teaching and learning and some wished they could be taught cosmetology and agricultural science at school. These important observations led students to feel empowered to question and challenge their own educational provision and to agitate for a different kind of learning experience. Additionally, both staff and students were able to make *links* between their lives and the lives of people throughout the world (DCSF 2009). This awareness of how other teachers and students live, study and work, produced a deepened sense of longing for home and a heightened appreciation for home and for the facilities at their disposal (Woolf 2007). This was especially noticeable amongst UK participants.

Both staff and students were surprised at the sense of community that existed within schools and the involvement of the local community in the life of schools. This was observation that could be 'lost' based on how the data has been presented, although it is one that should not be ignored. On its own, this sense of community is indicative of broader communitarian tendencies in Malawi and Jamaica compared with England. Nevertheless, these observations led both staff and students to commit to challenging practices at school back home (Pariola and Pariola 2006).

Perplexity and Change

Staff and students marvelled at how creative teachers were; how resilient teachers and students were; and how well students were learning. This was an important observation across all four countries and across all four tours. Despite severe lack of material resources and a shortage of material and equipment, students in Albania, Malawi and Jamaica were stretched by their teachers' creativity, underpinned by their desire to be lifted from poverty through education. Many students and staff from England struggled to keep back tears as they observed learning environments that were markedly different to their own. Some also felt guilty for wasting some of their resources and/or for not taking better care of resources they had. Similarly, Jamaican teachers and principals marvelled at the quality and availability of resources available to students and staff in England and wished they had 'even a tenth' of what staff/students in England have. This paradox simultaneously places upon participants two things: an understanding of the *economic, cultural, political and environmental influences* which shape our lives (DCSF 2009) and a sociocultural understanding of another place and space, not previously had (Sachau et al. 2010) and not possible from remaining at home or from textbooks. This first-hand experience of schooling outside their own cultural and physical space (Taylor 1969) was as 'eye opening' as it was challenging for them, prompting students and staff to committing to developing a 'worldly mindset' (Mintzberg 2004) and cultural connectivity (Harrison 2006).

Armed with new knowledge of context, staff and students are empowered to *engage* in thinking and acting across cultures (Bikson et al. 2003) with one student from England describing herself as an 'honorary Jamaican' and pledging to return. Staff and students did not want simply to return to their home countries and back to their previous lived experiences. Instead, they wanted to connect with staff and students in tour countries, and to find ways of developing and sustaining new friendships and collaborative partnerships, underlining Sutton and Rubin's (2004) suggestion that study tours can lead to deeper understanding of [our] global interdependence.

Contextualised Capital

The confluence of three kinds of capital is illuminated earlier. Personal capital illustrated in spades in the way participants have reflected on their experiences; the evidence illuminates the social capital generated as a result of the methodology of this project; and the analysis mentioned earlier demonstrates the decisional capital that has emerged, with the data revealing participants better able to make sense of their contexts having been exposed to different contexts. Their capacity to generate knowledge was enhanced through the design of the programme and the reflective methods demanded throughout it.

Collaboration was promoted, because of the admiration that developed and sense of community that grew, that enabled communities of practice (Wenger 1998) to emerge. This in turn increases capacity because of the growing capital. Yet, what is particular in this type of knowledge production is the experiential element and the mobilisation of the knowledge being so contextualised. The students and the adults are in the location together. They are making sense of where they are and where they come from simultaneously. They are contextualising and decontextualising the educational case studies. Capacity for school improvement is being built through this holistic approach, which recognises the perplex complexities of inter-cultural understanding, that in turn demands change of oneself and one's perspectives.

This third theme, therefore, builds on the previous two and finds a perspective on the globalisation problematic. It is a perspective that recognises the methodological power of the study tour programme and how through international collaboration comes added value to the home school. There are huge challenges to such a perspective towards a school curriculum and pedagogy for globalisation becoming 'mainstream'. The most obvious is cost. Another challenge is the 'performativity' (Ball 2012) agenda prevailing in many schools making this type of programme seem the least of their priorities. However, it is a change that the evidence does demonstrate makes a difference to young people's lives and consequently should make a difference to the leadership of schools. 'But before any of these changes can happen . . . we first have to stop looking away' (Klein 2015, p. 10).

CONCLUSION

At the time of planning the study tour to England in 2013, there were no plans to engage in other tours. It was the success of the initial study tour that led to further tours being organised to (and between) other countries. It is significant the data provides triangulation amongst all four countries and the different participants.

The objectives of the study tours have been achieved. There has been a narrowing of the gap between peoples and places and there has been a cultural introduction (and immersion) for participants, not obtainable from textbooks. It should also be noted that through transformational leadership, tour organisers provided participants with the infrastructure for capacity building that connects homes, workplaces and civic spaces through the school networks (Wilkins 2013).

This study is an example of research that impacts because the data collected came from participants' completing diary entries regarding their observations on tour and how they perceive the tours have impacted on them. It did not seek to measure actual outcome (Chieffo and Griffiths 2004); thus, concerns about the validity of self-reporting, in particular in relation to perceived change to understandings, could be expected.

Undoubtedly, those preferring more positivist methods of research would criticise that this study was conducted with small cohort sizes, and hence only descriptive and qualitative indications can be drawn from our results. Quantitative data, such as responses to Likert-scale questions, may have strengthened the results but depth of finding comes from qualitative design. To have used closed questions for data gathering would have undermined the ethnographic integrity of the participants' reflections. Confidence comes from the less structured way of collecting the data. Indeed, in the words of Etherington (2004), 'Auto/ethnography is a word that describes both a method and a text' (p. 140).

We therefore propose that the diary entries of participants are sufficient. The notion of auto/ethnography being method and text is in how the research process aims to make tangible the issue of capacity building through study tours. A deconstructive approach is taken to understanding participants' experience, and a clear conclusion is that their voice is contributing to knowledge production.

These findings however, important as they are for the field of education, are not generalisable but instead should be seen as providing an 'index of generalisability' (Miller 2012b). We conclude that this is a field of research that is worthy of further exploration and would champion the idea that more institutions of learning adopt the methodological approach to intercultural learning that is illuminated within this chapter. A longitudinal study in various schools would provide evidence of impact on school development and subsequent improvement.

References

Allen, D., & Young, M. (1997). From tour guide to teacher: deepening cross-cultural competence through international experience-based education. *Journal of Management Education, 21*(2), 168–189.

Anderson, P. H., Lawton, L., Rexeisen, R. J., & Hubbard, A. C. (2006). Short-term study abroad and intercultural sensitivity: a pilot study. *International Journal of Intercultural Relations, 30*(4), 457–469.

Ball, S. J. (2012). *Global education Inc. new policy networks and the neo-liberal imaginary.* Abingdon: Routledge.

Bikson, T., Treverton, G., Moini, J., & Lindstrom, G. (2003). *New challenges for international leadership: lessons from organizations with global missions.* Santa Monica, CA: RAND.

Brokaw, S. C. (1996). Planning, organizing, and executing short term international exposures for U.S. students of marketing and business: an alternative method. *Marketing Education Review, 6*(3), 87–93.

Burns, J. M. (1978). *Leadership.* New York: Harper & Row.

Business students flock to DePaul study abroad seminars in Cuba, Chile, Greece, Thailand, Hong Kong in December. (2002, November 18). Ascribe Newswire.

Chieffo, L., & Griffiths, L. (2004). Large-scale assessment of student attitudes after a short-term study abroad program. *Frontiers: The Interdisciplinary Journal of Study Abroad, 10,* 165–177.

Commins, T., Cheuthai, P., & Travichitkun, R. (2010). Study tours: enhancing the international mobility experience. *Asian Journal on Education and Learning, 1*(1), 44–54.

DCSF (Department for Children Schools and Families). (2009) *Beyond current horizons.* http://www.beyondcurrenthorizons.org.uk. Accessed 1 May 2016.

Dimmock, C. (2012). *Leadership, capacity building and school improvement.* Abingdon: Routledge.

Etherington, K. (2004). *Becoming a Reflexive Researcher London.* JKP.

Fullan, M. (2004). *Leadership and sustainability: systems thinkers in action.* Thousand Oaks, CA: Corwin Press.

Gibbon, M., Limoges, C., Nowtny, H., Schwartzman, S., Scott, P., & Trow, M. (1994). *The new production of knowledge.* London: Sage.

Hallinger, P. (2003). Leading educational change: reflections on the practice of instructional and transformational leadership. *Cambridge Journal of Education, 33*(3), 329–352.

Hargreaves, A., & Fullan, M. (2012). *Professional capital.* Abingdon: Routledge.

Harrison, J. K. (2006). The relationship between international study tour effects and the personality variables of self-monitoring and core self-evaluations. *Frontiers: The International Journal of Study Abroad, 13,* 1–22.

Klein, N. (2015). *This changes everything: Capitalism vs. the Climate.* London: Penguin Books.

Lewis, T. L., & Nisenbaum, R. A. (2005). The benefits of short-term study abroad. *The Chronicle of Higher Education, 51*(39), B20.

Miller, P. (2012a). Editorial on 'educational leadership in the Caribbean & beyond'. *Journal of the University College of the Cayman Islands, Special Issue, 6,* 1–3.

Miller, P. (2012b). *Professional lives in transition: shock, turbulence and adaptation in teacher identity reconstruction.* Germany: Lambert Academic Publishers.

Miller, P., & Potter, I. (2014). Teacher CPD across borders: reflections on how a study tour to England helped to change the practice and praxis among Jamaican teachers. *International Journal of Education and Practice, 2*(1), 9–20.

Miller, P., Bennett, K., Carter, T. S., Hylton-Fraser, K., Castle, M., & Potter, I. (2015). Building Teacher Capacity through an International Study Tour: Impact and Evidence. *International Studies in Educational Adminstration, 43*(1), 19–33.

Mintzberg, H. (2004). *Managers not MBAs: a hard look at the soft practice of managing and managing development.* London & New York: Financial Times Prentice Hall.

Nowotny, H., Scott, P., & Gibbon, M. (2001). *Re-thinking science.* Cambridge: Polity Press.

Nueman, W. L. (2006). *Social research methods qualitative and quantitative approaches* (6th edn), USA: Pearson Education Inc.

Orahood, T., Kruze, L., & Pearson, D. E. (2004). The impact of study abroad on business students' career goals. *Frontiers: The Interdisciplanary Journal of Study Abroad, 10,* 117–130.

Pariola, J. S., & Pariola, A. G. (2006). Expanding the parameters of service learning: a case study. *Journal of Studies in International Education, 10*(1), 71–86.

Pence, H., & Macgillivray, I. (2008). The impact of an interventional field experience on pre-service teachers. *Teaching and Teacher Evaluation, 24,* 14–45.

Porth, S. J. (1997). Management education goes international: a model for designing and teaching a study tour course. *Journal of Management Education, 21*(2), 190–199.

Sachau, D., Brasher, N., & Fee, S. (2010). Three models for short-term study abroad. *Journal of Management Education, 34*(5), 645–670.

Sikes, P. (Ed.) (2013). *Autoethnography.* Sage Benchmarks in Social Science Series— 4 volumes. London: Sage.

Sutton, R. C., & Rubin, D. L. (2004). The GLOSSARI project: initial findings from a system-wide research initiative on study abroad learning outcomes. *Frontiers: The Interdisciplinary Journal of Study Abroad, 10,* 65–82.

Taylor, H. (1969). *The world as teacher.* New York, USA: Doubleday.

Tucker, M., & Weaver, D. (2013). A longitudinal study of student outcomes from participation in an international study tour: some preliminary findings. *Journal of University Teaching & Learning Practice, 10*(2), 1–14.

Wenger, E. (1998). *Communities of practice: learning, meaning and identity.* Cambridge: CUP.

Wilkins, R. (2013). Professional strengths in school leadership: collaborating for knowledge generation, problem solving and policy influence. *Education Today, 93*(4), 308.

Williams, T. R. (2005). Exploring the impact of study abroad on students' inter-cultural communication skills: adaptability and sensitivity. *Journal of Studies in International Education*, *9*(4), 356–371.

Woolf, M. (2007). Impossible things before breakfast: myths in education abroad. *Journal of Studies in International Education*, *11*(3), 496–509.

Paul Miller, PhD, PFHEA, is Professor of Educational Leadership and Management at the School of Education and Professional Development, University of Huddersfield, UK. He is President of the Institute for Educational Administration and Leadership, Jamaica (IEAL-J); a member of Council of the British Educational Leadership Management Administration Society (BELMAS); a member of the Board of the Commonwealth Council for Educational Administration and Management (CCEAM). He is an Associate Editor of *International Studies in Educational Administration and Educational Management Administration & Leadership*. He has taught in secondary schools and universities in both Jamaica and the United Kingdom, and his work in educational leadership and management is predominantly framed with compara-tive and cross-cultural perspectives. He is Principal Fellow of the Higher Education Academy.

Ian Potter is Executive Headteacher of a large 11–19 comprehensive school in the south of England and previously was a Deputy Headteacher in Milton Keynes having started his career as a teacher in 1987 in Bedfordshire, following his training in London. Ian's research interests include distributed and system leader-ship. He co-coordinates the International School Leadership Development Network researching Social Justice Leadership in schools across the world. He is a member of the BELMAS Council and is its International Affairs Coordinator, a member of the BERA Conference Committee and an Honorary Assistant Professor at the School of Education at Nottingham University, UK.

INDEX

© The Author(s) 2017
P. Miller (ed.), *Cultures of Educational Leadership,* Intercultural
Studies in Education, DOI 10.1057/978-1-137-58567-7